More Praise for
Think Like Your Customer

W9-AWG-757

What top business leaders are saying . . .

"Starting with what your customers need and want, rather than what you have to sell, is key to sales success. This book will show you how to identify your customer's business objectives before the sales cycle even starts. Stinnett provides the insight to deliver real business value to your customers."

Bill McDermott, CEO and President,
SAP America, Inc.

"Even after thirty-five years in this business, I found Think Like Your Customer *to be loaded with powerful and proven advice, which I began putting to use immediately. This is a very practical guide to better understanding how your customers think."*

Bill Zeitler, Senior Vice President and Group Executive,
Systems and Technology Group,
IBM Corporation

"This book will teach you how to sell 'business results' instead of just products and services."

Gerri Elliott, Corporate Vice President,
US Enterprise Group,
Microsoft Corporation

"If you want to move from selling a product to understanding your client, from a one-time sale to career-long selling relationships, and from solutions focus to business issue resolution, then you've found the right book."

Craig Wrigley, Senior Sales Coach,
EDS

"Bill Stinnett has provided an approach that enables delivering full value to the customer, an approach that is essential for success today."

David Alexander, Sales Effectiveness,
Accenture

"Bill Stinnett's Business Value Hierarchy is the framework of a powerful method to successfully penetrate accounts and earn access to key C-Level executives. This book will help you take your game to the next level."

Jim Follett, Chief Operating Officer (and acting CEO),
NOP World

"Bill Stinnett's sales models and techniques have had a positive impact on our day-to-day sales activities. Using these ideas, we've been able to break down barriers that stood between us and several important new customers."

Gregg D. Tiemann, President,
Intertek, **ETL Semko** Division

"Bill's Business Value Hierarchy concept is absolutely brilliant! It has become a part of every executive presentation we give. It has enabled us to get in front of higher-level decision makers and has played a major role in closing a number of substantial new sales opportunities for our team."

Roxanne Leap, Executive Vice President,
Analytic Insights Group,
Information Resources, Inc.

"Bill Stinnett's unique approach to the sales process—which is really all about your customer's buying process—is just one way *Think Like Your Customer will help improve your sales results. His philosophy of selling has completely transformed how we engage executive decision makers.*"

Sanjay Pingle, Executive Vice President,
Medsite, Inc.

"*Stinnett's approach focuses on the individual buying motives of your customer, an essential ingredient of every successful sales campaign. These ideas and approaches have helped our sales management team immeasurably.*"

Randy Verdino, President, IT Services,
Computer Horizons Corporation

"*This book is a winner!! Bill has done an excellent job in pulling together the sales process and providing actual tools that salespeople can put to use immediately to begin shortening their sales cycle and increase their closing ratio. I particularly like his tips on thinking about the sale by seeing things through the prospect's eyes, versus from our own perspective.*"

Jim Clary, President and CEO,
Mullin Consulting, Inc.

"*Stinnett will cause you to rethink conventional sales strategy that focuses on product attributes and benefits, and reminds you that,* 'It's all about the customer!'"

Dave Doherty, Vice President, Marketing,
Arrow Electronics

"Think Like Your Customer *sits on my desk as a daily reference for improving our sales and selling team. A must-read for our entire commercial organization.*"

Nick La Magna, Director of Sales,
Huntsman Petrochemical Corporation

What top business educators are saying . . .

"I've never seen anything quite like this. Page after page, Mr. Stinnett manages to connect with your intuition making you feel like his ideas are your own. The result is enlightening, compelling, and powerfully motivating. You'll want to stand up and go sell something right away!"
Luc Wathieu, Associate Professor,
Harvard Business School,
Harvard University

"Reading this book is like taking a guided tour through the mind of your customer! Bill Stinnett masterfully explains what value is, how value is created, and how to sell value by linking your offerings to your customers' goals and objectives."
Mohanbir Sawhney, Professor,
Kellogg School of Management,
Northwestern University

"As someone who teaches both marketing and sales, I appreciate that Bill Stinnett has placed his focus squarely where it belongs . . . on the customer. This book will challenge you to understand why *customers buy,* how *customers buy, and offers suggestions on how to use these insights to sell more effectively."*
James M. Lattin, Professor, Graduate School of Business,
Stanford University

"Great sales and marketing require great customer insight. Think Like Your Customer *provides an innovative and rigorous look at how corporations operate—think, feel, function, and behave—as potential customers. The book's many insights are quite refreshing and its old truths well worth retelling. A highly recommended read for any sales and marketing manager."*
Michel Tuan Pham, Professor, Graduate School of Business,
Columbia University

"Think Like Your Customer *puts into writing many of the tools and techniques I used at McKinsey to help our clients improve their selling effectiveness. Stinnett presents practical ideas and concepts that can be used by CEOs, Marketing VPs, and Sales Managers to sell higher within their customer's organization and accelerate their customer's buying process."*

Robert A. Garda, Executive-in-Residence,
Fuqua Graduate School of Business,
Duke University
Former Senior Director and Head of Marketing Practice,
McKinsey & Company

"Think Like Your Customer *is a comprehensive analysis of the complex process of personal selling and buying loaded with lots of practical wisdom. This book will be invaluable to any sales executive who wishes to excel."*

Vithala R. Rao, Professor,
Johnson Graduate School of Management,
Cornell University

"Think Like Your Customer *is written for every sales professional and senior executive who wants to succeed by creating real measurable value for their customers. Bill Stinnett has developed a process to unlock the secret of understanding customer value creation that is easy to understand and implement."*

H. David Hennessey,
Professor of Marketing,
Babson College

"Bill Stinnett brings new meaning to the old adage of 'think before you act.'* Think Like Your Customer *is a refreshing look at the all-important sales process that emphasizes strategic action based on thoughtful reflection. Reading this book will change the way you think about selling."*

Paul N. Friga, Assistant Professor,
Kelley School of Business,
Indiana University
Coauthor of *The McKinsey Mind*

"The test of any book on sales strategy is how many times you say to yourself while reading, 'Huh, I never thought of it that way before.' Think Like Your Customer *is full of those moments. Stinnett's rock-solid approach is based on time-honored sales insights, which he has updated for use in today's fast-paced, complex business environment."*

Paul Nolan, Editor,
SalesForceXP

"Use Think Like Your Customer *to keep your customers forever!"*

Tony Parinello,
Bestselling Author of **Selling to VITO**

*"*Think Like Your Customer *isn't the best way to think, it's the ONLY way to think. Buy this book and make the conversion before your competition does!"*

Jeffrey Gitomer,
Bestselling Author of **The Sales Bible**

"This authentic book will teach you a sound, step-by-step approach to walking in your customer's shoes. Learning and practicing these principles will elevate you to the pinnacle of sales success."

Willis H. Turner, CSE, President, and CEO,
Sales & Marketing Executives International, Inc.

"Bill Stinnett has written a book that turns the selling process on its head. It's all about understanding not only your products and services, but also why people buy them, how people buy them, and how customers perceive value and risk."

Jack Covert, President and Founder,
800-CEO-READ

THINK
LIKE YOUR
CUSTOMER

A Winning Strategy to Maximize Sales by
Understanding How and Why Your Customers Buy

BILL STINNETT

McGraw·Hill

New York   Chicago   San Francisco   Lisbon   London   Madrid   Mexico City
Milan   New Delhi   San Juan   Seoul   Singapore   Sydney   Toronto

The McGraw-Hill Companies

Library of Congress Cataloging-in-Publication Data

Stinnett, Bill.
    Think like your customer : a winning strategy to maximize sales by understanding how and why your customers buy / Bill Stinnett.
        p.   cm.
    Includes index.
    ISBN 0-07-144188-3 (alk. paper)
        1. Consumer behavior.   2. Selling.   3. Customer relations.   4. Customer loyalty.
    I. Title.

HF5415.32.S75   2004
658.8'342—dc22
                                          2004019679

3 4 5 6 7 8 9 0   FGR/FGR 3 2 1 0 9 8 7 6 5

ISBN 0-07-144188-3

McGraw-Hill books are available at special quantity discounts to use as premiums and sales promotions, or for use in corporate training programs. For more information, please write to the Director of Special Sales, Professional Publishing, McGraw-Hill, Two Penn Plaza, New York, NY 10121-2298. Or contact your local bookstore.

This book is printed on acid-free paper.

"If you want to catch a fish, you have to think like a fish."

DAD

Contents

Acknowledgments

I am grateful for this opportunity to thank several very special people who have directly or indirectly contributed to my work and to my life. First of all, to my immediate family: my dad and mom, my brothers, Gerald (Jerry) and Jim, and my sisters, Glenda and Gloria. Thank you for setting a high standard to live up to.

My thanks go to the entire team at Sales Excellence, Inc., but especially to Avanya Manasseh, Wes Beckwith, and Brad Smith, who have all contributed greatly to the success of our company and of this book.

I want to thank my former managers and mentors: Larry Smith, Herb Anderson, Sandy Elam, Ed Krolick, Michael Copperwhite, Marv Kaufman, Shawn Hardy, Dave McKenna, Mark Smith, Mark Rossini, Jim White, Doug Brooke, and John Iuliano.

There are also several very special clients who have had a profound impact on my company and on my career. These include, but are not limited to, Roxanne Leap, Paul Bates, Helen Hoedt, Sue Hamilton, Hugh Ujhazy, Kim Dienstmann, Paul DeStephano, Bob Compagno, Joe Ciringione, and Rick Abbate.

I believe I owe a debt of gratitude to those who have laid the foundation of sales doctrine upon which the material in this book is based. This elite group includes Dale Carnegie, Frank Bettger, Zig Ziglar, David Sandler, Mack Hanan, Neil Rackham, Robert Miller and Stephen Heiman, Jim Holden, Michael Bosworth, Anthony Parinello, Jeffrey Gitomer, Rick Page, and many others.

I want to thank Donya Dickerson, my editor at McGraw-Hill, for her incredible patience and steady support throughout this entire project. Many thanks to my agent Jeff Herman. I am also grateful for three true professionals, whom I greatly admire, who have always been willing to share their experience and advice along the way: Nancy J. Stephens, Steve Waterhouse, and Alan Weiss.

And to several very close friends who have supported me through so many endeavors: Jeff Bernier, Tim Schmidt, Dave Rohlf, Ken Plasz, Jim "Smitty" Smith, and Charlene Kelly. I deeply appreciate each of you! You have meant more to me than I have ever been, or shall ever be, able to express.

Introduction

When I founded Sales Excellence, Inc., my intention was to develop and offer training and consulting services to help executives, sales managers, and salespeople learn *how* to do all of the things that every book and seminar on sales had already told them they should be doing. There were already several very successful and widely used sales methodologies on the market, and over the years I had attended seminars and read books on just about all of them. I thought that rather than trying to re-create or repackage what had already been done, our company would provide what I called "skill-specific" training on various aspects of professional sales such as prospecting, negotiation, reaching and selling to executives, developing business and financial acumen, and so on. We developed a curriculum that goes deep into targeted subject matter in a series of one- or two-day workshops, as opposed to trying to teach everything about selling in a five-day seminar. This approach was designed to effect substantial changes in the way participants think about selling, which results in marked and lasting changes in behavior.

We work with our clients to determine what specific knowledge or skill-sets can offer the greatest opportunity for improvement. We then develop a custom workshop focused on achieving specific learning objectives that support, and are congruent with, whatever processes and tools they are already using. We find that nearly all of our larger clients—which now include the likes of Microsoft, General Electric, and EDS—as well as many of our midsize and smaller customers, already use one of the popular sales methodologies such as Strategic Selling®, Solution Selling®, or SPIN Selling® as their core sales process infrastructure.[1] Most of them also have some kind of Customer Relationship Management (CRM) system in place to manage accounts and opportunities. They hire us to help maximize the return on those investments by making their sales force more effective at executing the processes they already have in place, while adding tools and structure where needed.

In some cases, of course, our role becomes much more broad and strategic, providing overall sales process consulting and infrastructure for sales force management, depending on what we and our clients decide is the right approach. But in order to streamline the customization process and maximize the impact of our workshops, we established a five-step diagnostic process for engaging each new client, which involves a great deal of discovery up front. As we worked with a wide variety of sales teams from every conceivable industry, we began to recognize some very interesting patterns.

The Discovery

As part of our discovery process with new customers, we use a carefully chosen series of questions to determine whether we can help, and if so, how. We seek to understand their major goals and objectives and what initiatives are currently underway to achieve them. We ask how they measure their business performance, as well as how they measure the productivity and effectiveness of their sales organization. Once we understand what they want to accomplish, and how they will measure the results, we then brainstorm about their ideal outcomes for sales training. My favorite question is, "If you decided to bring us in to train your sales team, what would you want your people to be willing or able to do the day after the training that they weren't willing or able to do the day before?" Here are a few examples of what we consistently hear:

• "We want our people to be able to really capture our prospective customer's interest on the phone and get them excited about what we can do to help them."

- "We want our people to be better able to determine which opportunities are worth working on and which ones we should seriously consider walking away from."
- "Our competitors often beat us on price. We want our people to be better at communicating the value of the products and services we bring to market, instead of just listing the features and benefits and ending up competing on price alone."
- "We want our people to have the confidence to call on senior executives, especially those at the C-Level (i.e., CEO, CFO, COO, CIO, etc.), and be able to have business conversations with top decision makers."
- "We want our people to be better equipped to handle negotiations so that we don't have to give away so much profit just to win or keep the business."
- "We want to become a valuable partner to our customers instead of just being one of their vendors."

It became apparent that there weren't a thousand, or even a hundred, different challenges our prospective clients were struggling with. Most of their concerns fell neatly into eight or ten different buckets. So we developed our workshop programs to specifically address these issues and called them *Power-Prospecting for New Business*™, *Qualification and Pipeline Management*™, *Selling Business Value*™, *Selling at the C-Level*®, and so on. But we soon found that it was futile to try to teach our participants prospecting skills, for example, without the foundational knowledge of *why* a prospect would want to buy their products or services in the first place. Likewise, we couldn't teach the skill of competitive positioning without first addressing *how* a prospective buyer perceives value and risk. And we certainly couldn't teach the techniques involved in bringing business to closure without an understanding of the corporate budgeting and acquisition process.

In short, there is a body of knowledge, which I call "How and Why Customers Buy," that needs to be learned before any specific techniques or approaches will be effective. This material, or at least a portion of it, has become the backbone of all of our workshops, regardless of the specific subject matter being covered. This foundational body of knowledge has now become the book you hold in your hands.

The Process

In almost every team of sales reps we work with, we see a variety of backgrounds and experience levels. There are usually a few reps who are brand-new to the company. Others have been with the company for a while but are new to sales. Some have been around for several years. And a few, who are frequently the top performers, have been on the job fifteen, twenty, or even twenty-five years. Their experience has been earned through a career marked by success, failure, and a lot of hard work.

I have come to believe that the greatest benefit of this experience is a better understanding of the industry and the marketplace in which their customers compete. They know their customer's business—in some cases, better than their customers do. They have a large number of industry contacts, which certainly helps with referrals and networking for new opportunities, but I also observe an uncanny ability to know where to spend their time to maximize results. They just seem to work much smarter than the newer guys do.

There are exceptions, but generally speaking, the more experienced sales professionals aren't twice as good at executing any particular task or technique. They seem to simply be better at understanding how customers think. They have learned, probably the hard way, how to determine which ones *can* buy. They've also learned how to get the ones who can buy to do the things they need to do in order to buy. The concepts and approaches in this book are offered for the express purpose of accelerating the acquisition of this kind of experience.

We will explore, in the first five chapters, *why* customers buy. Then, and only then, will we look at *how* they buy. I believe that until we understand why, and until our customer understands why, the how doesn't matter much. The first half of the book focuses heavily on the way customers see the world, how they perceive value, and what motivates them to buy. The second half deals primarily with how individuals and organizations make buying decisions, as well as how we interact with them and ultimately influence the decision and buying process.

All of the ideas presented here are based on a set of basic, yet very powerful, tenets (strongly held beliefs). Together they form the foundation of our philosophy of selling. I have no way of proving that they are universally true. I can only claim that they have been consistent in every situation I have encountered over a twenty-year career in sales and sales management. Those who attend our workshops consistently confirm these beliefs with their own experiences. These tenets appear throughout the book, set out from the regular text, for emphasis and easy review.

Although, in retrospect, these ideas will probably seem like common sense, many of them do represent a departure from the mainstream of selling theory, which has long been accepted as gospel. Everything I will propose here is presented with the intention of *changing the way you think* about selling. It will require a transition for some, and for others, a complete transformation.

The Results

For those who are willing to make the voyage, the rewards are tremendous. The ultimate outcome is an increase in gross revenue. This will be accomplished in three major ways:

1. Maximizing sales velocity (i.e., how fast opportunities flow through our sales pipeline and how many we can manage at one time), which also improves the utilization of sales resources.
2. Increasing average deal size, or the wallet share (share of spend) we achieve with each customer, while at the same time minimizing price erosion.
3. Increasing customer loyalty and customer retention, which in turn drives down our overall cost of sales.

For the individual, this approach will maximize your own income potential and your ability to manage your time, as well as your return on time invested. It's bound to make you happier, too, because seeing positive results and having more time, either to reinvest in your work or to do other things, brings a feeling of being in control of your life and your destiny.

If what has been described here sounds good, you shouldn't be surprised to learn that there is a substantial investment required. Be prepared to invest *more* time and effort up front, while you are learning how to make these ideas work for you. Your return will come in the future. At first, you'll probably be uncomfortable with some of these suggestions. You might even experience some failure along the way. Rest assured, this is part of the process and a sure sign that you are changing and growing.

As you read and study, I encourage you to stop from time to time when you hit an "aha" moment and think about how you can apply that new idea to a current sales opportunity. In our workshops, participants use a separate piece of paper we call a "Best Ideas Sheet" to capture good ideas as they come to them. I encourage you to try something similar, using a separate sheet of paper, as you work your way through the book.

Once you have a list of a dozen or two dozen ideas that you think are good, then prioritize them by which ones you think can help you the most, and figure out how you can put these ideas to use. Your list of "Good Ideas" can then be pinned to the wall, or carried around in a day planner, so you can review them and think about them every week, or even every day.

If you reread this book in six months or a year, I believe you will find yourself applying these ideas far more than you might at first imagine. The main reason is that what is written here is the truth. It simply makes sense. Now let me be clear: I don't take credit for any of these truths. I didn't make them up. They have been there all along, waiting to be observed. My life's work has been to recognize them and organize them in an effort to advance my own career and yours.

I would wish you luck if I thought it would help. But I have come to believe that luck has very little to do with success. Instead, I wish you energy, stamina, and a burning desire to achieve. With these things, and the willingness to learn, and grow, and *change the way you think*, success is yours for the taking.

PART I

WHY CUSTOMERS BUY

CHAPTER 1

What Customers Think About

When I was a kid, I loved to go fishing with my dad. We always had a lot of fun. The only thing that wasn't very fun about it was that he could normally catch fish all day long and I couldn't catch anything. Well, as a nine-year-old kid I could get pretty frustrated, and it usually wasn't long before I resorted to my standard incessant question, "What am I doing wrong? What am I doing wrong?" His advice was always the same. He said, "Son, if you want to catch a fish, you have to think like a fish." I remember being even more frustrated then because, *"I'm not a fish!"* I didn't know *how* to think like a fish. Besides, I reasoned, how could the way that I think influence what a fish does or doesn't do?

As I got a little older I began to understand what my dad was really trying to say to me. What he meant was I needed to learn to think *about* what fish think *about*. So, I decided to do some reading and research. I went to the library and found some books on fish. I subscribed to several fishing magazines, and I even joined the local bass fishing club and started attending the monthly meetings. I learned all kinds of things.

Did you know that a fish is a cold-blooded animal? Therefore, fish are very sensitive to water temperature, and generally speaking they would rather be in warmer water as opposed to colder water when they can. Water is usually warmer in direct sunlight than in the shade, but fish don't have any eyelids and the sun hurts their eyes. Shallow water is usually warmer than deep water, and it tends to hold a wide variety of food sources. But even if there is adequate cover (a boat dock or a thick growth of lily pads), so that they feel safe moving into the shallows, fish always position themselves so they can quickly escape to deeper water to avoid predators or threats of any kind. As I took the time to learn and understand more about all the different things that concern fish, I became much more effective at finding and catching them.

Later on, when I entered the business world, I remember hearing my first boss say, "Although we each have different titles and responsibilities here in this company, we are really all in sales. We all need to think like salespeople." I also started attending sales seminars and I read a number of books on sales. They all seemed to revolve around the thought, "Here's the way top salespeople think." I appreciate the point that my former boss and those trainers and authors were trying to make, but it didn't completely make sense. My dad never once said, "If you want to catch a fish you need to think like a *fisherman*." What he said was, "You need to think like a *fish*."

In my work as a speaker and trainer in the field of sales performance and business profitability, I teach business professionals, and especially those in sales, to quit thinking like salespeople. What we all need to do is to start thinking more like *customers*! Admittedly, this is not always the most natural thing to do.

As I built my own professional career, I managed to work my way into a very uncomfortable position. I had sought out opportunities to sell enterprise-wide solutions and long-term services engagements with price tags in six and seven figures in order to maximize my own income potential. But because of the cost and the scope of the things that I sold, I had no choice but to deal with business owners and senior executives. This meant I often had to engage people twice my age—some of whom made more money every month than I made in a year—and help them arrive at my conclusions.

It quickly became glaringly apparent that if I was going to be effective dealing with, for example, the chief financial officer (CFO) of a major corporation, then I was going to have to think like a CFO. And for me that was a problem. I didn't know how to think *like* a CFO, because I had never been one. But in time, with determination and a ton of personal effort, I did learn to think *about* what CFOs think *about*. And so can you. This book will show you how.

Your Customer's World

With the exception of those who make their living as purchasing agents or secret shoppers, most people aren't professional customers. Rather, they are professional engineers, accountants, human resource managers, customer service reps, chief executive officers (CEOs), or whatever. They spend their time thinking about the things that are most important to them and to the people they care about, are responsible for, and accountable to. They think about family issues, the weather, where to go for lunch, an upcoming sports event, or whichever global calamity dominated the morning news. While they're at work they also spend at least part of their time thinking about their jobs, their responsibilities, and their objectives, as well as the expectations and obligations placed on them by themselves and others.

While there is no way we can know everything our customers are thinking about, one thing is relatively certain: they're not spending a whole lot of time sitting around thinking about being our customer. In fact, dealing with vendors and suppliers is considered by many to be somewhat of a pain. Even those who frequently deal with outside vendors typically see it as a means to an end, and unless they work in procurement, it is just one of the many hats they wear each day.

Your customers, or those you hope soon will be, are busy. They are deluged with correspondence of every kind. They've got 150 e-mails in their inbox, eleven unplayed voice-mail messages, and a stack of papers on their desk that need to be dealt with ASAP. No wonder when we call it seems as if we are interrupting them. We are!

Imagine for a moment that you are one of the executives on your prospect list. What are some of the things that might occupy your mind? If you were in their position, would you make the time to take a phone call from a salesperson you didn't know? A general manager who attended one of our workshops recently shared his perspective with the team. He said, "Sometimes I do end up talking to salespeople on the phone . . . when I'm expecting a call from someone else and I accidentally pick up the wrong line."

Our customers (or clients) really aren't that much different than we are. Wouldn't it stand to reason that if we spend most of our day thinking about how to keep our boss happy and how to take better care of our customers, our clients probably spend most of their day thinking about how to keep *their* boss happy and how to take better care of *their* customers? If we could figure out how to help them do that, and then communicate to them that we could, we might find a lot less resistance.

At some point in my career, I came to the realization that . . .

> **In the business world, everybody has customers—
> those who buy, use, or benefit from whatever it is
> we produce or deliver—and serving our customers
> is the most important thing we do.**

For those of us in professional sales, our customers are the people outside our company who buy what we sell. But for many people in a corporate setting—whether department managers or individual contributors—their customer is their boss or some other "internal customer" who "buys" whatever they produce at a predetermined contract rate (a salary) and then uses that work product to serve and satisfy yet other internal customers within their company.

A design engineer's customer might be the manufacturing department that uses his blueprint as a guide to making a new product or component. The accounting department's customers are the various internal or external consumers of the financial data, reports, and analyses that they produce. The CEO's customers are the shareholders who "buy" a little piece of the company (i.e., shares of stock) based on the promise of favorable returns, which they hope will result in dividends and/or an increase in the value of each share of stock.

Learning to *Think Like Your Customer* requires each of us to look beyond how we interact with, deliver value to, and serve our own customers. We have to begin to think about how our customers, in turn, interact with, deliver value to, and serve *their* customers, whoever they may be. Only then can we truly begin to see ourselves the way our customers see us and understand how the products and services we bring to market can impact and add value to our customer's world.

A Partnership

Just about every company and every sales leader I meet and work with tells me, "We want our clients to think of us as more than just a vendor. We want to build strong partnerships with our clients." You know what? Your clients want that too! They wish somebody would come along who could help them identify the business problems that are keeping them from reaching their goals, help them determine which ones are the right problems to solve, and then roll up his sleeves and help them to achieve their desired business results.

Partnering with customers is not complicated, because . . .

> **The essence of partnership is working together
> toward a common goal or objective.**

Building a vendor-client partnership is based on working together with our customer toward the common goal of better serving *their* customers. We do this by helping them to deliver higher-quality products and services, faster and more cost-effectively than *their* competition. Selling something is actually a small part of it. In fact, if that's all we want to do, our customer will probably smell it a mile away. Buyers have a sense of discernment—to varying degrees, of course—but they can usually tell whether we are there to help them or to help ourselves.

Despite our good intentions, and our desire to follow the advice of author Stephen Covey, who said, "Seek first to understand, and then to be understood," many of us have been conditioned to start every introductory meeting with a quick overview of, "Who we are and what we do."[1] The truth is, our prospective customers are far more interested in who they are and what they do. We'd probably be better off if we quit trying to impress them with facts about us and instead impress them with what we have taken the time to learn about them.

What if we stopped talking about what we do long enough to learn a little more about what they do and how they do it? What if we took the time to find out what their customers have been asking them for lately, or what they think their customers could really benefit from, but they haven't yet figured out how to deliver? If we could brainstorm together about how we could help them to better serve *their* customers, or how we could help them better compete with *their* competitors, then partnering with us would be the only sensible thing to do.

To be perceived as more than just another vendor who will probably end up wasting their time, we will have to behave entirely differently than the other twenty-two vendors who will call them that day. We will have to come to the table with more than a glossy brochure and an "elevator pitch."

If we want to build strong partnering relationships with our clients and earn access to decision makers and senior executives—such as those at the C-Level (CEO, CFO, COO, CIO, etc.)—we should start by investing the time to learn more about their world, their business, their goals and objectives, as well as the obstacles standing in their way of achieving them. Only then can we effectively articulate how our products and services can enable them to reach those goals and objectives, be more competitive in the marketplace, and produce more business value.

One of the most important truths of selling, which we must accept and should constantly remind ourselves of, is . . .

> **Nobody wants to buy what you sell. What they want are the business results they can achieve by utilizing what you sell to pursue their own goals and objectives.**

Most of the things that you and I sell are not *ends* unto themselves. More often they are a *means* to an end. To develop a well-rounded understanding of your customer's business and the *ends* they are trying to accomplish, you'll probably have to talk to and interview several people who work there. Once we do earn access and get in front of a decision maker, we can't afford to waste their time or ours. We should start by doing some research before we even ask for the appointment. In the next section, we will look at some of the things we can learn *before* our first meeting with our customer.

Your Customer's Business

Some of the best resources from which to learn about your customer's business are the various corporate reports that all publicly traded companies, and many private companies, produce and make available to the public. By reading key sections of these documents, you can get an overview of your customer's business model, their high-level business strategy, their primary goals and objectives, and even some of the tactics they intend to employ to pursue these goals and objectives. The more you know about their business, the more likely you'll be to ask intelligent questions that lead to productive conversations.

Not too many years ago, it took a fair amount of time and effort to find and review enough information on a company to provide a good understanding of their business. Today, it's as close as your laptop. To make the most of this book, I'd like to encourage you to select a target prospect account, preferably one that is publicly held, so you can easily get plenty of information about the business.

If you sell only to privately held companies, see if you can find one of your prospect's direct competitors that is publicly traded to use as your case study account. You'll still be able to gather a lot of information about the market your customer competes in, as well as what particular challenges they are likely to face from their direct competitors.

Go to your target prospect's website and find the Investor Relations section, which is usually under About Us. You'll probably see subheadings such as Management Team, Mission, Frequently Asked Questions (FAQs), Stock Performance, Press Releases, and so on. All of them are worth review, but there are a few documents in particular that you'll want to look at closely. Take a minute to download or print the following documents:

1. The most recent Annual Report
2. The most recent SEC Form 10-K
3. The 3–5 most recent press releases
4. The 3–5 most recent news articles

1. The Annual Report

An Annual Report is a collection of corporate information and financial reports that most publicly held companies release approximately ninety days after the close of their fiscal year. The first page or two of most Annual Reports features a "Letter to the Shareholders" from the chairman of the board or CEO. This letter acts as an executive summary to the rest of the report and is a great place to start your research. In it, they normally provide a quick snapshot of the company's performance over the past year as compared to previous years. It also often contains the outlook for the future and sometimes offers details about the company's primary objectives, their plans for the future, and how senior management intends to carry them out.

Many companies' Annual Report takes on the look and feel of a sales brochure. That makes sense, because its primary purpose is to educate and inform investors who might want to buy their stock. It can also be a great resource for the sales professional who'll take the time to read it. You can normally learn about the relative performance of the various divisions or segments of their business, as well as some of their initiatives surrounding quality, safety, and corporate citizenship.

The Annual Report also contains at least the three primary financial reports: Income Statement, Balance Sheet, and Statement of Cash Flows. Learning to read and understand these key financial statements, as well as knowing exactly how you can impact your customer's financial results, is a vitally important skill-set for selling business solutions.

In Chapter 4, we will look more closely at how what we sell translates into economic business value.

If you have a financial background, or have learned how to read financial statements in college, you will have an edge on those salespeople who do not. Either way, don't get bogged down trying to analyze all the numbers. Just catch the spirit of what is being communicated. As you browse the Annual Report, what you want to learn are the answers to several general questions:

- Is this company growing and investing for the future? Are they just trying to hold on? Or are they losing ground in the marketplace and/or downsizing?
- Is this company expanding into new product lines and new markets? Or are they divesting (selling off) certain segments of their business to become more focused and streamlined?
- Are they making money and profit? Or are they losing money?
- If you owned or were managing this business, would you be excited and likely to embrace change and take chances on new ideas? Or would you be hunkering down, cutting back, and avoiding risk however possible?
- If you had some money to invest, would this be a good company to invest in?

The answers to these kinds of questions can give you an indication of how receptive your prospective client might be to the kinds of business solutions you bring to the table. It can also give you an idea of their appetite for investment in new business processes and technologies designed to support and propel growth, contain or drive down costs, or help them accomplish more with less infrastructure.

Don't forget to look in the very back of the Annual Report, where you will normally find a list of the senior officers and the board of directors. This is a great resource with which to begin constructing an organization chart that shows the various people you will likely need to interface with during your sales campaign. Make particular note of any executive biographies that may mention where these executives used to work. They might have come from another company that has experience with your company, either good or bad. Also, note any members of the board of directors who happen to work for companies that might already be on your company's client list.

2. The Form 10-K

An even better source for detailed corporate information than the Annual Report is a document that all publicly held companies are required to complete and file with the Securities and Exchange Commission (SEC) within ninety days of the close of each fiscal year. It's what the SEC calls a Form 10-K. If for some reason your case study account doesn't post their latest Form 10-K on their website, you can get it from the Securities and Exchange Commission website (www.sec.gov). You can query for it in the section called EDGAR (Electronic Data Gathering, Analysis, and Retrieval).

Companies tend to be far more forthcoming in the 10-K report than in the glossy Annual Report. They have to be. There is a standard format in which the SEC requires companies to disclose a broad variety of information to current and potential shareholders, which includes details about the company's financial performance, all properties owned by the corporation, any pending legal actions they may be faced with, as well as any potential threats or exposures to risk that management believes could substantially impact the company's ability to achieve its stated objectives.

This report contains a wide variety, and often an overwhelming quantity, of financial reports. Here again, don't get bogged down by the numbers. Invest most of your time in Part I, Item 1, which contains what the SEC calls a "narrative description" of the business. Companies are given some leeway in the presentation of this information, but topics common to many 10-K reports include:

Business Overview	Risk Factors Affecting the
Business Strategy	Company's Business
Industry Overview	Intellectual Property
Business Operations by	and Licensing
Segment or Division	Employees

Products and Services	Environmental, Health,
Markets and Marketing	and Safety Compliance
Research and Development	Executive Officers of
Competition	the Company
Government Regulation	Corporate Governance

3. Press Releases

Press releases serve the function of communicating information that the company wants the world to know. They often include:

- Quarterly financial reports
- The hiring or promotion of senior executives
- New product releases
- Announcements relating to mergers and acquisitions
- Major sales made to "household name" customers

One effective strategy for finding new business opportunities is to monitor your prospective customer's press releases. When something important happens—so important that your customer decides to issue a press release about it—this is a great time to initiate correspondence that mentions or relates to the press release you just read. Press releases almost always carry a quote by, or mention the name of, certain company executives or other personnel who might be receptive to hearing from you on a relevant topic. This also helps you further build your prospect list and organization chart.

We should also make it a habit to monitor our customer's press releases any time we are engaged in an active sales campaign. Changes in company leadership, the announcement of an upcoming merger, or missing a quarterly earnings estimate can all have a major impact on the conditions of a sales opportunity. Always try to stay as up to date as possible to reduce surprises of any kind.

4. News Articles

News articles in which your customer's senior executives have been quoted can also be very useful. Many of these kinds of comments tend to be forward-looking and may contain information about the outlook for their particular company or for the industry in general. They also frequently drop a few hints about their company's plans for the future, using the opportunity to communicate to both existing and potential investors. This can help us keep abreast of what's happening within our customer's business and help us to prepare for an upcoming meeting or telephone call.

You will probably agree that this kind of information would be very valuable to know before you try to get an executive on the phone, or before you drive or fly over for an introductory visit. We don't have to memorize the company's entire 10-K report. All we are looking for are a few items of particular interest that we can use to ask questions that stimulate conversation and discussion. As you read through, be on the lookout for information you can use, such as:

- What is their business model? How do they make money?
- What different lines of business are they in?
- Are they diversified in many product lines or focused on one thing?
- What segments or divisions of their business are growing?
- What segments or divisions are underperforming?
- Where do they see the greatest opportunity for growth?
- What markets do they serve geographically, demographically, or by industry segment?
- Who do they see as their primary competitors?

As a general rule of thumb, we should never ask an executive, or any key decision maker, a question that we could have found the answer to on the company website. Instead, we should ask questions based on the knowledge we have acquired *from* the information on the website, as well as other sources.

There are a myriad of other resources available on the Web ranging from industrial-strength, subscription-based content providers to free research information on sites like Yahoo (www.yahoo.com) and MSN (www.msn.com). Some of the subscription-based services, such as Lexis-Nexis (www.lexisnexis.com), serve the academic community, and most colleges offer access to their students and alumni. It's worth checking with your alma mater to see if you can get free or highly discounted access to one or more of these resources.

With some general knowledge of our customer's business, we can start to frame the questions we need to ask in order to learn even more. What we're looking for in all of this is a deeper understanding of our customer. We want to understand their business model, which I define as "How a company uses its assets to serve its customers and make a profit for its owners or shareholders," or more simply put, "How a company makes money." We want to understand their strategy for doing whatever it is they do *better* than their competition. And we want to understand the goals and objectives they are currently pursuing, as well as the business problems that are keeping them from reaching those goals.

Your Customer's Goals and Objectives

Once we have this knowledge we can position our solutions as the means to help them accomplish the goals and objectives they already have, because . . .

> **It's a lot easier to sell somebody something if it's positioned as a way to help them achieve a goal or an objective that they already want to achieve.**

We should certainly talk to our customers about new ways of doing business and new approaches that they could use to make their business even more profitable and more efficient in the future. But let's not overlook what they are trying to accomplish now—what they've got the time and money to act on *right now*—and help them accomplish those things. We should remember . . .

> **There will always be more business opportunities to invest in than there are time, money, and resources to invest in them.**

Our customers can't act on every good idea they have or that we as vendors present them with. They have to pick and choose. That picking and choosing can be quite complicated. Short-term goals, like containing costs by freezing wages, are often in conflict with long-term goals, like increasing morale and employee retention. Most companies have hundreds of great ideas and projects that are never acted on because they invest their resources in others they think are better or demand more urgent attention.

Corporate managers develop a list of goals and objectives through a process of valuation and prioritization, either formal or informal. Factors that influence prioritization could include:

- Return on investment of money, time, and other resources.
- Availability of those same resources.
- Competitive threats.
- Market opportunities.
- Stated objectives or promises to various stakeholders.
- Alignment with company values and mission.
- The personal or professional agenda of any particular person involved in the prioritization process.

Whatever their process, business managers end up with a list of prioritized goals and objectives for their business unit, department, or for the company as a whole, that looks something like the one in Figure 1.1. There may be hundreds of projects that all make the first cut and are deemed viable by certain standards, but companies seldom have the resources to fund them all.

Figure 1.1 Your Customer's Prioritized Goals and Objectives

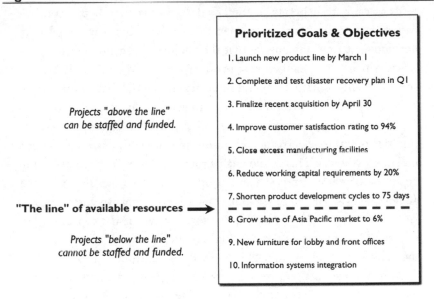

Projects "above the line" can be staffed and funded.

"The line" of available resources ➤

Projects "below the line" cannot be staffed and funded.

Prioritized Goals & Objectives

1. Launch new product line by March 1
2. Complete and test disaster recovery plan in Q1
3. Finalize recent acquisition by April 30
4. Improve customer satisfaction rating to 94%
5. Close excess manufacturing facilities
6. Reduce working capital requirements by 20%
7. Shorten product development cycles to 75 days
8. Grow share of Asia Pacific market to 6%
9. New furniture for lobby and front offices
10. Information systems integration

A line has to be drawn, above which are projects that can be staffed and funded and below which are others that cannot. If economic conditions tighten or revenue and profit lag behind projected forecasts, the line has to be moved up. Just because money is budgeted in August for an investment the following May doesn't necessarily mean your customer will actually have the money in their bank account when May comes around.

In order to maximize the likelihood of our success, we need to do one of two things. We have to make sure that the project—which the purchase of our products and services is part of—ends up above that line. Or we have to position our products and services solutions to support the execution of one of the goals or objectives that is *already* "above the line."

Notice, in Figure 1.1, "Information systems integration" is quite low on the list. It's not only "below the line." It even ranks lower than "New furniture for the lobby and front offices." If we happen to be in the systems integration business, we could be in trouble, that is if we continue to sell what we do as "systems integration."

What we should do is start positioning our ability to integrate systems as a way to help our customer's design experts to better collaborate with their manufacturing experts. In this way, they can cut product development time and ensure that they achieve their number one priority, which is to "Launch new product line by March 1." The same solution will contribute to number seven on the list, which is to "Shorten product development cycles to seventy-five days."

We could also position our systems integration services as a way for our customer to electronically communicate with *their* customer's inventory systems. This would enable them to dramatically improve the accuracy of their forecasts and production plans, resulting in the achievement of goal number four, which is to "Improve customer satisfaction rating to 94 percent." The more we can tie the capabilities of our solutions to our customer's highest-level business objectives, the more likely it is they will be able and willing to acquire them.

When money is tight, we see a lot of company managers practicing what I like to call "corporate triage." They really only treat the life-threatening wounds, and they let a lot of the little ailments go untreated. In an effort to contain or reduce costs, scheduled upgrades in equipment are often postponed, as long as it doesn't interrupt business operations. Likewise, new market opportunities might have to be passed up because of a lack of sales or marketing resources. A certain manufacturing problem, even one that is costing the company money, may go unaddressed if there are eight bigger problems that are costing even more.

When it comes to allocating resources and prioritizing which projects to invest in, we should remember that business managers are faced with a difficult decision . . .

The question is not whether any particular investment is good or bad, but whether it is better or worse than every other possible use of available capital and resources.

Our job, which is no small undertaking, is to learn enough about their business to answer the question, "What are the chief issues and concerns our prospective client is faced with? And of all the things they already know they need to do, which ones are they compelled to act on now, and which ones do they have the resources available to do something about?"

We are valuable to our clients in direct proportion to our unique ability to help them solve problems and achieve their business goals. So it's up to us to find out, first through our research and later through discovery:

- What exactly is this particular customer or prospect trying to accomplish?
- What are their goals in terms of revenue and growth?
- What are their goals for expanding into new markets?
- What are their goals in terms of on-time deliveries?
- What are their plans to reduce raw materials and finished goods inventories?
- What are their goals in terms of cost containment?
- What are their goals to reduce labor costs and overtime pay?
- What are their goals in terms of cash flow management?
- What are their goals in terms of workforce productivity?

This is just a small sample of the areas in which our customers have probably *already* established goals that they are trying to achieve. From here we will need to:

1. Understand these goals and objectives.
2. Understand how they rank and prioritize them.
3. Figure out what, if anything, our products and services can do to help them achieve each one.
4. Propose a plan of how we think we can help them solve the problems that stand between them and the achievement of these goals.

As we endeavor to understand how we can help our customer, it might also be helpful to know the answers to the following questions:

- What are the projects and initiatives that are already underway?
- What are the projects and initiatives that are planned for the near future?
- What is the criteria and rationale for how they prioritize their list?
- Who would be involved, and whose approval would be required, if they decided they wanted to re-prioritize the list?

Any particular project or problem that happens to appear at the top of the list for the director of information technology (IT) might be near the bottom of the list for the plant manager, and it may not even show up on the list of the CEO. To galvanize and bulletproof our sales campaign, we should take the time to ask whatever questions are necessary to understand the prioritized goals and objectives of each person we meet or who can influence our customer's buying decision.

Part of our job—as was illustrated in the earlier example—is to help the director of IT translate the value of systems integration into the kind of value that plant managers and CEOs care about, such as shorter product development cycles and improved customer satisfaction ratings. We may also have to help plant managers and CEOs understand how their corporate-level initiatives are made possible, or perhaps made more effective, by certain functional capabilities, such as systems integration. We will go much deeper into the concept I call "translating business value" in Chapters 4 and 9.

The Diagnostic Approach

What has been described here represents a major departure from the way many of us have been taught to sell. This approach takes the focus *off* the product or services solutions that we sell. Instead, it puts the focus on the business results that our clients are trying to achieve and the business value they can produce by using our products or services to pursue their business goals and objectives.

This method, and the discovery process that it requires, is what I like to call the "diagnostic approach." It stands in stark contrast to the outmoded and archaic manner of selling that we have come to refer to as "broadcasting." We've all seen the broadcast approach in action. Most of us (including me) are even guilty of falling into it from time to time. It's where the salesperson describes their product and services solutions, and their company, in intimate detail to make sure their customer hears all the advantages and benefits, as well as exactly how their solutions can be used in the customer's business. It's then left up to the customer to determine whether or not any of those benefits or functional capabilities happen to line up with the problems they are trying to solve or the business goals they are trying to achieve.

Our customers shouldn't have to do that for themselves. In fact, we can't afford to leave it up to them to connect the dots between our functional capabilities and their goals. They don't know enough about how our solutions work, or the different ways they can be implemented, to effectively map our capabilities to their desired outcomes and results. That's *our* job to do!

The diagnostic approach, which is at the foundation of everything in this book, requires that we engage in research and discovery ahead of time, so that when we do earn the right to sit down with senior managers and decision makers, we can ask intelligent and informed questions about what they are trying to accomplish and how they are currently going about it. Only when we understand that can we offer sound recommendations on how our products and services could be used to achieve those goals and objectives faster, at a higher rate of return, or with greater predictability, than they could otherwise achieve without them.

I believe that when we engage customers, we should be less like salespeople and more like doctors. We should take the time to get a good history, understand what's going well and what's not, conduct a thorough examination, and carefully arrive at a "diagnosis" that our prospective client can truly have faith in.

Imagine walking into your doctor's office for a standard check-up. You've been feeling pretty good lately except for one sore knee that's been bugging you for a while. You're seen into the examination room

and seated comfortably on that cold table in one of those flattering little outfits affectionately referred to as a johnny. After a wait, the doctor walks in and says,

> *"Hello there, my name is Doctor Johnson. Let me tell you about penicillin.*
> *Penicillin is the most exciting drug . . . This thing will solve just about any*
> *problem you've got. It's been around for over one hundred years, and it's*
> *been proven effective with millions of patients all over the world. I've*
> *prescribed it myself to hundreds of patients with tremendous success. Let me*
> *show you a list of people in your town who have taken penicillin. I know*
> *one woman who was on the verge of death, but after taking penicillin, she's*
> *up and about and planning to run the Boston Marathon next year. It's safe,*
> *it's effective, and best of all it's available right now at your local pharmacy.*
> *Should I put you down for one bottle or two bottles of penicillin today?"*

People usually get a good laugh out of this in my workshops. But
how different is this from some of the "Introductory Overview" slide
presentations you've seen lately? Do our customers want to sit through
all those bullet points about "Who we are," "How many offices we
have," or "Where our founder went to college"? Is that really what they
care to hear about?

My critics say, "Bill, that's how you build credibility." Nonsense! You
build your credibility by demonstrating your knowledge of *their* industry, your knowledge of *their* business, and your ability to ask intelligent
questions, diagnose problems, and discuss possible solutions to the problems that stand between your client and the achievement of their goals
and objectives.

No doctor would dream of pitching you on penicillin as in the example above. A good doctor walks in and starts asking questions . . .

> *"Good morning. Why have you come to see me today?"*

> *"Well, Doctor, I'm here for my check-up and I'm feeling pretty well except*
> *for a sore knee."*

Does she go right to the knee? No. She saves that for last. She takes
you through the whole examination: heart rate, temperature, blood

pressure, eyes, ears, nose, throat, and so on. She checks your reflexes. Then she gets out the stethoscope:

"OK. Breathe deeply"

. . . the whole nine yards. Then, and only then, she says . . .

"Tell me about that knee. How long has it been hurting?"

"About two weeks."

"Did you do anything that may have caused an injury to it: sports, dancing, a fall, or something?"

"No. Not that I can think of."

"Well, did it hurt more two weeks ago and less now? Or did it start hurting just a little two weeks ago, but now it's getting worse?"

"About the same all along, I guess."

"Do you have any family history of knee or joint problems, arthritis, etc.?"

. . . she takes the time to really diagnose.

No wonder we have so much faith in doctors. When they finally do get through with the examination and write the prescription on the little piece of paper, you don't even ask any questions, do you? You can't even read the thing! But you take it right down to the pharmacy and whatever they give you back you just swallow it, no questions asked. Wouldn't it be great if we could sell like that? I'm not saying we can ever be as trusted as doctors, but we can work toward that. And it starts by being willing to quit broadcasting and start becoming an expert diagnostician.

If we intend to be perceived as something other than a "salesman," and move beyond the status of supplier or vendor toward becoming a partner or an advisor, we have to do some things differently than our competitors do. The other vendors will be trying to get within earshot of an executive decision maker so they can deliver their "message" or their "elevator pitch." What you and I will do is conduct enough research and preparation to craft two or three well-informed "elevator questions." Your prospective customers will quickly recognize the difference.

At this point in my workshops, someone almost always asks, "Bill, do we really need to invest all this time to get to know our customer's business to this level of detail?" All I can say is that if you don't invest the time, somebody else will. But you're not going to invest this much effort for every single prospect. In fact, the more proficient you become at analyzing and evaluating sales opportunities, the more you will be screening out the ones you think aren't worth investing your time in. The return on your time and effort will be just like in every other endeavor in life. Eighty percent will appear to be completely wasted. But if you will go ahead and invest the 80 percent anyway, the other 20 percent will make you rich!

CHAPTER 2

What Customers Really Want

The role of a business manager, whether a CEO who leads a vast enterprise or a director of research and development (R&D) who leads a small team of engineers responsible for new product development, is to leverage all available resources to pursue and achieve his or her goals and objectives. Through this process, business value is created. What all managers want, then, is to accomplish all they can with the resources they have available, or to maximize the value that their unit is able to create in any given period of time. In short, they want results.

Managers know that in order to reach their goals and objectives, they will have to take certain risks. They will have to invest resources—in the way of time, money, and manpower—using a reliable strategy in pursuit of the right goals in order to achieve their objectives. Sometimes the investment of resources involves buying goods and/or services that they will employ to achieve the results they want. That's where you and I come in.

I often begin my workshops by asking participants a very important question: "What is selling?" The answers I hear reveal a lot about how participants see themselves and how they think about their work. Within the answers, I often hear words like "convincing" and "persuading," but I also usually hear "helping" and "providing." In most sessions, some person eventually repeats the sentence that has somehow become universally accepted as the correct answer to this question: "Understanding your customer's needs, and fulfilling those needs."

Once this phrase is uttered, no one else will say a word. The whole group just nods.

I must admit, it's pretty hard to argue against this definition. No one could deny that there is tremendous value in fulfilling your customer's needs, whether they be professional needs or personal needs. But is it really enough that our customer has a need? Or that we fully understand that need? One of the major tenets on which this book is based, which is sometimes a little tough to accept at first, is . . .

**It's not enough that your customer has a need,
because needs go unfulfilled every day.**

One of my favorite questions to ask a group is, "Have any of you in the room ever had a personal need in your life go unfulfilled?" It always manages to draw a laugh. The answer is so obvious. If we have personal needs that are going unfulfilled, then wouldn't it stand to reason that there are probably corporate needs going unfulfilled, too? Of course there are! The practice of corporate triage—which we discussed in Chapter 1—basically reminds us that companies have to prioritize projects and investment opportunities because they don't have the time or the money to pursue them all. Some needs are simply left unfulfilled, either temporarily or permanently.

I wish I had a dollar for every time a prospect looked at me and said, "Oh, we know we have a problem, and it's costing us thousands of dollars every month. We know that we *need* your solution, and it's also clear to us that it is far superior to anything your competition has to offer. But right now we are so busy with so many other projects . . . if you would just come back and see us in six months, we would probably be ready to move forward."

Of all the times I have heard this and have gone back to see them in six months, I can't remember any of them ever buying anything. I regularly poll my audiences to see how many have heard these same words, and how many have gone back in six months and actually sold some-

Figure 2.1 The Customer Results Model with a Gap

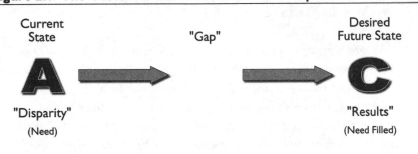

thing. So far, I have found two cases out of thousands where the customer *did buy* the second time around. Many needs go unfulfilled forever. It's up to us to look beyond our customer's needs if we are to understand *why* customers buy.

Needs vs. Results

We find our customers at what I like to call point "A." It's a *current state*. They probably have all kinds of needs, whether or not they recognize them as such. But what we are looking for is what I call a *disparity*. It might be a need, problem, pain, obstacle, or it might be an opportunity of some kind that they have not yet recognized or taken advantage of. It could be seen as a "gap" between where they are now and where they would like to be, and it might take us coming along and letting them know that there *is* a better place to be before they can envision it. We are looking for a customer who already has, or will let us help them to create, a vision of a *desired future state* that is better than the current state they are in now. I like to refer to this desired future state as point "C." See Figure 2.1.

We should do all we can to understand point "A" (the customer's current state), by asking key questions to learn . . .

- Are they happy with the way things are going right now?
- Do they recognize any needs that they feel must be addressed?

- Is there a disparity between where they are now and where they would really like to be?

We need to understand the circumstances surrounding point "A" because they can give us valuable information and ideas about how our customer got to that point and what they might be able to do to get away from it. But we should spend just as much, if not more, of our time and effort trying to gain a better understanding of point "C," where their need is fulfilled and the disparity or the "gap" no longer exists. It is "C," after all, that they *want*. This is a vital distinction. Identifying and pointing out needs or deficiencies is easy, but helping our customer think about and vividly imagine what their world might be like at point "C" is how we move from demand fulfillment to demand creation.

If we've done our research up front, we can craft a few key questions that help lead our customers to arrive at our conclusions. If, for example, you sell market research and analytic services, which help companies make smarter decisions about entering new markets—as does one of my best clients—you might pose a question like this:

> *"I read in your Annual Report that you are planning to expand into several new international markets over the next couple of years. If everything goes as planned, how many different countries will you be in by the end of next year?"*

This information will help us to understand where they are going and how aggressively they are planning to expand. If we want to learn more about their specific plans and lead them even closer to our conclusion, we can follow up with a question like this:

> *"How will you decide which markets offer the best upside revenue potential, with the least capital investment, or the least downside risk in terms of market acceptance?"*

Another excellent line of questioning that can help us better understand our customer's desired point "C" is to ask what I call a "prioritizing question." Here's an example:

"Your last 10-K report mentioned three major competitive threats as you see them:

1. ***Globalization:*** *Giving some of your overseas competitors an edge because they are able to operate at a lower overall cost basis than you are.*
2. ***Commoditization:*** *Resulting from so many players offering nearly identical products at lower and lower prices.*
3. ***The Rate of Technological Advancement:*** *Rendering any new product you bring to market obsolete in 90 to 120 days.*

Which of these do you consider the most worrisome?"

A question like this should always be followed by three more crucial questions:

1. "Why do you think that?"
2. "How do you plan to respond to that threat?"
3. "What would be the ideal outcome if everything went as planned?"

Your customer has plenty of plans and initiatives they are already committed to pursuing. They've already got plenty of goals and objectives, and plenty of problems that are standing in their way. We just need to learn what those plans and goals are.

If your customer is more focused on solving a particular problem than achieving a specific goal, we could ask:

• "What is the highest level objective you are trying to accomplish?"
• "What is the desired result you are trying to achieve?"
• "What do you see as the most valuable outcome of solving this problem?"

Once we get a good understanding of what "C" looks like to our customer, then and only then can we properly position our products and services at point "B," as the mechanism or the vehicle that takes them from "A" to "C" as shown in Figure 2.2.

I want to emphasize that our "B" only has relevance as it pertains to enabling our customers to arrive at "C." Because the honest truth is . . .

There is no value to our customers in *our* product or service solutions, but only in *their* desired outcomes or results.

This model reinforces a change in the way many of us think about selling. This is not the traditional selling of products and services, features and benefits, or even solutions to problems. What we are talking about selling here are *results* . . . results that contribute real value to our customer's business or to their personal lives. I have heard it said that customers don't buy what they need; they buy what they want. What this "Customer Results Model" illuminates is that . . .

Customers buy what they need so they can get what they want. They don't want a solution; what they want are results.

I like to ask my workshop participants, "Can your prospect *tell* whether you are focused more on "B" (the things you sell) than "C" (their business goals)?" Everybody seems to agree that customers can tell quite easily. "How is it possible that they can tell?" I ask. The answer is "By the things we say and do and especially by the questions that we ask."

In a complex buying decision, which carries a substantial degree of inherent risk, customers almost always buy from the seller who . . .

1. Best understands their ideal point "C."
2. Provides the simplest and most reliable plan to help them get from "A" to "C."

Figure 2.2 The Customer Results Model

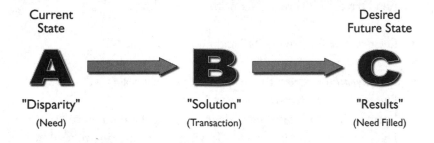

3. Makes them feel most confident about reaching "C" on time and on budget.

. . . not necessarily the vendor who offers the lowest price.

I am always willing to pay a little more to buy from someone who takes the time to understand what I am trying to accomplish, helps me evaluate my options, and then helps me select the right solution. You're probably the same way. Most of your customers are too.

Action Drivers

If selling were simply a process of understanding our customer's goals and objectives and then coming up with a way to help them achieve them, then we would win every sales opportunity we engage in, wouldn't we? Unfortunately, there are a few other factors involved. Customers don't pursue every "C" they can imagine because they don't have enough time and money to achieve them all. They have to choose among the available options by assessing which are the best ones to pursue right now. It is a process of valuation or prioritization as we discussed in Chapter 1. Now let's take a closer look at some of the variables or criteria used in that valuation process.

To position our "B" (our product and services solutions) in the best possible light, we have to understand not only what our customer's "C" is, but also the conditions and the *drivers* that surround their desire to leave "A" and move toward "C." I like to refer to these conditions as "Action Drivers." There are six of them as follows:

- Their *motive* for leaving "A" and moving toward "C"
- The *urgency* to arrive at "C"
- The *payback* or *return* they expect when they reach "C"
- The *consequences* for staying at "A"
- Their available *resources* or their *means* to make the trip to "C"
- The perceived *risks* involved in leaving "A" or moving toward "C"

Understanding these Action Drivers, and the degree to which your customer feels them, isn't as complicated as it might sound. It's really just asking more of the right questions. Next, we will go through the six Action Drivers offering sample questions to better understand each one.

When you are meeting face to face with your prospective client, or even while you are conducting research ahead of time, be on the lookout for the presence of these Action Drivers. When you find a customer who has a desired point "C" and is driven by these six Action Drivers to arrive there, then you've got a real opportunity on your hands. If you can get your prospect to start talking about his goals and objectives, all you have to do is remember to ask some variation of the questions that relate to the six Action Drivers.

	Questions Beginning With	Relate To
1.	"Why . . . ?"	Motive
2.	"When . . . ?"	Urgency
3.	"How much . . . ?"	Payback or Return
	"How many . . . ?"	
4.	"What if you don't . . . ?"	Consequence
5.	"How would you . . . ?"	Resources or Means
	"How do you plan to . . . ?"	
6.	"Is there any downside . . . ?"	Risk
	"What are the obstacles . . . ?"	
	"What could go wrong . . . ?"	

I'm not so worried about the structure of your questions (open-ended, closed-ended, either/or, etc.), as much as with the *substance* of your questions. By asking these questions, you are asking about the things that really drive buyer behavior and enable you to better understand the quality of the sales opportunity at hand.

These drivers could be strictly business related, personal, or both. There could very well be a business motive *and* a personal motive, a business urgency *and* a personal urgency, as well as a business risk *and* a personal risk at play. A chief information officer (CIO), for example, may recognize a strong business motive to outsource as many IT functions as possible, in order to contain or cut costs. But she could also perceive outsourcing to be a personal risk because a smaller in-house IT staff means a smaller budget and perhaps less need for a CIO. If we listen closely and ask the right questions, we'll hear both personal drivers and business drivers that affect any individual's judgment and decision-making process.

1. Motive

Once your client acknowledges a need, problem, pain, obstacle, or some other description of the *disparity* that exists at point "A," and has also expressed an interest in moving toward a desired point "C," the most important question we should be asking ourselves is, "Why would they do this?" There is no single question that is more important in our quest to understand and qualify any sales opportunity.

Remember, reaching point "C" will require time, attention, and resources on your customer's part. And if it requires passing through "B" on the way and giving us some money as they go by, they're going to need a good reason to do it. I think it's safe to assume that . . .

If your customer can get from "A" to "C" without you, they probably will.

We want to know, as early on as possible, what would motivate our customer to hand us a large sum of money and then spend months and maybe even years implementing whatever solution we sold them. If they don't have a strong enough motive to leave the perceived safety of the status quo and venture into the unknown in search of a better reality, they might just choose to stay at point "A." To understand Motive, we need to ask, "Why . . . ?"

- "Why is this desired outcome so important to you right now?"
- "Why would achieving this objective be of value?"
- "Why does this disparity you've discovered constitute a problem?"
- "Why does this disparity exist?"
- "Why haven't you done something about it before?"
- "Why would you invest money to solve this problem rather than investing that money to address some of the other needs that the company has?"
- "Why couldn't you let someone else in the company worry about solving this problem?"
- "Why not just 'do nothing' and hope it works itself out on its own?"

2. Urgency

Just because a project or a new initiative is worth pursuing doesn't mean your customer has to act on it *now*. Even the biggest companies have limits on available resources. Priority is often determined more by urgency than by long-term importance or significance. Urgent problems have a way of siphoning resources away from more important projects and initiatives that don't pose as great of a short-term threat.

A lack of buyer urgency is one of the most troublesome issues that sales professionals deal with. Therefore, begin as early as possible asking your customer questions to determine or establish their level of urgency. These questions begin with "When . . . ?"

- "When would you like to reach this goal you have defined?"
- "When did you discover this obstacle to achieving your goal?"
- "When did you decide something needed to be done?"
- "When will this medium-size problem become a big problem?"

- "When do you think you need to take action to solve this problem?"
- "When does this project need to be underway?"
- "When would you like to start seeing results?"

Buyer urgency is often overlooked early in sales campaigns. Our assumption is that once they see and hear how great our solutions are, they will want to hurry up and buy them. Don't fall for this. Without an urgency that is driven by their desire to reach point "C," the sales opportunity can easily slip from one month to the next, one quarter to the next, and even one year to the next, indefinitely.

No amount of customer enthusiasm for, or interest in, your "B" can make up for a lack of urgency to reach "C." Some other project or some other initiative that demands more urgent attention can easily come along and steal away those highly coveted resources that were supposed to be used to buy your solution.

3. Payback or Return

Another major factor in establishing priority and resource allocation is the potential payback or the return on the time, money, and resources invested. Return, especially economic return, is evaluated on three different scales:

1. **Quantity:** How much return is possible?
2. **Speed:** How quickly can we expect those returns?
3. **Certainty:** How predictable are those returns?

Of course, *we* will be actively trying to determine the quantity, speed, and certainty of the potential payback so we can share our estimates with our client. This will become a crucial component of our overall value proposition. But to position ourselves and our solutions effectively, we should always begin by finding out what return or payback *our customer* expects or anticipates when they arrive at point "C."

We help to quantify payback or return in their mind by asking questions that begin with "How much . . . ?" or "How many . . . ?"

- "How much time could you save if you decided to move forward with this initiative?"
- "How many people would that free up for other projects?"
- "How much extra warehouse space could you lease to someone else if you were able to reduce your inventories by 20 percent?
- "How many more customer orders could you handle each day using this new system?"
- "How many days could we drive out of your product development cycles if we could cut your product testing time in half?"
- "How much money could be freed up for reinvestment if we were able to help you reduce your average accounts receivable cycle from forty days to thirty-five days?"
- "How much do you think this problem is costing you each month?"

At the end of the day, any investment has to be worth making. And as I pointed out in Chapter 1, it has to be better than the other possible uses of available resources. Unfortunately, it doesn't really matter how we think our clients should invest their resources; what matters is how *they* think they should. Our job is to find out *how* they think and *why* they think that way.

4. Consequence

You may have read or heard that "motivation comes from within." That might be true, but consequences come from without. How else can we explain certain behaviors? Do you suppose that every February 14, millions of men all simply wake up with an uncontrollable urge to buy flowers? Is it sheer coincidence that millions of Americans, every April 15, simultaneously have the inspiration to file their personal income tax returns?

Psychologists have found that our desire to avoid loss is much stronger than our desire for potential gain. One famous study found that most people would much sooner take $500 for sure, than take a fifty-fifty chance of winning $1,000. Likewise, far more people who had $1,000 would take a fifty-fifty chance of losing it all, as opposed to just handing over $500. In our minds, and the minds of customers, losses loom larger than gains.[1]

Because of this fact, the potential consequence of inaction is often the most reliable Action Driver of all. If we can identify a consequence that matters enough, to enough of the people involved in the decision, the likelihood of that decision going our way is substantially increased. We will look much more closely at consequence in Chapter 7 as we explore the "Anatomy of a Buying Decision." As we converse with customers and learn about their goals and objectives, we can look for Consequence by asking questions beginning with "What if . . . ?"

- "What if you just put this project off until next year?"
- "What if you just kept doing it the same old way?"
- "What if you just did nothing? What would happen?"
- "What if you put this off another month? What would that cost you?"
- "What if you decided you wanted to move ahead with this but you couldn't get it approved?"
- "What if your finance department didn't release the funding for another ninety days?"

Occasionally, in a seminar, I get a little push back on this one. "Bill, you should never ask a customer something like that," they say. "You don't want to put the idea in their head that it's OK to delay the purchase." Let's not be naïve. Companies don't buy on impulse. In fact, that's the main reason companies institute buying policies that require a documented evaluation plan, multiple bids, a cost justification, and an elaborate approval process. There are multiple checks and balances put in place specifically to reduce the likelihood of buying something without considering all of the potential consequences and risks.

In a complex buying decision involving many decision makers and influencers, the question of "Can we put this off for a while?" is one of the most basic questions they will ask. And if they still have to buy something but *can* wait until next quarter to do it, they probably will. I'd rather find out early on that there is little or no consequence for them to just stay at point "A." Then I can better prioritize my time, set expectations within my company, and go to work figuring out how to identify and leverage some *other* time-bound trigger that represents some sort of consequence to one or more of the people involved in the decision.

5. Resources or Means

Sometimes, when we meet a prospective client who shows an interest in us and what we sell, we assume that if they decide they want to buy, we've got a deal. Well, that's not all there is to it, I'm afraid. We've already talked about limited resources and unlimited opportunities, as well as the process of prioritization and allocation.

When we discover what looks like a new opportunity to help our client achieve an objective using one or more of our products or services, let's also make sure they actually have the means to acquire it, implement it, and make use of it. Some of the most embarrassing memories of my career resulted from my naïve assumption that once I convinced them they *should* buy, they were automatically *able to* buy. The question we need to answer is, "Do they have the money and the manpower to get to point "C" if they want to?"

I remember one beautiful August morning a number of years ago when I received a phone call from the CFO of my number one prospect at the time. I had invested ten months on what promised to be a multimillion-dollar sale of enterprise software applications, and I thought to myself, "This is the call I've been waiting for."

I had sat across the table from him months earlier, with my boss and his boss flanking, looked him in the eye and said, "I know your company has been struggling financially, and I know you are turning things around. But we will be investing thousands of dollars and hundreds of man-hours in this process of mutual discovery, and I need to know if there is any scenario under which you will not be able to afford to make this investment." His reply was an emphatic, "No. This is a strategic investment for us. We see this as part of our turn-around strategy, and we have to get this done." His boss, the CEO, was nodding in support.

On that August morning phone call, after I had invested all that money and time, the CFO said, "Bill, we just called your primary competitor and told them we are sorry, but we've decided to go with you." Have you ever had the feeling you're about to hear a really big "BUT"?

"But," he continued, "I also just spoke with the bank and they want to see two more quarters of growth and execution on our strategic plan before they will provide us with the letter of credit we need to take advantage of the financing you arranged for us."

I'm sure that you've already guessed; they never did buy. In retrospect, I still think that it was that CFO's responsibility to contact the bank to make sure they would provide the letter of credit before he allowed his people to invest their time—and waste our time—in an elaborate selection process. But it was clearly my responsibility to know whether or not he had done that.

People in my workshops often wonder why I tell stories about deals I lost. It's because I've learned a lot more from my losses than I have from my wins. This particular disaster stirs emotion in me to this day, but I've been far less shy about asking resource and means questions ever since. You have a right, and indeed *a responsibility*, to ask all the questions about Resources and Means you can think of. Make sure that if you're going to invest your selling time, they've got the resources to buy and use your solutions by asking "How . . . ?"

- "How do you plan to accomplish this particular objective?"
- "How do you see your project plan rolling out?"
- "How would you manage a project of this size and scope?"
- "How would you fund a project like this if you decided to move forward?"
- "How does an investment of this magnitude get approved? Does your board of directors get involved?"
- "How would you cost-justify an investment like this? Is there an elaborate capital budgeting process you have to go through to get approval?"

- "How could we both be sure that your bank will provide the letter of credit you would need to take advantage of the financing we've arranged for you?"

Hindsight is a wonderful thing.

6. Risk

I like to remind salespeople that there are always three elements of competition in every deal. First, there are those who sell what you sell, the other vendors or suppliers your customer will consider as a source. Second, there are all the other projects that will compete for the same limited capital dollars. It is possible that our primary competition for the $300,000 our customer will need to buy new networking equipment is a new advertising campaign designed to boost revenue this quarter. Third, and perhaps the most formidable of all, is the risk of taking action as opposed to doing nothing.

When the individuals within the company feel confident about the future, such that they expect to meet or exceed their revenue and profitability forecasts, then our primary competition for capital are the other investments they are considering. But when our customers feel the future is less certain, and they are worried about being able to meet their obligations, sometimes doing nothing—or at least doing nothing *new*—is the smartest thing they can do. The element of risk can be the fiercest competitor we ever go up against.

Risk is present to some degree in any investment situation. In Chapter 10, we will talk more about managing and mitigating both actual and perceived risk. For now, let's just be sure to ask our customers the questions that can reveal to us how sure they feel about their chances of arriving at point "C" unscathed and achieving the results they want to achieve. Some good risk-related questions are:

- "What do you see as the risks involved in this endeavor?"
- "Is there any downside to starting this project right away?"
- "What are the obstacles to your success as you see them?"
- "What could go wrong?"
- "What could be done to reduce the likelihood of that happening?"

If we can understand the risks our customer perceives earlier in the process, we'll have more time to deal with them by mitigating or eliminating actual risks or influencing our client's perception of them through education and positioning.

Recognizing Future Objections

The issue of handling and overcoming objections always seems to be a hot topic among the sales teams I work with, and I have included several proven techniques for dealing with objections in Chapters 3 and 10. But the best way, by far, to deal with an objection is to recognize it and handle it before it becomes an objection.

In our workshops, we dedicate a whole segment to the topic of overcoming objections. We start with a clean flip chart or whiteboard and ask the group to name every possible objection they have ever heard or can think of. Some examples include:

- "We've decided to just keep things the way they are for now."
- "We are too busy with other projects right now."
- "We have depleted our budget for this quarter."

Some of them are rather unique and others are downright comical:

> *"We wouldn't want to automate this process because several of our best people would be out of work."*

Or . . .

> *"If we provide our people too much training, they'll start looking for a better job."*

Once we list every objection that the participants can imagine, we break them down into groups. There are two major kinds of objections: (1) objections about buying *in general*, and (2) objections about buying *from you specifically*. Once we separate the two and look more closely, we see that the objections to buying from you specifically can be quite varied and have to do with matters of choice. Many of these objections refer to what I call "Choice Drivers," which we will explore in depth in Chapter 7.

When we look at the list of general objections, we normally see that every one of them is directly related to the absence of, or a weakness in, one of the six Action Drivers. The overwhelming majority of all the objections you will ever hear reveal one or more of the following:

1. Lack of Motive
2. Lack of Urgency
3. Lack of Payback or Return
4. Lack of Consequence
5. Lack of Resources or Means
6. Excessive Perceived Risk

Wouldn't it be a good idea to find out early exactly what objections, potholes, roadblocks, or brick walls we might encounter down the road? I encourage you to memorize this list of Action Drivers and their related questions so you can weave them into every customer conversation. Some people find it easier to memorize:

1. Motive
2. Urgency
3. Return
4. Consequence
5. Means
6. Risk

Others prefer to remember the first word or two of the related questions:

1. "Why . . . ?"
2. "When . . . ?"
3. "How much . . . ?" or "How many . . . ?"
4. "What if you don't . . . ?"

5. "How would you . . . ?" or "How do you plan to . . . ?"
6. "Is there any downside . . . ?" or "What could go wrong . . . ?"

However you do it, make asking these questions as natural, and as much a part of your normal discovery process, as asking for their phone number and their e-mail address. The value and importance of these six questions is second only to the questions that reveal your customer's vision of an ideal point "C." Without the answers to these six questions, which illuminate your customer's *desire to reach* point "C," you really can't understand much at all about *why* your customer would buy.

The Customer Results Model (i.e., "A," "B," and "C"), and the six Action Drivers (along with their related questions), are absolutely foundational to everything presented throughout the rest of this book. I encourage you to quickly review these two ideas presented in this chapter to make sure you are comfortable with them before moving on. You may also want to come back to them whenever you feel the need to in the future. Yes, they're just common sense. That's what makes them so powerful and important. But that doesn't mean that we don't need to remind ourselves of them from time to time.

Everything in this chapter relates to better understanding what your customer really wants and the reasons they want it. It's all part of what most sales professionals would call qualification. The value of sales qualification is in determining the "quality" or close-ability of each sales opportunity in our pipeline in order to prioritize our efforts and properly allocate sales resources. Therefore, answering a question like, "How many do they want to buy, and when do they want to buy them?" hardly scratches the surface of what we should know. What we really need to know is *why* they would want to buy something in the first place and *how* they could buy it if they wanted to. That's why I decided to make this entire book about "How and Why Your Customers Buy."

Unless we have a clear understanding of these two basic elements, we have not really qualified an opportunity, because either of these can make or break any deal. It is actually very common to discover that your buyer hasn't yet *fully* considered both of these things and all of the specific details of each. To conduct a bulletproof sales campaign, we'll need to understand—and help our clients understand—all of the variables we have discussed in this chapter and many more.

I happen to believe that . . .

**Qualifying sales opportunities is not difficult.
What is difficult is accepting what you learn when
you do qualify.**

It might be tough to take when you discover that your customer has no real urgency to buy right now, or despite their motive and their urgency, they simply don't have the means to take action. But I'd rather find out now than the last two days of the quarter, wouldn't you? I've heard it said that "ignorance is bliss," but in my experience it doesn't pay much.

CHAPTER 3

How Customers Perceive Value and Risk

There is an equation that governs commerce, and business in general, that we need to understand backward and forward. I call this the "Value Equation" because at its most fundamental level . . .

**Buying and selling is trading one kind of value
for another.**

Our customers need the functional capabilities that our products and services can provide in order to achieve their goals. Since it's our job to sell those products and services, we arrange a trade. We deliver *value* to them, and they deliver *money* to us, as is shown in Figure 3.1.

Like an algebraic equation, this exchange has to balance. The value we deliver needs to be at least equal to, if not greater than, the money we are asking for. It doesn't really matter to our buyer whether or not *we* think the trade is balanced. What matters is whether or not *they* think it is.

If your customer thinks that the value of what you are offering is not equal to or greater than the money you are asking them for, they probably won't buy. In order to balance the equation, the customer's proposed remedy is almost always "lower the price." But is that the only way this equation can be brought into balance? Another way to balance the trade is to increase the value on our side of the equation. But we should always remember that . . .

> **It's not the actual value of what we sell, but the customer's *perceived value*, that really matters.**

This perception is, of course, a subjective opinion, but it's the only opinion that counts. We have to accept that the buyer's perception of value governs all of their decision making and behavior. In this chapter we will explore how our customers perceive value, as well as the things we can do to influence that perception, by looking at:

1. The kinds of value our customers want to derive from a relationship with us and our company, which I call the "Denominations of Value."
2. The things we bring to the table that provide that value, which I call the "Sources of Value."
3. How the two tie together in our customer's mind.

Understanding Value

Despite our best efforts to define and quantify value, the process of valuation remains very subjective. There are standards that can be used to quantify the economic value of an asset (normally based on the cash flow that the asset can be used to produce over a certain period of time), but there is no standard for desirability. A free market economy sets a standard for the value of any product or service based on supply and demand and how much any individual or organization is willing to pay for it. What is highly valuable to one, though, might not have the same appeal to another. The reason for this is very simple . . .

> **Value is in the eye of the beholder, and each person perceives it differently.**

Figure 3.1 The Value Equation

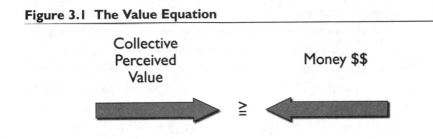

Not just every company, but every person within every company has his or her own unique perception of value. That perception has been established over a period of many years by their own set of beliefs, their background, their upbringing, their education, and their experience. It is further colored by their perspective from the position they occupy. Their individual roles and responsibilities can cause them to see value in a completely different way than someone filling a different role.

When a company is faced with a complex buying decision that may involve multiple decision makers and influencers, it is actually the *collective perceived value* of all the individuals involved in a decision that will ultimately be weighed against the money we ask them for. A design engineer, for example, may perceive our solution as a means of improving his ability to collaborate with the manufacturing department, thus making his job much easier. His perception of value will be combined with that of the controller who may see our solution as an unnecessary luxury and an unjustified expense. The collective perceived value is based on the average perception of all of the people involved.

A perception of value is not static. It changes over time, and it can change rapidly with the introduction of new information or when framed in a new context. This means that a person's judgment and decision-making criteria will be different based on each judgment or decision they are faced with. The reasons they decided to buy or not to buy a new piece of manufacturing equipment yesterday will probably be entirely different from the criteria they use to decide whether or not to hire three new office temps today.

What we need to know is what constitutes value to them right here, right now, on the particular project or decision at hand. Research can give us clues, but to get a real understanding of how your customer sees value, you'll have to ask them some questions.

In Chapter 2 we talked about asking your customer questions to discover more than just their needs but also their desired results. We also talked about the questions that reveal both their desire to leave point "A," the current state your customer is in when you find them, and what drives them toward "C," their desired future state where they have achieved the results they are looking for. Now, we will turn our attention to what point "C" actually means to your customer and what value they hope to derive when they get there.

The Eight Major Denominations of Value

There are at least eight major kinds of value that your customer may be interested in deriving from a relationship with you and your company. Now, there could actually be sixteen or twenty-seven, but there are at least eight. Some of them are tangible and measurable, and others exist only in your buyer's mind. I refer to these as the Denominations of Value, and they represent the various outcomes or outputs that our customers might want to "get out" of an investment in our product and services solutions. Economic Value or a financial return on investment is one of them. The others include Time Value, Quality Value, Guidance or Advice Value, Political or Image Value, Relational Value, Simplicity Value, and Emotional Value. In Figure 3.2, we can see how these various denominations are interrelated, like the many facets of a cut and polished gemstone. This diagram is also meant to remind us that value can look very different based on who looks at it and the angle or position from which they look.

Our task is to understand what kind of value the individual or the group we are selling to is hoping, or expecting, to derive when they reach point "C," so that we can position our "B" as the ideal solution to provide it. This involves questioning and understanding on a much deeper level than most would-be vendors and suppliers are accustomed to.

For each of the Denominations of Value, there is a corresponding denomination of risk. As we endeavor to better understand the way our customers see value, we should remember that . . .

Figure 3.2 The Eight Major Denominations of Value

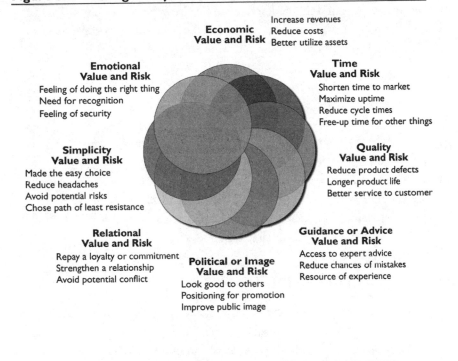

Economic Value and Risk
Increase revenues
Reduce costs
Better utilize assets

Emotional Value and Risk
Feeling of doing the right thing
Need for recognition
Feeling of security

Time Value and Risk
Shorten time to market
Maximize uptime
Reduce cycle times
Free-up time for other things

Simplicity Value and Risk
Made the easy choice
Reduce headaches
Avoid potential risks
Chose path of least resistance

Quality Value and Risk
Reduce product defects
Longer product life
Better service to customer

Relational Value and Risk
Repay a loyalty or commitment
Strengthen a relationship
Avoid potential conflict

Political or Image Value and Risk
Look good to others
Positioning for promotion
Improve public image

Guidance or Advice Value and Risk
Access to expert advice
Reduce chances of mistakes
Resource of experience

Value and risk are two sides of the same coin.

Risk, as it will be used here, refers to the possible downside of leaving the status quo of point "A" and venturing out in search of point "C." While a prospective customer may believe that they can save money, or derive Economic Value, by switching suppliers from you to your competitor, they will hopefully also understand that they may have to give up some Quality Value. They might choose to take the Quality Risk if the increase in Economic Value is great enough, but only to a point. They might be willing to accept a few more defects or mistakes, but not so many that it begins to impact their ability to serve their customers at a required minimum level. Likewise, your customer might be willing to wait a little longer, or incur some level of Time Risk, in exchange for the Quality Value of obtaining the best service available.

The exact mix of value and risk that any buyer may desire, or be willing to accept, can only be determined by the buyer themselves. One of the things that we can do to maximize the value of our offerings is to eliminate as much risk as possible from the equation. Simply put . . .

Any decrease in perceived risk is, in effect, an increase in perceived value.

So, as we look at the various kinds of value our customers may seek, we should look not only at how we can maximize the value we deliver to our customers, but how we can minimize risks as well. Now, let's look at each of these eight in more detail.

1. Economic Value and Risk

It would be great if every customer considered only the economic outcomes and financial ramifications of their buying decisions. It's the most easily measured and probably the most tangible denomination of value there is. Unfortunately, they don't. Economic Value is usually only one of several aspects of value they consider. The question is, "How can we position what we sell to be perceived among the options as offering the greatest Economic Value or the lowest Economic Risk?"

We might use examples and metrics of how we've helped other clients to derive Economic Value by effectively earning more profit. Case studies of the payback and return that our current clients have experienced are extremely useful for this. Of course, we may also offer to assist them in producing a return-on-investment analysis, a cost justification, or a business case of their own to help validate the investment in our solutions.

We should be prepared to offer some kind of proof or evidence of the Economic Value we can deliver, because most customers will consider the economic impact of a purchase or investment. There are exceptions. Occasionally, a buyer decides to operate with a "money is no object" mentality. But for the most part, business managers making complex business decisions make investments for the express purpose of increasing revenue (selling more), reducing costs (spending less), or better utilizing their assets (doing more with less). We will explore Economic Value in great detail in Chapter 4.

2. Time Value and Risk

There seems to be a universally accepted premise that "time is money," but time is often far more valuable than money. If it weren't, FedEx probably wouldn't exist because it's cheaper to send things parcel post. The value of time can be enormous, as is evidenced by how much consumers are willing to pay in interest charges to buy things on credit.

The question for us is, "How can we help our customers gain time?" We should take a look at our customer's specific situation, depending on their business model and the things that we sell, and ask questions like:

- Can our collaboration solutions help them share design ideas and information with subcontract manufacturers and effectively reduce time to market?
- Can the high quality of our products, or the availability of our service specialists, help them to maximize uptime and reduce downtime in their manufacturing plant?
- Can our business-process consulting or systems-design consulting help them to drive time out of their product-design cycles or to reduce payment-collection cycles?
- Can they hire us to help them implement our best-practice business processes and thereby free-up time to do other things?

Remember, most customers are cautious. It's only natural to assume that if something is done faster, some other kind of value might have to be sacrificed. Make sure your buyer doesn't inaccurately assume that faster means lower quality, less reliability, or the risk of higher costs in the future. Always position yourself considering both added value as well as reduced or "managed" risk.

3. Quality Value and Risk

The business world seems to be on a ceaseless quest to improve the quality of everything they do. The widespread adoption of Six Sigma and other quality initiatives is evidence that quality is a top-of-mind issue for almost every company today. Here are four ways we might deliver Quality Value to our customers, depending, of course, on what you sell and who you sell to:

- Can our systems be used to reduce the number of defects or mistakes made in manufacturing?
- Can we implement a process that reduces the number of errors made in billing and collections?
- Can our state-of-the-art diagnostic equipment improve the quality of medical care and improve the quality of the patient experience?
- Can our customer use our components to make higher-quality machines that last longer and require less maintenance?

The area of quality is one of the first to be impacted when companies try to reduce costs. If you want to occupy the position of the "high quality" solution, make sure to point out to your customer the Quality Risk they are likely to face if they choose to go with your "low cost" competitor.

4. Guidance or Advice Value and Risk

Customers frequently look to vendors for advice on which solution would be best suited to solve their problems and to achieve their goals. To some buyers, this is the most important denomination of value there is. This is especially true for the buyer who doesn't know what all the options are and doesn't have time to learn. Many clients will gladly pay a premium price to the supplier who they feel "really understands" what they need and takes the time to educate them on why they make the recommendation that they do.

In order to use this to our advantage, we—or somebody on our team—must possess the knowledge and experience needed to make the right recommendation. We demonstrate our expertise in part by using the diagnostic approach to selling and avoiding broadcasting as much as possible. This emphasizes our intention to fully understand the issue at hand before we make any kind of recommendation. This makes our customer more confident that when we do offer an opinion, it will be tailored to their specific situation and not just a general recommendation based only on our desire to sell something.

Once in a while, you'll come across a customer who uses you for ideas to solve his problems but then—once he has the value of your expertise—buys from someone else who is a little cheaper. Don't be shy about reminding him that "This might not be the last problem you ever have. So, the next time you need some help, please call me back, and I'll help you again. Except next time, buy from me. Would that be fair?" Always keep it positive. Never burn a bridge, but help your customer understand that guidance or advice can provide tremendous value, and it is part of the overall package you bring to market.

5. Political or Image Value and Risk

It has probably never happened where you work, but I did hear once about a customer who actually let his own political motives (i.e., desire to look good to his boss) influence whom he decided to buy from. Surely, that has never happened to you, has it? Unfortunately, it happens to all of us.

Some customers use a buying decision as a way of advancing their own agenda or acquiring more clout and political influence within their company. What we have to do is try to figure out how to use this to our advantage. We should try to determine how the buyer can "look good" for deciding to buy from us instead of our competitor.

Always be on the lookout for situations that might pose a political threat to anyone in your customer's organization involved in a buying decision. We should be very careful to never make one of our customers "look bad." If we can recognize a situation where one of the decision makers perceives some risk to her image or political standing, perhaps we can do something to try to alleviate that risk or at least bring her perception of it into perspective.

We should also recognize that the resolution of any buying decision that includes many different people reaching some form of agreement will always involve some degree of compromise and trade-off. Take care that some of your customer's buying committee members don't trade their vote of "YES" on your project for something else they want more. You and I will never know all the back-channel communiqués that go on among and between decision makers and influencers, but let's not be oblivious to how corporate politics can impact a deal in which we invest our precious time. Learn and understand the agenda and motives of as many of the different players as you possibly can.

6. Relational Value and Risk

Sometimes a customer decides not to buy from us in favor of their brother-in-law or someone they already have a relationship with or whom they have dealt with before. It is completely normal for a buyer to favor a vendor or supplier they know, like, and trust. Frankly, it should be expected. We, of course, want to develop a good working relationship with as many different people as possible within our client's company. Relationships based on a consistent, pleasant customer experience make people feel safe about doing business with us.

We should also try, when possible, to get other people within our company involved with the personnel of our client's company. The more relational ties we build with our customer, the tighter the bond between the two organizations becomes. This is especially important in the case of our best customers, with whom we really want to develop a partnership. We can't afford to base everything on any one person on either side because if (or rather when) that person gets promoted, quits, retires, or gets fired, it can be very difficult to salvage the relationship between the two companies.

Customers value relationships with vendors and suppliers to varying degrees, but they also value their relationships with their coworkers. For this reason, the judgment of one decision maker or influencer can be swayed by someone else involved in the decision process. Your internal champion might back down or be persuaded by someone else who happens to be a champion for another supplier or vendor. Your guy could side with your competitor just to avoid the Relational Risk of an internal conflict. But this works both ways.

A purchasing agent may just love doing business with your competitor. But if you can meet and build a relationship with the director of manufacturing on whose behalf she is buying, she will then have to consider her relationship with the director as she makes her buying decision. Likewise, our great relationship with the vice president of advertising might lead us to believe we have that new ad campaign deal all sewn up. But we could be surprised to learn he ultimately decided to go with the other vendor to preserve his relationship with the marketing communications director, who simply did not like us for some undisclosed reason. When assessing how any particular player in a buying decision thinks, make sure to consider all the relationships within and even outside the company that they might take into consideration before making their decision.

7. Simplicity Value and Risk

Simplicity Value is the label I use to describe the value customers derive when a task is made easier, simpler, or is eliminated altogether. I don't know how many millions of dollars in revenue I've booked by figuring out and selling creative ways to make my customer's life easier, but it's a lot! Simplicity Value can result in a savings of time, reduced chances of making mistakes, less hassle, less stress, or fewer headaches, either now or in the future.

Simplicity is one of the reasons it can be difficult to unseat an incumbent vendor. Sometimes it's easier for your customer to just keep working with the same supplier they've always worked with. To displace an existing vendor, we have to overcome the inertia of the status quo by getting creative about the Economic, Time, Quality, or some other kind of Value we can deliver that their current supplier does not.

The flip side, Simplicity Risk, is surely one of the most common reasons that sales aren't made. Nobody wants a hassle, and most buyers are glad to pay a little more to avoid one. Make sure your customers understand how simple and easy it is to work with you and your company. You might also need to carefully remind them of how painful life could be with a vendor who doesn't offer all the convenient services that your company does.

8. Emotional Value and Risk

Most decision makers would probably never admit it, but Emotional Value and Emotional Risk play a major role in the way we all think and make decisions. It could easily be argued that our personal emotional needs drive our pursuit of, or desire for, each of the other forms of value, as well as our aversion to all forms of risk. Our emotional need for security and admiration drives our pursuit of Economic Value, as does our need to feel important and successful. Guidance or Advice Value serves our emotional need to feel safe and more likely to avoid the humiliation of failure. And our need to believe that we "did the right thing" can cause us to overlook a potential gain in Economic Value or to incur the Relational Risk of disagreeing with, or voting against, someone whose goodwill we value highly.

I have found, however, that we can't really openly talk about these things with prospective customers. I admit that I've never asked a CEO, "Can you share with me a little more about your emotional needs?" but if I did, I doubt it would have gone over very well. Instead, we have to learn to listen for it within and between the things they say.

Many business executives who are considered great leaders and great decision makers rely heavily on their "gut," their "instinct," or how they feel about a tough decision they face. This is strong evidence that emotions do play a role in good decision making. People tend to make judgments and choices based on emotions and then justify those judgments with logical arguments.

Our job is to ask the right questions, and then listen closely enough to our customer that we begin to hear their perception of, and need for, Emotional Value, so that we can position ourselves as the ideal vendor or partner to deliver it. Throughout the balance of this chapter, I will explain exactly how this is done.

Breaking value and risk into these eight denominations helps us to think more carefully about what our customers think about, what they really want, and what value they hope to derive from their relationship with us as a vendor or a partner. Now let's turn our attention to what we bring to the relationship that will deliver the value our customers seek.

The Three Major Sources of Value

When a customer is faced with a significant buying decision, one in which there are many options of what to buy and who to buy from, there are always at least three different variables they take into consideration. I call these the three major Sources of Value. The first I will call the *solution*. It is comprised of the actual products or services your customer needs to implement and utilize in order to achieve their desired business results. Second is the *company* that supplies those products or services. And third are the *people* who work for that company and who make, sell, and deliver the products or services the company provides. Figure 3.3 shows how these three interrelate and together form the total package we bring to market.

There are plenty of buying situations today, especially with the advent of online shopping, in which the people element seems almost irrelevant. In the sale of a commodity or a low-risk tangible product, many customers aren't overly concerned about the quality of the people who are involved, or the stability and longevity of the company they buy from. Until something goes wrong, that is. Then the people and the company make all the difference.

In a complex multimillion-dollar transaction, which will define a long-term partner relationship between two companies for years to come, the caliber of the people and the reputation of the company may well be the most important criteria. There is a continuum then, delineated mostly by the presence of perceived risk, along which solution, company, and people have varying degrees of significance and importance to your customer. Now, we will look at each of these sources of value separately.

1. Your Company

What value do your customers perceive in doing business with your company, as opposed to your toughest competitor? Are there any differences? What do those differences mean to your customer? In our workshops we do a very popular exercise where we ask participants to take a close look at their own company from their customer's point of view. The question we ask is, "What are the things about your company that might be important to a customer?" We can't truly know until we ask our customer exactly what matters to them, or what makes us different or better. But we can speculate.

As participants offer up attributes and characteristics of their own company that they think might matter, or that they have heard their customers mention, we capture them on a flip chart. It is amazing how little the list varies from industry to industry and continent to continent. Things like reputation, financial stability, and longevity always top the list, but we almost always hear other key characteristics as well, such as the size of the company, the location of their nearest office, or the breadth of their offerings (i.e., the quantity and variety of the products and services they provide). There seems to be a list of ten to twelve characteristics of a company, as shown in Figure 3.3, that customers typically think about, which is almost universal.

2. Your People

Please finish the following sentence with the first word that comes to mind: "People buy from people they _____." I'll bet the word you thought of was either "know," "like," or "trust." Regardless of which word it was, you affirmed perhaps the most enduring truth in selling. People matter. And the more potential risk a customer perceives in a transaction, the more they matter.

There are a couple dozen characteristics or attributes, as seen in Figure 3.3, of the kind of people that customers like to buy from. This list includes honesty, likeability, and trustworthiness. But it also includes business acumen (an understanding of how business works) and domain

Figure 3.3 The Three Major Sources of Value

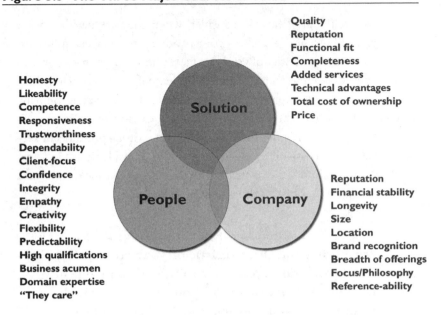

Honesty
Likeability
Competence
Responsiveness
Trustworthiness
Dependability
Client-focus
Confidence
Integrity
Empathy
Creativity
Flexibility
Predictability
High qualifications
Business acumen
Domain expertise
"They care"

Solution

People

Company

Quality
Reputation
Functional fit
Completeness
Added services
Technical advantages
Total cost of ownership
Price

Reputation
Financial stability
Longevity
Size
Location
Brand recognition
Breadth of offerings
Focus/Philosophy
Reference-ability

expertise (industry- or discipline-specific knowledge). So, customers care that you are a nice person, but knowing enough to be able to help them diagnose and solve business problems is very important, too.

Of all the characteristics of people shown in Figure 3.3, there is one that deserves special mention. I put it last on the list for a reason: I think it is probably the most important characteristic of all. The most fascinating attribute of any individual you or I might meet—whether or not it is in the context of a sales transaction—quite simply is "they care."

I've seen customers buy from a supplier with an inferior product because that supplier demonstrated that *they care*. I've seen customers pay substantially higher prices to a particular vendor over another because the customer believed *they care*. And I've seen buyers take huge risks to go with an unproven partner because they genuinely felt that *they cared* more about making sure the client achieved their desired goals and objectives. Over the years, I have used this philosophy as a major competitive strategy. The good news is, you can too.

3. Your Product and Services Solutions

The third area your client will consider, when they are deciding what to buy and who to buy it from, is your product and services solutions. Some of the characteristics of your products and services that your customers might take into consideration include quality, functional fit (i.e., does it do what they need it to do), the added services that accompany and add value to your product, and any technical advantages that your products or services might offer that your competitor's products or services don't. Your customers will also, no doubt, consider price.

While price almost always matters to some degree, one of the most important takeaways of this discussion is that . . .

Price is but one characteristic of your product and services solutions. And your solution is only one of three major sources of value you bring to the table, and which your customer will consider when deciding what to buy.

There are a variety of ways that your company, your people, and your solutions bring value to your customers besides just "a low price." In fact, one way to look at this is to imagine your "price" being placed on one side of the Value Equation (shown earlier in Figure 3.1), and *all* of the other characteristics and attributes of your company, your people, and your solutions placed on the other side. That's a lot of value to consider. Many of those things matter much more to your customer than the price, whether they will admit it or not.

You may have noticed here that I started the discussion of these three major sources of value by looking first at your company, then at your people, and last at your product and services solutions. There is a very good reason for this. This is exactly what we should try to do when talking with our clients, too.

For years, I was in the habit of asking the worst question you could possibly ask a prospective customer:

"On what will you base your final decision?"

Or . . .

"How will you decide which solution is the right one for you?"

You already know what every customer on the planet is conditioned to say in response, don't you? "Price!"

Then we say, "Is price your only concern?"

Then they say, "Oh no, we also need to make sure that it is the right functional fit, and that it meets our needs, etc., etc., etc."

But by then it's too late. They've already driven that stake in the ground around price so they can always come back to it and use it as leverage later. Asking that question also causes your customer to focus primarily on the characteristics and attributes of your solution, as opposed to your company and your people.

Somewhere along the line, I realized that I was asking the wrong question. I discovered that if we can have a discussion about the characteristics of the ideal *company* our customer likes to work with, and the kind of *people* they like to do business with, the edge of the price issue is not quite as sharp.

It will take a little practice to start your questioning and positioning around your *company* instead of your product and services solutions, but once you get the hang of it, you'll never go back. As you're getting comfortable with this, you might try framing the discussion by setting the price issue aside on purpose, like this:

"I'll assume that you want the best value for your money, and you certainly don't want to overpay for whatever you decide to buy. Let's lay that aside for a minute. What are some of the criteria that will influence your decision about the right company to partner with on this project?"

Using this kind of an approach will help you lead the conversation in the direction that you want it to go, and it will help your customer see— and better appreciate—all of the good things other than "a low price" on the other side of the value equation.

The Lens of Perception

Part of our job as sales professionals revolves around our ability to understand how customers think. The more we can understand the way our customers perceive value, the better we can position our solutions to help them derive the value that they seek. It is important for us to remember that . . .

> **Customers don't choose one vendor over another accidentally; they choose for specific reasons that they value.**

Like an investigative reporter, or a detective trying to solve a complex mystery, we endeavor to understand what causes our customer to see the world the way they do. The better we can understand the way our customers think, the more influence we can have on what they think about.

Our customers see the world through a lens that colors their perception and the way they interpret value. This lens creates a perception of the world and everything in it that our customer accepts as reality. Their perception seems to be the truth to them, and in fact, it is the truth to them. But what we think is truth and what they think is truth could be two different things.

When we come to the marketplace with our company, our people, and our solutions, each of these three has unique characteristics that distinguish us from our competitors. But every individual or decision maker who might be asked to evaluate our company, our people, and our solutions will see a completely different picture, filtered by his or her own lens of perception.

Figure 3.4 The Lens of Perception

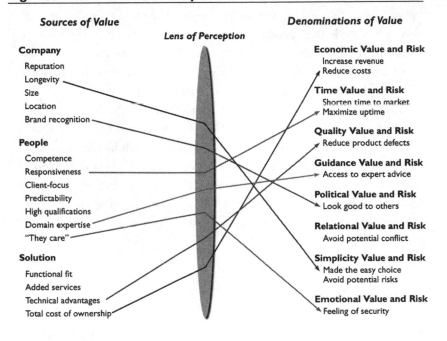

The Three Major Sources of Value model, shown in Figure 3.3, contains a list of the vendor attributes customers consider that are incredibly consistent from customer to customer. But how your customer prioritizes them, in terms of which are most important, and *why* they think those particular attributes are important is as unique as their fingerprint.

Figure 3.4 depicts this lens of perception, and how the various characteristics of our company, our people, and our solutions could be interpreted by an individual customer. Your customer might believe, for example, that since your company has been around a long time, that means you are a safe and easy choice, which adds an element of Simplicity Value to the reasons to buy from you. The same customer might believe that since you and your field service team are very responsive, it means that they can derive Time Value in the way of more uptime and less downtime by partnering with you, as opposed to the other vendor who is not as responsive.

The arrows in Figure 3.4 show how the things that your customer believes about your company, your people, and your solutions refract through their lens of perception to become perceived in the various denominations of value that they care about. What we have to keep in mind is that every single decision maker and influencer you interact with sees you through his or her own lens of perception.

Looking at this model emphasizes the folly of the broadcast approach to selling. No matter what information you choose to broadcast about your company, your people, and your solutions, it will be "hit and miss" at best. It usually only takes a few misses before your customer "tunes you out" and nothing else you say gets through. We have to learn how to draw out information about our customer's perception of value through our conversations and questioning. Then we can position ourselves accordingly.

Intelligent Positioning

In our workshops we teach a technique we call "Intelligent Positioning," which makes this concept of how your customer perceives value incredibly useful. We teach participants to start out every introductory meeting with questions. Some of the questions are designed to reveal our customer's business disparity. Others are meant to discover more about their desired business results, their goals and objectives, or their motive, means, and urgency to achieve them. But before we begin to position our products and services as solutions to business problems, we should use our discovery process to learn some things about how our customer perceives value by asking questions such as:

> *"Laying aside the details of products and services for a minute, have you given any thought to the kind of company that you would like to partner with on this project?"*

Or . . .

> *"What are some of the characteristics of the kind of companies you like to do business with?"*

Now, if you've looked at the Three Major Sources of Value model in Figure 3.3, you already know what they are going to say. But even if their answers are exactly what you would have guessed, the fact that you asked them these kinds of questions sets you apart from your competitors, who just show up and "talk at them."

Regardless of which specific characteristics or attributes of an ideal vendor they happen to mention, you earn the right to ask another question. It is this follow-up question that really matters, because . . .

Far more crucial than *what* is valuable and important to your customer is *why* it is valuable and important to them.

Asking questions in a way that helps your customers to clarify what is important to them helps you understand the characteristics by which they will evaluate you as a vendor. Asking "Why?" tells you which denomination of value they believe these characteristics relate to. It enables you to tie the strengths of your company, your people, and your solutions to the particular denominations of value they care most about. Here's an example of how Intelligent Positioning sounds in practice:

"Mr. Johnson, what are some of the things that matter most to you when evaluating a new vendor or supplier?"

"I'd say that the vendor's reputation is key."

"Why is that the first thing that comes to mind?"

"Because we have bought from a few vendors who weren't around a year later."

"So, is it financial stability that you are referring to?"

"Yes, but also I'd say the size of the company matters."

"Why is the size of the company important to you?"

"Because we have operations in several countries and we need a vendor that can support us all around the world."

"So, worldwide support is important."

"Yes."

"Why is it important?"

"Because when we have a machine down, I need someone that can get there and get it running again ASAP."

"Is there anything else from a company standpoint that is more important than that?"

"I need to know that they will stand by their commitments."

"Why do you say that?"

"Because I need to know I can count on them to do what they say they will do."

"Of all of these, which is the most important to you?"

"Probably the last one. I want to work with a supplier I can rely on."

"So, integrity is the most important thing of all?"

"Yes. I would say so."

Now we have something to work with! This customer seems to think that the key characteristics of the right company to partner with include:

- A strong reputation.
- Financial stability.
- Highly responsive global support.
- People of high integrity.

The denominations of value that he believes these characteristics represent are:

- **Simplicity Value:** Selecting a vendor that is proven and low risk
- **Emotional Value:** Not having to worry about replacing the vendor again in a year

- **Time Value:** Having someone "on-site" to quickly handle any problems
- **Relational Value:** Knowing that the vendor is reliable and will do what they say they will do

Using this approach, we can position our company against an understanding of exactly which factors this customer thinks are important as well as *why* they are important to him, like this:

> *"Well, Mr. Johnson, you'll be happy to know that we currently support many clients with global operations and we've been doing so for over twenty years. One of the reasons that clients choose to work with us is our worldwide support network that ensures we can have a person "on-site" at your facility anywhere in the world within twenty-four hours. When the time comes, I'd like to introduce you to a couple of our long-term client/partners and have you ask them confidentially whether or not we have been true to our word. Would that be all right with you?"*

This is very different than reading the bullet points on a slide presentation announcing:

- Founded in 1982
- 6 international offices
- Over 800 customers
- Global support

Another important facet of Intelligent Positioning is that it enables us to change the way we position ourselves based on what we learn about our customer's perception of value. I could ask two different people, working for the same company, "Does the size of a company matter to you as you evaluate potential partners for this project?" and get a "Yes" from both. But when I ask, "*Why* does the size of the company matter to you?" one person might say:

> *"Because we want to work with a* big *vendor who can support our global operations."*

We don't necessarily have to be the global market leader to do that. We could respond by saying:

"Well, you'll be happy to know we work with many clients with worldwide operations and our worldwide support network enables us to provide the highest-quality service wherever you do business."

Then we could walk right down the hall to meet with a different person in the same company, and ask them *"Why* does the size of the company matter to you?" and hear:

"Honestly, I am fed up with our current 'big' vendor, who won't return our phone calls and who treats us like 'a number.' We are looking for a company that's more focused on partnering with us to make sure we get what we need."

We're still the same company, but in this context our response could be:

"You'll be happy to know that our company philosophy keeps us very client-focused. I hope to demonstrate to you—as we talk about your business objectives and explore the ways we could possibly help you achieve them— that we are exactly the kind of company you will enjoy doing business with."

Intelligent Positioning is actually a microcosm of the Customer Results Model (points "A," "B," and "C"). We need to learn *what matters* and then *why it matters* before we can properly position our solution. In the alphabet, these three letters appear "A," "B," and then "C." But as they apply to Intelligent Positioning and the diagnostic approach, we start with "A," and then understand "C," before we position "B."

Preparing for Potential Objections

There may well be characteristics about your company or your products that frankly aren't that impressive. If we know there is the potential for an objection or issue with something about our company, our people, and our solutions that we *can't* change, then by all means let's prepare to handle it before it comes up.

There can't be that many bad things about your company, your people, and your solutions. But if there are some, you need to know what they are and be prepared to respond to any questions or objections you might get. Better yet, deal with them ahead of time because . . .

The best time to handle an objection is before it becomes an objection.

I was a sales rep for an enterprise software company during the late 1990s that enjoyed an excellent reputation for customer satisfaction and customer loyalty. That was great for the guys who managed existing accounts. My job, on the other hand, was "new business only."

We were a publicly held company that had a little issue with financial performance. Well, actually, we had missed our earnings estimate for several quarters in a row. Unfortunately, all my prospective clients knew about it. It might have had something to do with the fact that our primary competitor made photocopies of the article that talked about our poor performance and handed it out to all of them, as evidence we were "going out of business." Now I had a choice to make. I could wait for them to bring it up, and then try to make excuses, or I could bring it up myself and stand a chance of handling it.

While asking about their concept of a good vendor/partner, I made a point to ask:

> *"Mr. Johnson, I want to ask you about your idea of the kind of company you're hoping to partner with on this project. Do you mind if I ask you a very specific question? Is a company's financial performance ever a concern of yours when evaluating a new vendor?"*

> *"Yes it is."*

> *"Why exactly do you say that, Mr. Johnson?"*

"Well, we couldn't very well go with a company that might not be around to support us next year."

"I can certainly understand that. So, it's company stability that is important to you. You want a partner who isn't going anywhere."

"Yes. That's right."

"Well, you'll be happy to know that we've been in business for twenty-five years, we've got over 5,000 customers worldwide and over 1,000 in your particular industry. We've got $400 million in the bank and our outlook for the next three to five years is quite favorable. Now you also might have read that we missed our earnings estimate last quarter."

"As a matter of fact, I did."

"Well, the truth is, that's not the first one we've missed. Let's talk about why that happened and what the outlook is for the balance of this year . . ."

You get the idea.

If you've got a problem, learn to deal with it. Get your rebuttal ready and practice it a few times. Frame it, couch it, or whatever you have to do, but don't just sit there and wait for them to hit you upside the head with it. Get it out in the open, and if they've got a problem with it, you can help them get over it or move on to the next customer who can. I'd rather know *now* that there is a problem than after I invest three months of my life in an opportunity that goes nowhere. As one forty-year veteran of sales told me years ago, "Half of selling is figuring out who ain't gonna buy."

The Difference Between Apples and Oranges

It seems almost comical now to read some of the literature of the late 1990s in which some predicted the end of the sales profession as we know it. Many were convinced that once companies could buy everything they would ever need over the Internet, once they could look at a spec sheet and a picture, or even watch a video demonstration of a product all from the comfort and safety of their laptop, there would be no need for a salesperson anymore.

Today we know that the need for sales professionals who can diagnose a business problem, craft a vision of a solution, and put together a plan to use their products and services to help their clients achieve their business goals is greater than it has ever been.

Your customers are constantly looking for fresh ideas and new ways to achieve their goals and objectives. We should always keep in mind that we bring much more to the table than just a product or a service. The total package we bring is unique.

Customers who are considering or evaluating more than one vendor often talk about wanting to compare apples to apples. Well, I firmly believe that . . .

There is no such thing as apples to apples. Even if your competitor sells the exact same product that you sell, your *company* and your *people* make it different.

What we need to do is help our customers appreciate the difference between apples and oranges. Once you learn to ask questions that reveal how your customer perceives value and risk, and then position the total package of your company, your people, and your solutions in that context, no competitor will even come close.

CHAPTER 4

The Cause and Effect of Business Value

Early in my career, I took a sales position with a small technology reseller that sold software and hardware systems primarily to manufacturing companies. In those days, it wasn't uncommon for a workstation and a single-user license of software to run well into six figures. So, almost every sales opportunity required us to get involved with our customer's finance department to develop a business case or cost justification. Unfortunately, I had no financial background whatsoever. I didn't know a Balance Sheet from a Rap Sheet.

I read a book on selling that admonished the reader to "Sell higher . . . Learn to sell to decision makers . . . Understand what keeps executives up at night." Then the author offered a list of executive business issues like the one below:

Mergers and Acquisitions	Labor Costs
Revenue Growth	Inventory Management
Working Capital	Market Share
Operating Expenses	Return on Assets
Leveraging Human Capital	Customer Satisfaction
Earnings per Share	Accounts Receivable
Time to Market	Order Fill-Rates
Product Quality	Managing Risk
Customer Loyalty	Materials Costs
Cash Flow	Workforce Productivity
Shareholder Equity	Knowledge Management
Profit Margin	Disaster Recovery

Does this help you any? It didn't help me very much. I was at a loss to understand the relative importance of all of these things. I could read English, but I had no context or frame of reference for understanding what these words really meant. I didn't even know which ones were good (i.e., a company would want more of) versus which ones were bad (i.e., a company would want less of). So, I went out and bought one of those little books of business definitions, but I soon figured out this wasn't all I needed to know either. Even if I had been able to memorize all of those terms and their definitions, was I going to just blurt them out at random in the general direction of an executive? I doubt that would have earned me much credibility.

Business acumen (an understanding of how business works) is more than just knowing words and their definitions; it's understanding that poor inventory control has a negative impact on order fill-rates. When order fill-rates fall, customer loyalty suffers, as do accounts receivable. When accounts receivable get out of hand, cash flow is impacted. Then a company might have to dip into lines of credit to cover short-term obligations, and the interest that has to be paid on that borrowed money erodes profitability. I call this the "cause and effect of business."

In addition to the financial measures that make up the line items on financial statements, businesses track their operational and financial performance by a myriad of other measures and metrics. Some of these are not so much measures as they are initiatives or objectives, such as improving quality, fostering better customer service, or leveraging intellectual capital. Companies are constantly trying to apply metrics and standards to these somewhat "soft" measures, and any particular company might have their own unique way of managing to these objectives. In this book, we will call all of these metrics, measures, initiatives, or objectives "elements of value." We will assume that if something can be improved, increased, reduced, or decreased, and if doing so is either "good" or "bad" for the company, then it is an element of business value. And the first truth for us to acknowledge is this . . .

Every element of value has one or more causes and one or more effects.

When any one of these measures moves in either direction, it has an effect on others in either a positive or a negative way. That subsequent movement has yet other effects on certain other elements in the value structure. The chain reaction can be quite substantial, as in the example above about the effects of poor inventory control. As we develop our business acumen and our understanding of how business works, we are developing a knowledge of "what causes what" in business. This knowledge of business cause and effect is what moves us from amateur to professional status in our customer's eyes.

Learning the Cause and Effect of Business

Learning business acumen can be turned into an academic exercise, complete with memorization and testing, but this only serves to reinforce the *theory* of cause and effect. While there is tremendous merit in developing a thorough understanding of the *possible* forces at work in a hypothetical business scenario, its practical value can be somewhat limited. It is very helpful to explore possibilities, such as the three principle causes of customer attrition, or the four major effects of increasing forecast accuracy; but a scenario or a case study is only an example of what *might* be causing a certain business problem, or what effect that problem *might* have on the overall performance of a company. What is far more useful is learning what is *actually* happening within your customer's business, and more specifically what *they think* the causes are and how they see the effects impacting their overall success.

Understanding Causes

The best way I know to begin learning business acumen is to start by really listening to what your customers are talking about. If we are stuck in constant broadcast mode, waiting for them to take a breath so we can deliver our "messaging," we probably won't learn very much at all. Slow down just a little, listen to what your customer is saying, and when you hear them mention that their company is having problems with *customer satisfaction*, for example, ask a simple question: "What do you think is *causing* this problem with customer satisfaction?"

By asking about the causes of any element of value, we hear back how our customer thinks the element can be impacted, for better or worse. Let's assume for a minute that you or I already know that there are three, or four, or six different ways to cause an increase in customer satisfaction, for example. That's not the point. What we really want to know is *what our customer thinks* will cause an increase.

Perhaps our customer tells us that "improving customer service" is one of the ways they think they can increase customer satisfaction. In that case, Figure 4.1 shows the relationship of these two measures.

Note the two little arrows in the upper left-hand corner of this diagram labeled "Causes" and "Effects." Whenever you hear your customer talking about a problem they are having with any element of value, you can gain a better understanding of that problem and its broader impact by asking questions about its *causes and effects*. Here are some possible questions for this customer satisfaction example:

> **Question:** "What do you think is *causing* this problem with customer satisfaction?"
> **Answer:** An issue with customer service.

Or . . .

> **Question:** "What *effect* is this issue with customer service having on your business?"
> **Answer:** A problem with customer satisfaction.

Now note the two little arrows in the upper right-hand corner of this diagram and their associated questions "How?" and "Why?" When your customer starts talking about a goal they are trying to achieve, or an initiative they are focused on, we can get a better understanding of their thinking and of how they see their business by asking questions beginning with "How?" and "Why?" This applies to the diagram in Figure 4.1 in the following way:

> **Question:** "*How* do you think you could increase customer satisfaction?"
> **Answer:** By improving customer service.

Figure 4.1 The Relationship of Causes and Effects

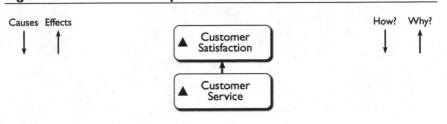

Or . . .

Question: "*Why* is improving customer service so important?"
Answer: To maintain or increase customer satisfaction.

Earlier, we said that each element of value has one or more causes and one or more effects. To get a broader understanding of how our customer sees their business, we will have to ask, "What *else* might be causing this problem with customer satisfaction?" Or, if we are exploring the possible ways to improve customer satisfaction, we should ask not just "How?" but also "How *else*?"

Perhaps you could ask, "How else do you think you could improve customer satisfaction?" or "Are there any other possible *causes* of this problem with customer satisfaction?" As shown in Figure 4.2, there could be many different causes of poor customer satisfaction, ranging from a sharp edge on a plastic baby toy (poor product quality) to how long a customer has to stay "on hold" when calling to place an order (poor customer service). The ▲ alongside each element of value indicates the direction of movement that is *generally* considered "good."

As we are learning this approach and building our own business knowledge, curiosity and a desire to learn makes us naturally inquisitive. But as we get more knowledgeable about how business works, we have to guard against assuming that we already know—or that our customer already knows—the major causes of customer satisfaction, and thereby incorrectly assuming that these questions are unimportant. Asking our customer "How?" and "Why?" they are planning to pursue a certain goal, or asking about the possible causes and effects of the business problems they face, is an integral facet of our diagnostic approach.

Figure 4.2 The Causes of Customer Satisfaction

Listen for what your customer thinks they already have a good handle on, as well as areas where they are not so sure, worried, or maybe even at a loss. If they recognize a business problem, or have identified a certain goal or objective, they've already got some ideas about what they want to do to solve the problem or reach the goal. We should try to understand what they already think *before* we start offering recommendations of any kind.

The real magic of the diagnostic approach is more than simply learning about our customer's business in order to offer a solution to help them achieve their desired results, because . . .

**More important than our need to understand is
our customer's need to feel understood.**

We will talk more about this in Chapter 5, but one of the major reasons for listening and asking questions is to help our customer arrive at a place where they are ready to hear and have faith in our suggestions or recommendations. Jumping to conclusions, or rushing to offer a solution, is almost always perceived as proof that we are more focused on "B" (selling something) than on "C" (our customer's business objectives). Even if our advice is exactly the same in both cases, our customers simply can't accept it as valid unless they feel we have taken the time to listen and fully understand them before we offer it.

Figure 4.3 The Effects of Customer Satisfaction

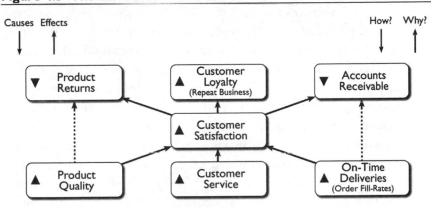

Understanding Effects

Now let's look at this from a different angle. What does an increase in customer satisfaction *cause*? Or put another way, what are some of the *effects* of an increase in customer satisfaction? For this we ask effect-oriented questions such as: "What are the *effects* of this problem you are having with customer satisfaction?" Or questions that begin with "Why?" such as: "Why is improving customer satisfaction so important right now?"

One of the effects or results of improving customer satisfaction is an increase in customer loyalty or customer retention. Another effect of having happy, satisfied customers is that they tend to pay their bills on time, or at least closer to on time than the disgruntled ones. This helps to keep accounts receivable down, or at least keep them under control. A third possible effect of higher customer satisfaction could be a reduction in product returns. Figure 4.3 illustrates these effects of customer satisfaction. The ▲ and ▼ represent an increase or decrease, respectively, and point in the direction that most companies would normally consider to be "good."

When your customer's customers are more satisfied, they tend to stay around. If they do remain loyal to your customer, instead of buying from the guy across the street, it reduces customer-acquisition costs, because it normally costs much less to keep a customer than to attract a new one. If a reduction in acquisition costs is good, "Why is it good?" Because it reduces overall costs and ultimately boosts profit. But that's not the only way that customer loyalty contributes to profitability. Another effect of customer loyalty (repeat business) is an increase in sales revenue. When combined with lower customer-acquisition costs, this also contributes to an increase in profit and earnings.

Let's not forget that a reduction in accounts receivable translates into a reduction in what finance managers call Days Sales Outstanding (DSO), which is a critical measure that nearly every finance executive and stock analyst watches closely as a factor of financial health. If a company can cut DSO, that frees up cash or capital for reinvestment, which drives asset utilization and profits. Figure 4.4 shows how—by following the trail of business cause and effect from bottom to top—an increase in product quality, customer service, or on-time deliveries is translated into profitability and earnings.

Using this "How and Why" approach, and the cause-and-effect relationships it reveals, we can build a model of any organization that depicts how they produce Economic Value. I call this model Business Value Hierarchy™ (BVH). It is a literal map of the approach your customer is taking to create value and achieve their business goals. It should be emphasized that this is a dynamic model, which means it will look different for each and every client you work with, it can change over time, and it will look dramatically different from industry to industry.

We can use BVH to visually depict the goals, strategies, tactics, or initiatives that any business is utilizing to execute their business plan. And because it's visual, it's easy to see the cause-and-effect relationships of the various strategies and tactics, as well as how these elements "roll up" to contribute to the company's higher-level goals.

A Model of Business Value

From an economic or financial standpoint, the purpose of every for-profit business is to produce a profit and a return on investment for its owners or shareholders. That's why they call it "for profit." Not every

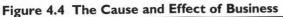

Figure 4.4 The Cause and Effect of Business

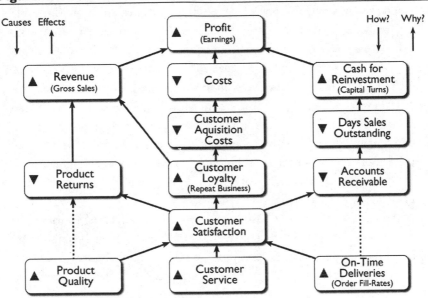

business is started for the sole purpose of profit, nor does any company endure long if their only objective is to maximize profits with blatant disregard for everything else. Most companies have a mission or a vision that looks beyond simply making money, and that seeks to produce a positive contribution to the world in multiple ways such as employment opportunities, charitable contributions, societal advancement, and so on. But if a company can't produce a profit, they won't be able to fund these noble causes for long.

When a private company earns a profit, it comes to the owner or owners in one of two forms: equity or cash flow. Equity is the value of, or worth of, a company equal to the sum of all of its assets minus all of its liabilities. So, if you or I started a business, one of the things that we might want as a return on our investment would be a company that would grow in value or equity over time. We might decide to pass the business on to our kids as an inheritance, or perhaps we could sell the company at a profit. We might even choose to sell shares of ownership (stock) to the public to fund growth or to "cash ourselves out" and retire.

When a company does decide to "go public" and issues an Initial Public Offering (IPO), you and I can buy shares of stock and become a part owner of that company. And what do we want as shareholders? We want equity and cash flow! The equity or worth of a share of stock would be the stock price. We buy it at $20 a share and we hope it goes to $30, or even $300, but preferably not $3. Cash flow would be synonymous with dividends (money paid to us as a shareholder when the company earns a profit). Investors who are young enough, or aggressive enough, aren't worried about dividends. They might simply choose to roll those dividends back in to buy more stock. But some people, especially retirees, do invest in stocks for the purpose of living on the dividends paid to them as shareholders.

A business owner or a business manager faces a host of factors that can have an impact on the equity and cash flow of their business: the general economic climate, consumer confidence, interest rates, the price of oil, government regulation, and on and on. But there is at least one thing that a manager can do to proactively impact equity and cash flow, and that is to earn a profit. So, "*Why* do we earn a profit?" To generate equity and cash flow. And "*How* does a business produce equity and cash flow?" By earning a profit. The next logical question is, "How do you do *that*?"

Your Customer's Goals

There are three major ways that a company can increase profits or earnings: (1) increase revenues (sell more), (2) reduce costs (spend less), and (3) better utilize company assets (do more with less). Everything else they do, and every other financial measure they track relates back to these three objectives, to the profits these three contribute to, and to the equity and cash flow that results. Figure 4.5 shows the cause-and-effect relationship between these high-level elements of value.

Most companies establish goals and objectives in each of these three areas. Read just about any Annual Report or Form 10-K and you'll see reference to your prospect's goals and objectives in the areas of selling more, spending less, and doing more with less. However, they never

Figure 4.5 Your Customer's Goals

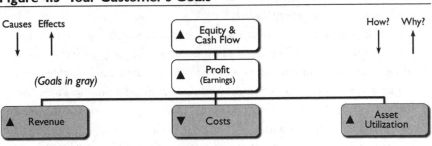

describe them quite that succinctly. It sounds a lot more impressive when you use fancy business jargon to describe strategic goals. Here are some examples of what you might read:

"Our objective is to expand our brand equity and global reach to maximize growth opportunities in emerging markets and further penetrate existing strongholds in domestic markets in which we maintain competitive advantage [i.e., they're going to sell more]."

"In order to maximize our profitability, we are constantly looking for new ways to reduce costs and expenses. Our commitment to continuous improvement focuses on maximizing workforce efficiencies while driving waste and errors from every facet of business operations [i.e., they're going to spend less]."

"We continue to leverage our core competencies for maximum results. Through our dual strategy of organic growth and selected mergers and acquisitions, we continue to streamline operations and divest of business segments and infrastructure which no longer fit the core focus of our strategic business plan [i.e., they're going to do more with less]."

However your customer chooses to express it, every company is constantly focused on the goals of increasing revenue, reducing costs, and better utilizing assets. In order for us to be successful selling business results (the achievement of these goals), we must learn to "Tie our functional capabilities (the things that our products and services do) to the achievement of our client's goals."

The problem with the sales approach of some technology companies, for example, is that when their salespeople engage a prospective customer, they talk about technology. Or when a professional services firm engages a potential new client, they talk about professional services. We have to break this pattern of behavior. As sales professionals, we need to quit talking about technology, or professional services, or whatever it is that we sell, and start talking about how those things will help our customers increase revenue, reduce costs, and better utilize assets. It's the difference between selling *technology* solutions as opposed to selling *business* solutions.

It is relatively safe to assume that every business wants to sell more, spend less, and do more with less. I've never seen a company that didn't. But we should try to learn the terms *they* use to describe these goals, because terms can vary widely, especially across industries. We want to learn to talk about our customer's business in their vernacular, using their specific lingo.

Take a minute to reread the "Business" section of your target account's 10-K report. How do they express their desire to increase revenue and sell more? What words and phrases do they use to describe their plans to reduce costs and spend less? Do they talk at all about any initiatives to better utilize their assets and do more with less? Some companies are more forthcoming with their business objectives than others. I have seen some that provide only a vague description of their business plans in their Annual Report or 10-K, and others that not only lay out their goals, complete with target numbers and metrics, but also the strategies they intend to employ to achieve them.

Your Customer's Strategies

By gleaning as much as you can from your reading and research, you can start to build a "skeleton" of the value model for your case study account. We fill in the gaps as we meet and interview the various people within the company. We can learn about the strategies that our cus-

Figure 4.6 Your Customer's Strategies

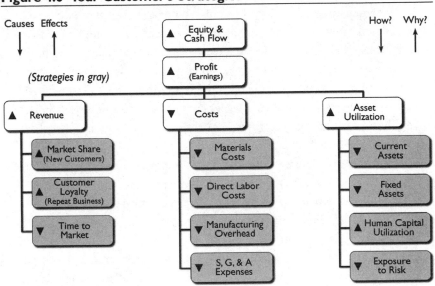

tomer is using, or plans to use, to reach their goals by asking, "*How* will you achieve your revenue growth objective?" or "*How* do you plan to control or cut your costs and expenses?"

Here again, we shouldn't be too assumptive. There are many different strategies that your client *might* use to pursue their major goals. Through our discovery process we want to learn which strategies they are *already* using or what they think would be the best way to achieve their goals. We could very well have several ideas or approaches that they have not yet considered or tried. There will be plenty of time to suggest or recommend these later. For now, try to learn what they have already done, are doing now, or are already planning to do.

Figure 4.6 shows an example of several strategies (in gray) that could be employed to achieve the goals of increasing revenue, reducing costs, and better utilizing assets. Two of the *causes* of increased costs, for example, could be a rise in either materials costs or direct labor costs. Therefore, one strategy for reducing costs would be to concentrate on lowering materials costs; another would be to focus on better managing and controlling direct labor costs.

We can add to what we already know about our customer's business by using questions like, "I read in your Annual Report that you anticipate doubling your revenue in the next five years. *How* do you plan to accomplish that exactly?" If we haven't been able to learn very much from our research, we might try using a question like, "Several of our clients in your industry have been actively seeking cost containment and cost avoidance opportunities in order to maintain profit margins in this highly competitive market. *How* has your company reacted to these kinds of pressures?"

Through a combination of research and questioning, you can begin to construct an understanding of your customer's business that will ultimately become a road map of exactly how to position your products and services, to whom within the company, and in the context of which goals and objectives. This BVH model will become a detailed depiction of how your client does business today, as well as the goals and objectives they are trying to accomplish going forward. In essence, it is a composite vision of what point "C" looks like for the various people, units, and departments within the company, as well as the enterprise as a whole.

I want to point out that the way these various elements link or tie together is not an exact science. They could fit together in dozens of different ways. We use our diagnostic process to discover how our customer *thinks* they link together. Let's look at one example in Figure 4.6.

This model shows reducing time to market as a strategy that supports the goal of increasing revenue, the idea being that the quicker we can get new products developed and on the shelves the more revenue opportunities we will capture. A different customer, or a different individual within your customer's business, may look at time to market not as a direct cause of increased revenue, but more as a cause of increased market share, which in turn causes an increase in revenue. So, what matters here is how your particular client sees these strategies, goals, and initiatives fitting together. Not everyone within a given company will see their business the same way. Your thorough understanding of your customer's business will actually be based on a composite of things you learn from, and about, all the different people you meet.

Your Customer's Tactics

In the example in Figure 4.6, we saw that our fictitious customer was focused on four different strategies for controlling or reducing costs:

1. Reducing materials costs
2. Controlling direct labor costs
3. Minimizing manufacturing overhead
4. Decreasing selling, general, and administrative expenses (S, G, & A)

Now, let's drill down another level to discover the causes of each of these, by asking questions such as:

> *"What are some of the causes you've identified that contribute to the problem of escalating materials costs?"*

Or . . .

> *"How will you go about reducing direct labor costs?"*

Figure 4.7 shows the Business Value Hierarchy™ model built downward one more level, illustrating several tactics (in gray) supporting each of the strategies this example company is using to pursue their major goals.

Moving downward to the next level in the BVH model provides more detail about their business and reveals more potential opportunities for improvement. They've already been thinking about the business problems that are keeping them from reaching their goals and objectives, long before we came along. We should try to learn what some of their ideas are, as well as which ones they've started in on, which ones have been put off, which ones have already produced positive results, and which ones have failed.

As I mentioned before, this level of understanding of your customer will require research and multiple meetings. It should be considered an ongoing iterative process, much like the development of an organization chart, which becomes more rich and complete with every meeting or interaction with the people within your customer's organization.

Your Functional Capabilities

The purpose of all this discovery process is to determine how the functional capabilities of your products and services tie to and support the tactics and strategies your client will use, or is already using, to reach their goals and objectives. Once you understand that, you can position your offerings in terms of producing the specific business results that your customer is already trying to produce.

Once you have an understanding of the various tactics your client plans to utilize to support the strategies they will employ to pursue their goals, the question becomes, "Where do the functional capabilities of your products and services fit in? Looking at your customer's value model, where do they need help? What exactly do your product and services solutions *do* that will enable them to take action on the tactics and strategies you've identified?" Once this is understood, you simply connect the dots between your functional capabilities (what your products and services do), and the tactics that your functional capabilities enable and support, as shown in Figure 4.7.

This figure shows how your functional capabilities, which in this example are the abilities to . . .

> *Increase Forecast Accuracy & Demand Planning . . . by collecting and distributing real-time data from multiple disparate sources such as retail point-of-sale (POS), warehouse management, distribution, manufacturing, and procurement systems, which enables the manufacturer to "solve" for the best possible production and distribution plan to properly balance supply with demand.*

. . . enable your customer to do four key things:

1. **Increase order fill-rates** (i.e., the percentage of customer orders that are filled and delivered on time, which many manufacturers call

Figure 4.7 Tying Your Functional Capabilities to Your Client's Tactics

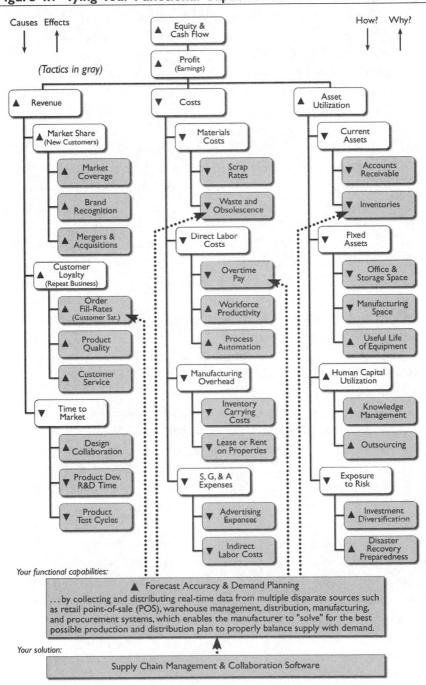

"customer satisfaction rating" or "customer sat.") by making the right products at the right time to meet customer demand.

2. **Reduce waste and obsolescence** by not overbuying raw materials or overproducing finished goods that will end up sitting around until they become obsolete and are ultimately discarded.

3. **Reduce overtime pay** by being able to better plan and anticipate proper staffing levels and reduce having to hold workers overtime to expedite shipments.

4. **Reduce inventories** by buying the raw materials that are needed *when* and *where* they are needed, as well as producing and completing finished goods *when* and *where* they need to be completed to meet customer demand.

Your solution, which in this example is a "Supply Chain Management & Collaboration Software" solution, is not what your customer needs or wants. What they *need* is the ability to improve forecast accuracy and demand planning. By connecting the dots and tracing the business effects up through the BVH model, we can clearly see what this particular customer *wants* to achieve:

1. Increased order fill-rates, increased customer loyalty, and increased revenues

2. Reduced waste and obsolescence, reduced materials costs, and lower overall costs, which drives profitability

3. Reduced overtime pay and lower direct labor costs, which also lowers overall costs

4. Reduced inventories, which converts current assets to cash that can be reinvested and improves their return on assets

Let me emphasize here, that what we "connect" are the functional capabilities of what we sell, not the products or services themselves. The name you choose to give your product or services means nothing to your customer. What matters are its functional capabilities, *what your products and services can do*, to support the tactics and strategies they will use to achieve their goals.

This approach represents quite a change from simply positioning your products by their superior features and functions. It's also very different than reciting a prepared list of advantages and benefits, or offering a description of all the different ways your products and services can be used. What I have found is . . .

> **Benefits are only beneficial if they help your customer to produce the business value, or the business results, they already want to produce.**

You may be coming to market with, for example, a "whole new way" to get your client's product in front of potential buyers. So, in one sense, how can they already want something they don't even know exists? Well, they can't, obviously. But even after you introduce your new idea to them, they *still* don't want whatever it is that you sell. What they *want* are the business results they can produce by using it. So, we have to understand those desired business results, their desired point "C," before we can properly position our product or service as the ideal "B" to take them there.

Cross-Organizational Impact

As was mentioned earlier, each element of value has one or more causes, and one or more effects. Therefore, an increase or decrease in any particular element of value could have multiple different effects on one or more units or departments across a business enterprise. Because of the complex interrelationships between all of these elements, it is impossible to visually depict all of them in a two-dimensional drawing. Figure 4.8 attempts to show a few common examples as they relate to the sample BVH model we just created.

An improvement in order fill-rates and customer satisfaction, for example, not only increases customer loyalty, but it also tends to reduce or contain accounts receivable. It can also help to drive down advertising costs because it fosters more repeat business and word-of-mouth advertising. Likewise, reducing inventories frees up capital for reinvestment, but it also reduces inventory carrying costs and reduces storage space requirements, which, in turn, reduces the cost of lease or rent on properties.

Sometimes an improvement in one measure could have a negative effect on another measure somewhere else in the company. Reducing inventories is generally considered a good thing, but taken too far, it could have a negative impact on order fill-rates, which results in both customer dissatisfaction and problems with accounts receivable and collections. Likewise, expanding into new markets may increase gross revenues but at the same time could dramatically increase storage and distribution costs, as well as divert working capital and other resources away from important projects supporting domestic operations.

Whenever we are diagnosing and evaluating business projects that our clients are considering, and while we are crafting our proposal of what we think they should buy, we need to be constantly asking ourselves "Why should they do this?" and "Why *else* should they do it?" in order to validate the business impact to our primary contact *as well as* the cross-organizational impact on other constituents throughout the company. These same exact questions ("Why should we do this? and Why *else* should we do it?") are what your customer will be asking themselves before they sign your contract or issue a purchase order. If we can't come up with some pretty strong answers to these two questions, chances are they won't either.

Notice that, in Figure 4.8, the titles of the key corporate executives are placed near the elements of value that each of them is primarily responsible for. Also notice the tall shaded ovals behind the BVH model that designate the areas of the business that these executives oversee. The executive vice president of sales and marketing (or some variation of this title) is primarily responsible for revenue, and all the business activities that contribute to selling whatever it is the company makes or delivers. The chief operations officer (COO) is focused mostly on mak-

Figure 4.8 Cross-Organizational Impact

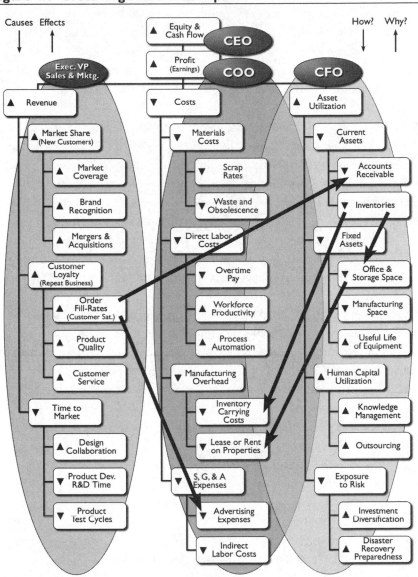

ing and delivering the products and services that are sold. The chief financial officer (CFO) has oversight of the care and use of the company's assets, which often includes—under his or her command—Human Resources, Facilities, and Information Technology (IT). There is some sharing of responsibilities across departments, but this illustration helps us to better understand "who is responsible for what" in the company.

It is vitally important that we develop our understanding of "who is responsible for what" because depending on the role of the particular person we are meeting with and selling to, we need to translate the value we can help our customer derive into the language they speak in their department. Let's take a closer look at the specific example in Figure 4.8.

If we have an opportunity to meet with an executive vice president of sales and marketing, we would probably want to start our questioning in the area of improving order fill-rates and customer satisfaction because that's the piece of the business they are primarily responsible for. For a meeting with the COO, or someone else in the operations department, we would probably do best to start by asking about containing or reducing materials or direct labor costs. If we have an audience with the CFO, we might be wise to concentrate our questioning on reducing accounts receivable, reducing inventories, and freeing up capital for reinvestment. This is not to say that these executives wouldn't care about issues or objectives outside their department, but this concept can help us focus on the issues or opportunities that are *most* important to the person we are meeting with.

We use cross-organizational discovery to learn more about other areas of the business, as well as who else within the organization might become an ally or an opponent to moving forward with any recommendation we might propose. Some examples of questions you could use while talking to the executive vice president of sales and marketing might be:

> *"Your plan to invest heavily in advertising to improve brand recognition seems to support your goal of increasing market share and top-line revenue. How will this impact the ability of your manufacturing and distribution departments to balance supply with demand?"*

Or . . .

> *"I can certainly see how better inventory management will enable you to reach your objective of increasing order fill-rates and improving customer satisfaction. Has your CFO done any analysis on how much capital could be freed up for reinvestment or how much she could save in carrying costs in the process?"*

Or . . .

> *"This new 'twenty-four-hour turnaround' service guarantee that you're planning to launch seems like a great competitive advantage. If your campaign is successful and you do increase sales by the projected 30 percent, how will that impact the staffing and logistics requirements of your field service organization?"*

If they know the answers to these questions, that's great! If they don't, this is one of the best techniques I know to build a case for why you should meet with some of those other managers and executives throughout the company to learn more about the broader impact of the project at hand. We will discuss this further in Chapter 9.

Practical Application of Business Value Hierarchy™

The concept of business cause and effect and the Business Value Hierarchy™ model can be used in a wide variety of applications, too many to be adequately addressed in one chapter. One workshop attendee asked me, "Isn't this BVH just a model for questioning?" In one sense it is, but it is much more than that. It is a model for *understanding* and depicting the way in which your prospective customer goes about creating business value. Of course, questioning is one of the ways we learn what we need to know in order to understand, so questioning is more the means than the end.

Understanding your customer's business isn't the endgame either. The endgame is using this knowledge and understanding to position your products and services as ideal solutions to specific business problems in order to influence your customer's decision criteria and buying process to close more business.

The following are just a few practical examples of the ways you can use the Business Value Hierarchy™ concept in your work.

Further Qualifying Opportunities

One major facet of qualifying sales opportunities is learning what "drives" our customer to buy something. As we use BVH to assemble a representation of our prospective client's business, we begin to see how the various groups, units, and departments work together to achieve shared objectives. By developing a model for "what serves which purpose" in the overall operation of the company, it becomes clear which groups or individuals have something to gain or lose and thus might play a role in any particular buying decision.

Sharing Knowledge with Your Team

Using the BVH model, you can more easily collect and share your understanding of your client's business with your management and other members of your sales team. Can you imagine how many words—written or spoken—it would take to communicate what is depicted in Figure 4.8? They say a picture is worth a thousand words. I seriously doubt a thousand words would come close to communicating what that illustration does.

A visual model like this can communicate a tremendous amount of information, perhaps some characteristics that could never be revealed by words alone. But more important, once we are all looking at the same picture, the quality of the dialogue and idea sharing among the team members improves exponentially. Used along with an accurate organization chart, it is very easy to see where certain responsibilities and concerns lay within the company, as well as who owns what element of value within your customer's business.

Positioning and Presentation

Over the years I have used the Business Value Hierarchy™ model as a mechanism to position products and services both in discussions and in presentations to customers, with great success. Today, many of my clients use it, in various forms, in presentations to their customers. One senior vice president (SVP) I had worked with in preparing a custom client presentation using BVH offered to attend a training session I was doing for some other executives within her company. We both felt it would be a great way to demonstrate the power of the concept in actual application with a real client, which happened to be one of the biggest foods manufacturers in the world.

She did a fantastic job of explaining how she and her team had used BVH to construct a model of her client's business strategy and how they leveraged the need and desire to get a broad and complete under-standing of their customer's business to gain access to many top-level executives. Several of her client's vice presidents ultimately invited her to present her findings and recommendations directly to their CEO. It was a smash hit, and the presentation led to a multimillion-dollar engagement.

She then showed my workshop participants the model that she had created for the client, which clearly revealed several great opportuni-ties to apply their analytic services to improve the client's business results. Then she went on to show the actual solution they had proposed to the customer, which included several studies and analyses that specif-ically addressed the issues that the BVH model had revealed.

One gentleman in my class felt compelled to burst out with, "Wow! This is one of the best business solutions I have ever seen. The way you positioned study X with analysis Y, and tied together with report Z, it's incredible! We need to take this solution to every CEO in this industry."

What had this gentleman missed? The reason the solution was so "dead on" was that the SVP and her team had done the research and discovery first—had fully understood point "C" if you will—and *then* presented the solution as the "B" that could take them there.

I suspect that if they had simply taken the same solution and broadcast the advantages and benefits to every CEO in the industry, they would have experienced a weak response at best. What makes a solution a great solution is that it springs from a thorough understanding of your customer's most important goals and objectives, as well as the unique challenges and business problems standing in their way.

My client used the BVH model and the diagnostic approach to better understand her customer's business. When she demonstrated that knowledge and understanding, and presented her solution in that context, she earned the right to present to the CEO, she earned their respect, and she earned their business.

Validation of Your Solution

Once you've done your discovery and are ready to "play back" to your client what you have learned in a presentation, it is sometimes helpful to use a more simplified or streamlined version of the BVH model. Figure 4.9 shows a "Value Pyramid," which is a powerful way to help your client understand exactly how the functional capabilities of your solution support the execution of their business plan.

Notice the "How?" and "Why?" in the upper right-hand corner that tie everything together. When done right, you should be able to use how and why to make this picture read like a narrative in your presentation. Here is an example of what a presentation like this might sound like:

> *"Over the last three weeks, you have shared a lot with us about your corporate goals and objectives. We don't profess to be able to solve all the world's problems, but we can certainly help you with your goal of improving gross margin from the current 25 percent to at least 30 percent. The question is 'How can we do that?'*
>
> *"We have determined together that the most effective way to quickly impact gross margin is by reducing materials costs. We looked at several different options of how to do that and concluded that the area of greatest opportunity lies in reducing scrap rates, which will reduce the waste of raw materials. The next question then is, 'How can we do that?'*

Figure 4.9 The Business Value Pyramid

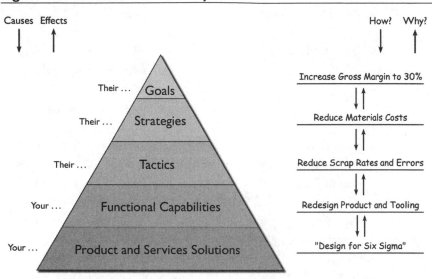

"*Again we considered the alternatives and have agreed that a slight change in the design of your product, as well as a redesign of the tooling used in manufacturing, could reduce or possibly eliminate the chance of machine operator error, and greatly improve the yield of product components that meet required specifications.*

"*So, 'How can we do that?' you ask. Our team of 'Design for Six Sigma' specialists has put together a plan . . .*"

Once you have explained the functional capabilities and how your solution does what you say it will do, you can tie it all back to their goals by working your way back up the pyramid with "Why?"

"*So, 'Why should XYZ consider this proposal?' The reason why a redesign is needed is for the purpose of reducing scrap and waste. Why reducing scrap and waste matters is that it can substantially reduce raw materials costs. And why should you worry about reducing materials costs? Because based on our estimates, which have been confirmed and validated by your materials manager and by your CFO, it is possible to reduce cost enough to increase gross margins from 25 percent to as much as 32 percent. If we begin today, we can have these design*" *changes complete, fully deployed, and in production within six weeks. Do you have any questions, or are you ready to move forward?"*

Please note, by looking at the left-hand side of Figure 4.9, that we are talking about *their* (your customer's) goals, *their* strategies to achieve those goals, *their* tactics that they will employ to make the strategies work, and the functional capabilities of *your* products and services solutions.

Another alternative for presenting the Business Value Hierarchy™ in a more streamlined and simplified way is shown in Figure 4.10. This model is used to illustrate how your solution offers one or more functional capabilities that facilitate the multiple tactics your customers may employ to support the strategies they will use to pursue their goals. Please note that the model will change depending on whom you are presenting to. If you are presenting to corporate management, you may choose to tie everything back to their primary objective of maximizing profits and the three high-level goals of increasing revenue, reducing costs, and better utilizing assets. On the other hand, if you are presenting to the executive vice president of sales and marketing, you can tie everything back to *his* primary objective, and the three (or five) goals he has established to ensure that the objective is met.

These two versions of the BVH model help to crystallize your client's understanding of what your product and services solutions can do to impact their business, without the clutter of all the various strategies and tactics you may have identified throughout your discovery process. Together these two diagrams form the backbone of the Executive Presentation format we teach as part of our Selling at the C-Level® workshop.

Training a Sales Team

BVH is a great mechanism to transfer domain expertise from those with a great deal of business acumen and industry knowledge to those who are new or who have less business experience. For use in our workshops, we have developed examples of a Business Value Hierarchy™ model for more than a dozen different industries including high-tech

Figure 4.10 A Simplified BVH Model for Presentation

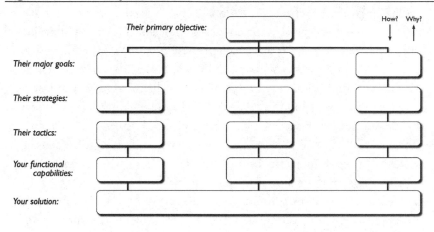

manufacturing, consumer packaged goods (CPG) manufacturing, retail, wholesale distribution, food service, financial services, telecommunications, engineering and construction, not-for-profit health care, and several different federal and local government agencies.

Even after doing hundreds of workshops, I am still surprised to see how excited and enthusiastic participants get when they see a sample BVH model for the industry they sell to. For most of them, the goals, strategies, and tactics identified are nothing new. They hear their customers talking about these things all the time. But being able to look at them in a hierarchical model that illustrates the cause-and-effect relationships between them, and being able to quickly see exactly how their own products and services can impact their customer's business, can be a major revelation.

We take participants through a process we call "Solution Mapping" in order to link the specific functional capabilities of their products and services to the business problems their clients are likely to be faced with. I firmly believe that for most of us . . .

It's not necessarily more *product* knowledge, but more *problem* knowledge that we need to develop.

Solution Mapping is simply taking each product or service that you sell, and first listing all of its functional capabilities (i.e., the things that it can do) and then translating those capabilities into what it will enable our customer to do. We look at each of these functional capabilities and ask, "*Why* would a customer want to be able to do this?" Then we look at each of the business tactics that a typical client in a given industry might be employing and ask, "*How* could we enable or help our customer to improve this particular aspect of their business?" Through a series of "Why?" and "How?" questions, participants begin to see the linkages between their capabilities and the tactics and strategies their customers use to pursue their business goals.

It is very important to point out that a pre-built BVH model, like the one in Figure 4.7, is only an example. It is based on a fictitious company and the things that this sample company *might* be doing to pursue their goals. Likewise, a solution map like the one described above, is only an example and should only be used for training and practice.

The real value of the cause and effect of business and the Business Value Hierarchy™ concept is not in developing a set of "cheat sheets" we can use to *presume* what strategies and tactics our client *might* want to employ in order to pursue what we *assume* to be their goals. The value is in facilitating business conversations and asking "How?" and "Why?" in order to construct a real understanding of our client's business, so that we can offer customized solutions that fit their specific situation and are designed to help them achieve the goals they already want to achieve.

Strategy Development and Clarification

For some of my clients, the BVH concept has become much more than a selling tool. If it is useful in modeling an understanding of our customer's business strategy, then it could be used to bring clarity to our own business strategy as well. Business Value Hierarchy™ is a great mechanism for brainstorming about all the possible ways in which we can impact a particular Key Performance Indicator (KPI) or achieve a particular business objective.

I regularly use a sales-specific version of the BVH model in selling our own training and consulting services, as well as in the consulting work we do to help our clients determine where they may need to invest resources to ensure that they produce the sales results they have promised to deliver.

Several of my clients who offer consulting services have also adopted the BVH model and use it as an integral part of every client engagement. They use the model to depict their customer's current business and brainstorm about other strategies and tactics that could help *their* customer achieve *their* business goals.

Business Value Hierarchy™ in Context

Like many of the ideas presented earlier in this book, and others still to come, BVH is a tool. You don't have to spend the time and effort to understand your customer this well. But it's worth it. It really doesn't take as much time as you think, once you get the hang of it. There is one very important truth about using these kinds of tools that I want to make sure to emphasize . . .

Whether you use these tools or not, you will probably get to know the top one or two opportunities in your sales pipeline this intimately anyway. You'll have to in order to win. The value of using tools like the BVH model is that you can reach this level of understanding much more quickly, with less chance of forgetting vital pieces of information, leaving you more time to leverage this knowledge to influence the customer's buying process.

Secondly, these tools make it much easier to organize your understanding of—and thus your ability to better manage—opportunities three through ten in your pipeline. Tools make you more effective and thus more efficient. Using tools like BVH, you will be able to better prioritize your time and efforts on the best deals in your pipeline, as well as be able to manage more opportunities at once.

Everything in this book is offered as a way to make your job easier, not harder. Finding one or even a handful of people within a company who have an interest in hearing about what you sell is easy. What's hard is spending a few months of your time trying to sell them something, only to discover that their interest was not grounded in, or tied to, corporate-level goals and objectives that were important enough to be funded.

You've heard it a thousand times. "You need to work smarter, not harder." Frankly, I always hated that statement. I actually felt insulted, because it seemed as if whoever said it was suggesting that I wasn't smart. I always thought to myself, "I'm obviously working as *smart* as I can!" After all, who in their right mind would choose to work *stupid*?

Perhaps a better suggestion than "You need to work smarter" would be, "You need to work, and make decisions, based on more of the right information." Because it's not intelligence we're talking about here; it's knowledge, insight, and understanding. The more you *learn* about your customer, the "smarter" you will be.

CHAPTER 5

The Value of Customer Relationships

Relationships. Isn't that what makes the world go around? In business and in life people tend to gravitate toward, associate with, and buy from people they know, like, and trust. I've never met anyone who can refute that. But what is the value of building business relationships with our customers and clients? Is it, as some have proposed, what it's *all* about?

Go to your favorite search engine, type in "relationship selling," and you'll find a number of books, tapes, videos, and seminars on the subject. Over the years I have met many accomplished sales professionals who attribute their success to "relationship selling." In many cases, they simply use this term to describe the process of understanding their customer and helping their customer to understand them. It's not rocket science. They didn't have to read any particular book or attend any particular seminar to learn the "secret formula" because *all* selling is relationship selling. But building relationships is *not all* that selling is. It's not *all* about relationships. There's more to the job than just making friends, because . . .

> A deep, meaningful, high-trust relationship with a client who has no *business disparity*, no *motive* to take action, or no *means* to take action even if they did have a motive, equals no sale. It's just a relationship.

Good business leaders make their decisions based on what they think is best for their customers, their employees, their owners or shareholders, and for themselves. That's the way it should be. Wouldn't it be a little unrealistic to expect an honest and intelligent business manager to commit his or her company to buying something that didn't add economic value to the company and its shareholders, just because they had a great personal relationship with a vendor? Has it happened? You bet it has! It's called corruption. But in today's climate of hypersensitivity to corporate ethics, it is simply not prudent to rely on the "brother-in-law approach" as an effective go-to-market strategy.

A great relationship is seldom what initiates or instigates a business transaction. A relationship, rather, is what facilitates cooperation, collaboration, and commerce. It makes it possible. A good relationship can make a prospective customer much more willing to share their goals and plans with you, explore possibilities, listen to new ideas, and engage in a process of mutual discovery. A strong relationship can also cause a buyer to take action to move forward with a project, or at least take a step *toward* moving forward, with one vendor or partner when they clearly would not be willing to take that same step with another. A high degree of trust in one supplier, compared to another, can make that supplier the vendor of choice, even if they charge a higher price. Trust can transform a vendor into a strategic partner.

Earning Trust

Trust is a belief that one person has about another person, or about an organization. It is a perception. It's a positive expectation that this other person or company can be relied upon, they will honor their commitments, they will treat us fairly, and "they care." We can have this belief about someone whether it is based on actual experience or simply on hope and assumption.

We willingly grant varying degrees of unearned trust to other people based solely on our own set of beliefs and expectations about the world. Many of us very quickly trust a doctor, or an airline pilot, or the complete stranger driving their car at sixty miles per hour in the opposing lane, with our very lives. But others of us have a hard time trusting anyone who stands to make a buck when we buy something. Your customers are the same way. They make certain judgments about people based on their own set of beliefs, biases, and opinions. We will never fully understand their reasoning.

What we can do, however, is learn how to earn trust. Much like respect, our customers are usually willing to grant us more when we earn it. But we don't simply go around earning trust for "no reason." Trust enables and empowers another person to take a chance on us, to take a risk. One of the tenets in Chapter 3 pointed out that reducing perceived risk increases perceived value, so . . .

> **Trust serves a purpose. It should exist, or rather *needs* to exist, wherever risk is present. Trust can offset risk. It facilitates action in the face of risk. Therefore, trust has value.**

Trust among work groups promotes teamwork and cooperation. Trust between employers and employees reduces turnover and boosts morale. Trust between ourselves and our customer fosters customer loyalty and repeat business as well as references and recommendations.

Trust, when it takes the form of our customer's belief that we can help them avoid future mistakes, adds Guidance or Advice Value to a relationship. The belief or the expectation that we can complete a project on time reduces the risk of being late and thus reduces the Time Risk in what we sell. As you can see, our ability to earn trust and develop business relationships can strongly influence how our customers perceive value and risk and thus is one of the most important skills of our profession.

I have never been comfortable with the phrase "building trust," because trust—like respect or admiration—is earned by one person and granted by the other. The other person has complete and total control of the granting—and can take it away at their discretion without notice. We can't build respect, or build admiration. They are outside our sphere of control. Trust is the same way. But trust *can* be proactively earned by establishing the right environment, and through a series of positive interactions.

The Right Environment for Trust

Whenever we meet somebody new, we instantly begin comparing all of the attributes and characteristics of that person with the things we already know and believe about people. It's not a conscious cognitive process. We don't have to remember to do it. It happens automatically whether we realize it or not.

Our mind likes to make sense of things and draw conclusions. We collect bits and pieces of information, which we observe and *assume* about another person, like so many million little pixels that make up a complete picture. Then we fill in any blanks ourselves as we form impressions of that person in our mind.

We never consciously ask ourselves, "I wonder if this person is honest?" We just collect the evidence and store it accordingly. We never think to ourselves—or much less ask out loud—"Is this person of strong moral character?" Instead we just collect the data, and based on what we observe and assume, we "feel" a certain way about someone.

But if we could hear the questions that our customers are asking themselves in their subconscious minds we would hear questions like:

- "I wonder if this person will really do what he says he's going to do?" which speaks to integrity.
- "Does she really believe what she is telling me, or is she just reciting her lines?" which speaks to honesty.
- "When we hit a rough spot in the relationship, will he do the right thing?" which speaks to character and ethical behavior.

The truth is, we can never truly know the answers to these questions. We can never really know another's disposition. We can only infer it from the things they say and do.[1] Our customers will trust us to the degree they *believe* we are worthy of trust. So, I say, "First, get your heart right," and realize that your long-term success is based on how many customers you help to become successful. When you internalize and believe that, you'll have no trouble communicating that to your clients. It will be communicated in everything you say and do.

Our customers won't come right out and ask us questions about honesty, character, and integrity. Nor will they ever consciously ask themselves. But the impression or perception they have of us will be formed in their mind by collecting the answers to these questions and dozens or hundreds more. In this chapter, we will look at four specific questions that every customer asks in the back of their mind. We need to be aware of these four customer concerns, and provide the answers to these four questions, so we can foster the right environment for trust.

1. Value Add: "What Value Do You Bring That Others Don't?"

Trust has value, but value also inspires trust. When a buyer believes that you offer superior value, they simply *want* to trust you more. When people want to trust, they start looking for reasons to believe. Conversely, if they're looking for reasons *not* to buy, they will probably find them.

When we talk about, and ask questions about, our customer's desired point "C," and the results they are trying to achieve, it is only natural for them to assume that we have their interests at heart. But if we spend more time talking about ourselves, and the products or services that we sell, our customer can only assume that we are more interested in ourselves than in them.

The more effectively we can communicate and emphasize the value of what we bring to the table, and how those things can be used to improve their business and their personal lives, the more our customer will want to find us trustworthy.

2. Motive: "What's in It for You?"

One of the things customers often wonder is why *you* think they should buy, buy now, and buy from you. They wonder, "What will you get out of this transaction?" This is a very natural and normal question, but for some buyers who are suspicious, skeptical, or paranoid, it can become an obsession. Here again people listen to the things you talk about, and ask about, to ascertain where your mind and heart are. So, we should keep our conversations and discussions on their outcomes and objectives (their point "C") as much as possible.

We should try to communicate, through our attitude and behavior as well as our words, that we are not in business to trick people into buying something. From time to time I have felt compelled to clear the air by telling a customer:

> *"Just so we both understand here, John, this is not my hobby. I do this for a living. This is how I pay the light bill. But I will never ask you to buy something if it's not in your best interest. If we get down to the end of this and you are not completely convinced that we are the right choice to go with, please don't buy anything from me. Is that a deal?"*

I've never yet found a customer who objected to that.

3. Competence: "Are You Competent Enough to Deliver on the Commitments You Make?"

The substance of a relationship is making and delivering on commitments. One of the things that anybody would naturally wonder is, "Are you capable of doing what you say you will do?" After all, we couldn't very well trust someone to do something that we weren't confident that they were *capable* of doing, could we?

People begin to gauge our competence in delivering on large commitments based on how we handle small ones. Something as trivial as forgetting to send an e-mail you promised, or failing to respond with some requested information may not seem like a major offense, but in the early stages of a relationship, it may be the only indication your customer has to judge whether or not you can be trusted to manage a million-dollar project.

We all make judgments about others using what psychologists call heuristics and biases.[2] These are mental shortcuts we use so that we can make sense of things faster and more easily. We take a small amount of information, the four corners of a painting for example, and by comparing that information with what we already know and believe about human nature, we guess at what the whole picture must look like. In everyday use, these shortcuts are amazingly accurate.

We don't have to see a dog to conclude how big he is or how far away he is. All we have to do is hear him bark, and based on the pitch and the volume, and a few hundred other little variables that only our subconscious mind understands, we guess that he is a little dog, perhaps a poodle, and that he is across the street in the neighbor's yard.

The problem with heuristics and biases is that they can lead us to premature conclusions. Just because a person shows up to a meeting without a pen, doesn't mean he or she is not management material, does it? Just because we forgot to confirm our appointment with the CFO's assistant, like she asked us to, doesn't mean that our firm wouldn't be a good consulting partner, does it?

The brutal truth is that our answer to—or our opinion about—these questions is irrelevant. Your customer can only make judgments based on the information that is available to them. They can't know that you really *meant* to confirm the appointment but didn't have time. We have to recognize that our customers can't trust us with big things if we don't demonstrate competence in the small.

4. Respect: "Do You Respect Me Enough to Deliver on the Commitments You Make?"

Trust and respect are closely related and have a reciprocal effect. It's impossible to trust someone we don't respect, or who is not respectable, but it's very easy and only natural to trust someone we do respect, and who we believe respects us. So, we should endeavor to earn the respect of our customers through our attitudes and our behavior, but also by showing respect to them.

If you want your customer to trust you, or to take a risk with you, please remember that . . .

Your customer can only trust *you* to the degree to which they believe you respect *them*.

If they don't think you respect them, how can they possibly trust you? It's only logical that if they believe you don't respect them, then you probably won't respect the commitments that you make to them, either.

For this reason, I am convinced that demonstrating respect is the most important thing we can do to foster the right environment for trust. In order to demonstrate our respect for our customer, we should:

Show Respect for Their Time

If we show up late, or talk too long, or don't call at a time they scheduled to hear from us, we are showing disrespect for their time, and thus a lack of respect in general. If there is one mistake we make too often it's not *ending* meetings on time. We have to break this habit. Period.

Talking on and on past the time we both agreed we would end says to your customer, "I care more about what I am saying than I care about you." The major cause of meetings that run too long is selling in the "broadcast" mode. We simply have to quit broadcasting! Later on, once you get so good at the diagnostic approach that your customer just won't stop talking at the designated ending time, just point to your watch and—when they take a breath—say, "I'm good to keep going if you are."

Show Respect for Their Ideas

If we are interrupting our customer, or finishing their sentences for them, or worse yet don't give them the chance to talk at all, we apparently don't respect or even care what they think. Now, we might have just talked incessantly because we were nervous, but it really doesn't matter *why* we did it. It still shows a lack of respect. Learn to get your customer talking and ask questions about what they say. More on this later in this chapter.

Show Respect for Their Position

We all want to sell to the CEO. But let's recognize that whomever we are talking to, their position is important to them. If we are interviewing the director of marketing, for example, chances are she went to college and maybe even earned an MBA to do what she does. She may have only been with her current company three years, but to go from analyst to director in that time might be a major accomplishment at her company.

Too often, in our haste to get to "the decision maker," we alienate the "gatekeepers" along the way. Please take my word for it; don't learn the hard way. Show the respect that each person deserves regardless of their title. When you talk with an executive assistant, treat them with the same respect and dignity you would show their boss. They may not carry the title, but an assistant to a top executive is likely one of the sharpest, most organized, and professional people at that company. One would have to be to earn that job! So, demonstrate respect for their position, no matter what it is.

Show Respect for Their Space and Their Property

When you walk into your customer's office, wait for them to show you where to sit. Be careful not to take their chair. Don't get too close to people. Some people get very uncomfortable when you crowd their personal space. Keep your conduct professional no matter how long you've known your customer.

Respect your customer's property and possessions. The things on their desk or office shelves wouldn't be there if they didn't have special meaning or value. Don't pick them up, or even ask to pick them up. You can still admire them or point to them without touching them. I remember one time asking about (without touching) an old slide rule sitting on the edge of a customer's desk. It happened to belong to his father, who had passed away earlier that year. It led us into a nice conversation about family and genealogy. I can only imagine what would have happened if I had been insensitive enough to pick it up and start messing with it.

Nobody likes it when we touch their "stuff," when we mess with the heater controls in their car, or push the things on *their* desk out of the way to make room for *our* PC. Be careful, and show the proper respect for your customer's space and personal property.

Show Respect for Their Views and Beliefs
Remove from your language and behavior all words and actions that your customer might find offensive. We've all made mistakes, but we should try to avoid as many as possible. Here are just a few ideas to consider:

- Be sensitive to religious beliefs by becoming aware of the holidays and rituals your client might, or might not, observe. Don't assume anything; just behave in a manner that shows the proper respect for their beliefs or customs, whatever they may be.
- Don't comment on politics or politically charged news and current events. Your client may not believe the same things you do, and you could offend them very quickly by making fun of a political figure whom they happen to respect and admire, for example.
- Purge *all* off-color language, jokes, and innuendo from your vocabulary, even if it's "just guys." The point is not whether they laughed at the joke or not; it's that highly respectable, and highly respectful, professionals operate on a higher level than that. Do what you want on your own time, but in front of customers, be a consummate professional.

The Power of Communication

Communication is where all trust and relationships begin. Without it, literally nothing is possible. But with it, anything is possible. Skills such as effective letter writing, public speaking, and presentation skills are very important for all sales professionals, but I believe that . . .

> **Communicating with your customer should be
> 80 percent listening and 20 percent asking questions
> so you can do more listening.**

Improving "listening skills" is one of the most popular requests we hear when we ask sales managers where their sales team needs the most help. So, I decided to include here a quick lesson in listening. Some will think this is overly simplistic, but I urge you to take this seriously. Sometimes it's the simple things—the ones that we think should be no-brainers—that we never get around to addressing. Always remember . . .

> **Trust is earned in listening, not in talking.**

So, to learn to earn trust, we all need to become better listeners. You might ask your boss or someone else on your team to critique you on your listening expertise.

If you want a real jolt to the ego, record *your side* of a few phone calls to customers, or, even better, record a live meeting with a client. Make sure to ask your client if they mind if you record yourself. I have recorded hundreds of customer conversations over the years and very few clients have ever expressed a concern with it. But what I have learned by hearing what my customers hear has helped me immeasurably.

A Lesson in Listening

Psychologists say that 93 percent of what we communicate to other people is nonverbal.[3] So, start your meeting off by telling your customer a few things without uttering a word. First, leave your laptop in your car. In fact, the less you bring in the better. If you've got a big shoulder bag, your customer has to assume it's full of something (brochures, literature, price lists, etc.) that you will use during your "broadcast." Why not try something a little different. Especially on your first meeting, just bring a notebook and two good pens. Let your customer know by what you *don't* haul into their office that this meeting is going to be a little different than the ones with their other vendors.

Next, open your notebook and write the company name, the name of the person you're meeting with, the date, and the time at the top. Keep your pen in hand, ready to write. You want them to know that you are there to listen, you are interested, and you are ready to take notes so you don't forget anything. By putting their name and the date at the top, you are communicating that these notes need to be labeled, so as to distinguish them from all the others you have. You will communicate to them that this is how you always operate—in listening and learning mode. The inference is that you will catalog these notes somehow, which communicates that you are well organized. They will probably even think that you must be working with a lot of different clients, since you need to label your notes so precisely.

Sit up on the edge of your seat, not laid back with your legs crossed or hunched over. Use a table to write on, if possible, instead of your lap. Now you are ready to start listening, and your customer will get the picture. Without exception, they will begin thinking about what they want to say, because it will be apparent that they will be doing most of the talking in this meeting.

You may need to start the conversation off with a few choice questions that you have prepared ahead of time, but whenever possible follow the five suggestions below:

1. Close Your Mouth

I know it seems overly simplistic, but you can't learn anything while you are talking. Salespeople tend to talk too much rather than too little. Learn to use silence in a conversation. When someone is talking to you and comes to the end of a statement, give him a second or two; he might want to follow up that comment with a little more detail or offer additional information you would have never thought to ask about. Leave more space in your conversations. You may be surprised what kind of information he decides to fill it up with.

One of my favorite questions to ask a prospective client—who I know is currently buying from my competitor—is, "What do you like best about working with XYZ?" No matter what they tell you about "The best thing about XYZ . . ." wait a full five seconds before you say your next word. Literally count one–one thousand, two–one thousand, . . . all the way to five. I realize it might feel like an hour and a half, but keep your mouth closed. Many times they will feel compelled to balance their endorsement with some less-than-glowing critique, which you could have never gotten them to tell you that by asking, "What *don't* you like about XYZ?"

2. Look at the Other Person and Smile

Eye contact is vital in good communication and earning trust. Don't have a staring contest with your customer, or burn a hole through their retinas. Just let your eyes roam around their face, coming back to their eyes every few seconds. If they use any hand gestures, let your eyes occasionally focus on their hands. Make sure that both your mouth and your eyes are smiling. People can see a fake smile a mile away, because it only involves your mouth. A real smile involves your eyes too.

While they are talking, try to block everything else out of your mind. Years ago I started using a technique—while listening to my customers speak—of subliminally repeating to myself, "You (my customer) are the most important person in the world right now." I repeat this in my mind every few seconds while my client talks regardless of whether it's in person or on the phone. This simple technique helps me stay focused and I definitely believe my clients can sense it too.

Listen with your ears *and* your eyes. If 93 percent of communication is nonverbal—and therefore only 7 percent is verbal—then you ought to be able to hear twelve or thirteen times as much information with your eyes as with your ears, right? While they are speaking, literally imagine that your eyes can hear. Look at them and listen with your eyes as intently as you can. Your customer will notice the difference, and so will you. I guarantee it. You try it and see if I am right.

3. Nod a Little

Encourage your customer to keep talking by nodding a little as the conversation goes along. Don't overdo this. You don't want to look like one of those little toy dogs in the back window of a car. Just acknowledge that what they are saying is making it through your eardrums and all the way to your brain. Once in while, when you hear something particularly interesting, silently say "Ahhhh" to yourself while raising your head slightly to signify that you heard it. You might also want to get your eyebrows involved a little on the really interesting bits. Again, don't overdo it, but remember . . .

Even when your customer is doing the talking, and your mouth is closed, you still have 93 percent of your capacity to communicate available.

Use it!

4. Become a Great Conversationalist

Great conversationalists, those who know how to get people talking and keep them talking, use a number of verbal sounds and certain words that encourage the other person to continue. Many of these "sounds" don't translate well into print, but I will do the best I can. There are certain voice inflections that make these sounds work, and even the actual words need to be delivered with the right intonation for maximum impact.

At just the right time in the conversation, when your customer takes a breath, encourage them to keep talking by mastering the use of these "great conversationalist" words, such as:

- Mmmmm
- Hmmmm
- Hmm!

- Ahhhh
- Huh!
- Oh?
- Wow!
- Really?
- Amazing!
- Seriously?
- Incredible!
- Is that right?
- Unbelievable!
- No kidding?

Try reading through this list a few times, saying them out loud if appropriate. Pay close attention to the punctuation, and notice how you can communicate a completely different meaning by changing the inflection or intonation just a little.

Practice using these words even when you have thought of some really impressive response to what your customer has said. Try using one of these "great conversationalist" words first, and then wait a few extra seconds to see if they have anything else to add. If not, then you can hit them with your insightful reaction. Sometimes just nodding a little and keeping your mouth closed will give your customer the nudge they need to keep going.

You can often prompt your customer to continue talking by repeating the last few words they have said using the right intonation to make a question out of them. Here's an example:

"I'm sorry, but this isn't the time for us to be looking at new consulting partners or new projects. Right now we are just buried with work; we've got more projects than we can handle."

"More projects than you can handle?"

"Yes, even if we had the manpower available, we'd be smarter to focus on some of the other projects under consideration."

"Other projects under consideration?"

"Yes, we've always got a half-dozen other things that we would like to do if we had the right resources."

"The right resources?"

"Yes, it takes more than just a few skilled people. What I really need help with is managing projects."

"You need help managing projects?"

You get the idea. The point is, give them a chance to talk, and encourage them to keep on talking.

5. Ask Clarifying Questions

We have already mentioned the importance of not just asking questions, but asking the *right* questions to better understand Motive, Urgency, Consequence, cause and effect, and so on. Prepare before you get on the phone or go to a meeting by crafting a few key questions to both start discussion and lead the discussion in the direction you want it to go. Whoever asks the questions actually controls the conversation.

Whenever you are in the middle of a conversation and you can't think of just the right question to ask next, or maybe you just need a clarification on what they have said, the best and most versatile question you could ever ask is, "Why do you say that, John?" Using your client's name makes the question much more personal, and often elicits personal opinions and perspectives.

As we have discussed, the answers to "Why?" questions tell us about Motive, they illuminate how our client perceives cause and effect, and they reveal more about our client's goals and objectives. They also simply communicate that we are interested in learning more and better understanding what our customer is trying to say to us. They communicate that "we care."

I urge you to weave this question into a customer conversation today, "Why do you say that, John?" Use this question a few times over the next few days to make yourself comfortable with it. I believe you will

Figure 5.1 The Trust Cycle

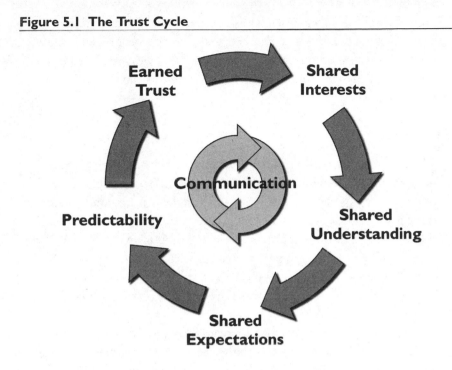

find it to be one of the most effective clarifying questions you can ask, and a surefire way to keep any conversation going.

The Trust Cycle

There is a cycle of human interaction that leads to trust and to strong resilient relationships. I call it the "Trust Cycle" as shown in Figure 5.1. It's a natural progression that happens whether we consciously attend to it or not, and it is constantly working for us or against us. It applies to every relationship in our lives and it illustrates how relationships evolve as we communicate and interact over time.

At the center of this model—and of all relationships—is communication, which acts as the engine that drives it. As we work our way around this model, beginning with shared interests, communication is the bridge that leads us to each new step in the progression. Only through communication can we even discover that we have shared interests to begin with. Thus, all relationships start and end there.

Shared Interests

The genesis of any relationship is some interest or some desire that two people have in common. It could be as simple as "we both like hiking" or "we both work at the same company." If there is no commonality, there is very little basis—and probably very little need—for a relationship. In fact, if we have nothing at all in common, we will probably never even come into proximity with the other person to start with. Yet, something as seemingly insignificant as two people being assigned to adjacent seats on an airplane can become the starting place for a relationship.

As we meet and begin to build a relationship with a new customer, we will no doubt discover many things we have in common. It's great when a buyer and a seller have shared personal interests, such as a love of baseball, skiing, or golf. But those commonalities are not what build a strong business relationship.

There's nothing wrong with golfing with a client, or taking them to a local sporting event. I know a lot of salespeople who love golf, and a lot of customers who do too. It's a great way for two people to get out of the confines and formalities of the office so they can relax and get to know a little more about each other. But you don't have to "wine and dine" your prospects to foster shared interests, and build business relationships.

Having shared interests with your customer happens when they want to arrive at their desired point "C," on time and under budget, and you want that too. Notice I didn't say they're interested in "C" and we are interested in "B," and therefore we have shared interests. That would actually be a conflict of interests! Your customer can tell if you have their interests at heart, and if you do, you have taken an important first step toward trust.

Shared Understanding

Through further communication, we move from shared interests to shared understanding. Your customer now knows some things about you, and you know some things about them, but you also understand the context of those facts. People are more than the sum of the labels that describe them.

Whenever human beings are involved, emotions are involved, as are personal interests and egos. The more time we can spend communicating with and listening to our customer, the better we can understand what makes them tick. But as pointed out earlier, feeling understood is more important than actually being understood.[4] The value of "face time"—the time we spend with our customer getting to know them—is directly proportionate to how much we can learn about them *and* to how confident they become that we actually understand them. Of course, this assumes we spend that time listening and learning as opposed to talking and telling.

How many times have you heard a customer say, "We decided to go with XYZ because they really seemed to understand what we were looking for and helped us find the right solution"? Understanding our customer shouldn't be random or accidental. It should be the result of a purposeful process of mutual discovery beginning with the very first phone call we make. Everything we do should be done to learn more about our customer and enable them to learn more about us.

Ultimately, we want our customer to understand that we are not just the same as every other vendor out there, because clearly we are not. No more so than they are just the same as every one of our other customers. So, a focus on understanding should be more than just a step in a sales process, it should be a philosophy of doing business. When it is, it will become your greatest differentiator of all.

Shared Expectations

Whether we are consciously aware of it or not, shared understanding leads to shared expectations. This is where this progression gets interesting. As we work together with our customers, they are naturally going to establish expectations about us. Those expectations can be based on actual experience, their own assumptions, or the way they *hope* to be treated. The problem comes when we don't understand their expectations or we make the mistake of believing they are exactly the same as ours.

Most of us seldom fail to meet expectations once they are set, but where we sometimes fall short is in making sure those expectations are set properly to begin with. We assume too much, our customers do too, and when our assumptions differ, expectations aren't met and relationships break down.

Now, it's not as if the second one little thing goes wrong the customer stomps their foot and says, "That does it. I'll never buy anything from that vendor again!" It's more like a little mark is recorded in the "minus" column; but those marks can add up if we're not careful. We can begin to take control of this and start proactively earning trust by leveraging opportunities to properly set and meet expectations. Every time we meet expectations, we score a little mark in the "plus" column, so we should take advantage of every opportunity we can to set expectations we know we can meet.

The next time you talk with your customer, and you make a commitment—no matter how small—take the time to make sure your expectations match theirs. When you say, "OK. I'll put some numbers together for you and get that over to you right away," realize that right away, to you, could mean next Monday. But they might have thought you would be faxing those numbers over that afternoon. This might seem like a small thing, and if you get the numbers over there Monday instead of this afternoon, it very well may be just a small thing. But you missed an opportunity to make it a big thing by not establishing shared expectations. Every little chance you have, set specific expectations. Instead of leaving things open-ended, try saying, "OK. I'll put some numbers together for you and get that to you right away. Will Friday be OK, or would Monday be better?"

How quickly you offer to get these numbers to your customer can communicate how highly you prioritize them, or how important they are to you compared to your other clients. But what's more important than how fast you turn it around, is that you establish shared expectations.

You might even want to get more specific than the day on which they can expect to see the numbers. For example:

"OK. I will get them to you on Friday. Will early afternoon . . . say 2 P.M. be alright?"

"Yes. That's fine."

"Excellent. What I will do is e-mail them to you at 2 P.M., and if you will be in your office, I'd like to give you a call. The call won't be to go over anything, but just to make sure you got the e-mail. Will that be alright with you?"

"Sure. Sounds good."

This is how you take a routine task and turn it into an opportunity to earn trust. Try to leverage every opportunity, regardless of how small or large, to properly set customer expectations. Then execute to the letter. Your customer can't help but be impressed.

Predictability

When we proactively set expectations, and we consistently meet those expectations, our customers begin to have more and more confidence in us. We become consistent, reliable, and predictable. We should be constantly on the lookout for ways to be found predictable, because . . .

Predictability is the natural precursor to trust.

We want our customers to feel that anytime they need us, we will be there, ready to help. We want them to know from experience that they can count on us, and when we say we're going to do something, we will move heaven and earth to get it done. We want to be "the rock" they can always turn to and know that we will come through for them, no matter what.

Sometimes, due to circumstances either within or beyond our control, we will discover that the expectations we have set cannot be met. What do we do then? Well, we certainly don't want to allow them to go unmet, so we have to take the time and the trouble to properly reset them. If we handle it right, most customers won't have a problem with it, as long as it doesn't cause a major headache or a negative impact for them. Of course, if our inability to deliver on time causes them to miss a deadline (or expectation) they've established with their customer, that's going to create a problem. The severity of the consequences will vary.

When we discover that we can't meet expectations, or even if we are concerned we may not be able to, we should let them know as far in advance as possible. Call them as soon as you can, and explain the situation. Find out what consequences might be associated with a change or a delay. I've found most customers very willing to work things out with you if you give them as much notice as you can and explore the consequences.

What damages your relationship and destroys trust is waiting until the last minute to notify your customer of a problem, or sending them an e-mail to announce a change in plans. If you have something important to tell them, talk to them in person or on the phone. Then you can get a sense of what kind of damage a delay or a change might cause, and you can come up with a solution together. Don't just make your problem *their* problem, by throwing it over the fence into their front yard. Call them and work out an acceptable solution together. That's what a true partner would do.

Working through problems together actually serves to further solidify and strengthen any relationship. When your customer sees you react and behave with character and integrity when something goes wrong, they feel more confident about relying on you the next time you encounter a problem together.

Earned Trust

When we ask our customer to take a risk with us, no matter how small, and we come through for them and meet our shared expectations, we earn a little trust. Unlike the unearned trust that people grant freely based on hope and positive expectation, "earned trust" is based on experience. Unearned trust can be revoked or taken away just as quickly as it's granted, but trust that we earn has an enduring quality.

This is not to say that earned trust is permanent, because we can certainly squander all the trust we've earned with one or more major transgressions. But when we build a business relationship on respect and predictability, we can weatherproof our relationship to stand up to the storms that inevitably come along.

When we have earned a level of trust with our customer, and communication is good, we tend to discover more and more interests that we have in common. That leads to deeper shared understanding, more shared expectations, and mutual predictability. We thus travel around the Trust Cycle again and again as we build our vendor/client partnership.

An interesting thing happens when we travel around and around this trust cycle with our customer over an extended period of time. At some point, our shared interests become each other's well-being. We start to look out for each other, and watch each other's back.

Unfortunately, we never get this far with most of our customers, or with most people for that matter. But with a few we do. I believe the more consciously and proactively we seek to earn trust, the more opportunities to build strong and enduring relationships we will find.

Not all of our customers want to build strong partnerships with their vendors. Maybe they don't understand that a great vendor relationship can bring them new business ideas that could add Time Value, new profit opportunities that could add Economic Value, as well as ongoing Guidance or Advice Value that could help them avoid embarrassing or costly mistakes.

Some customers, it seems, couldn't care less about your well-being, as long as they get a cheap price. That's OK. You and I are looking for a few great customers, who not only trust and respect us, but whom we can trust and respect as well. Because at the end of the day, business is a two-way street, and long-term, enduring relationships that bring measurable value to everyone involved are the foundation of business success.

PART II

HOW CUSTOMERS BUY

The Sales Process— Redefined

Despite all the lip service that has been paid to it, sales is the one area of business activity that has benefited the least from the application of process and process reengineering. While other departments, such as manufacturing and accounting, have been overhauled with Total Quality Management (TQM), Six Sigma, and a host of other management philosophies, Sales and Marketing have largely been left to fend for themselves.

Executives and business managers seldom look at a sales organization and ask, "What is this department capable of?" "How can we be more efficient?" or "What could be done to boost productivity and throughput?" More often, corporate goals and sales targets are established first, and then those expectations are simply *applied* to the sales organization who, in turn, divvy it up; sort of like "splitting the tab" after a group dinner in a restaurant: "How much does each of us owe?"

If the sales team achieves the goal, then everybody is happy. Never mind the details. Top sales performers are given free reign to do whatever they need to do to bring in business, and underperformers are replaced. As one sales professional put it, when speaking of his quarterly review with his boss and his boss's boss, "They don't ask how. They just ask how many."

The Value of Sales Process

Anything that we do over and over again can be made more efficient and more effective by developing and utilizing a standard process. It doesn't have to be complicated; it can be as simple as a series of steps and stages we *usually* work through to ensure that the outcome is as consistent, and as high quality, as possible. Using a defined sales process we can:

1. Leverage a common framework and pattern for planning, reviewing, and executing sales activities.
2. Communicate and strategize about sales opportunities with various team members using a common language.
3. Make fewer mistakes because we are reminded of the steps that need to be taken, which reduces the chance of forgetting important steps while in the heat of the battle.
4. Shorten sales cycles because we can usually work through the steps much faster if they are laid out ahead of time, than if we just "wing it" or make it up as we go along.
5. Shorten the ramp-up time for new hires who need to learn "how we engage clients" in our market.

Figure 6.1 shows a sample sales process that we use as an example in our workshops. Please note it is not my intention to suggest that you should adopt this as your process. On the contrary, I use this generic example to emphasize that this is *not* your process. Your process should reflect:

- How *you* find new opportunities.
- How *you* determine if the opportunity is worth investing your time in.
- How *you* engage in discovery to determine if there is a fit for, and a need for, what you sell.
- How *you* present your findings and your recommendations.

Figure 6.1 A Sample Sales Process

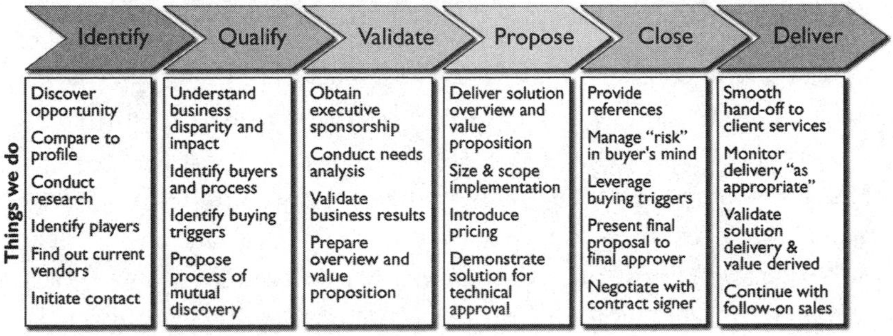
Identify
Qualify
Validate
Propose
Close
Deliver
Things we do
Discover opportunity
Compare to profile
Conduct research
Identify players
Find out current vendors
Initiate contact
Understand business disparity and impact
Identify buyers and process
Identify buying triggers
Propose process of mutual discovery
Obtain executive sponsorship
Conduct needs analysis
Validate business results
Prepare overview and value proposition
Deliver solution overview and value proposition
Size & scope implementation
Introduce pricing
Demonstrate solution for technical approval
Provide references
Manage "risk" in buyer's mind
Leverage buying triggers
Present final proposal to final approver
Negotiate with contract signer
Smooth hand-off to client services
Monitor delivery "as appropriate"
Validate solution delivery & value derived
Continue with follow-on sales

- How *you* bring business to closure.
- How *you* deliver what you've sold.

Your process doesn't have to be six steps or stages; it can be five, seven, nine, or whatever. However, what we do know is that the more detailed and granular it becomes, the less salespeople will want to use it. It's not because salespeople are lazy, or can't deal with structure. It's that every customer is different. Every sales campaign has its unique challenges, and what worked with the last client might be completely inappropriate for the next one.

It's funny, but after we win a sales opportunity and look back at it to determine why we won, it's usually a combination of many things that went right and all came together to make it happen. But when we lose, it often seems as if there were one or two specific things that went wrong. We think, "If we just could have known *this*, we would have done *that*, and maybe we could have won." Or worse, "I can't believe we did—or didn't do—*that* again! *That* happened to us before, and we should have learned our lesson." Developing an ever-evolving standard process to use as a guide helps us to be more consistent. It helps ensure that we not only do the right things, but also avoid doing the wrong things—hitting the same potholes and brick walls—over and over again.

The Problem with Sales Process

Unfortunately, not all companies that do take the time to observe, document, and develop a unified sales process see the results they expect, or that they would like. There may be several reasons for this:

- **Lack of support from sales management**—who don't promote and reinforce its use
- **Resistance from the sales team**—who perceive it as a way to "control" them or as "big brother" looking over their shoulder
- **It seems like overhead or busywork**—with too darn many forms or fields to fill out
- **It looks good on paper**—but it is not flexible enough to be useful in the real world

Any standard process we might choose to adopt, which is not flexible enough to support different types of sales campaigns and multiple sales strategies, or doesn't provide the ability to change gears in midstream when you need to, simply doesn't help your sales team close business. It may not be that your salespeople *won't* use your standard process; maybe they simply *can't* use it in a high percentage of cases.

The biggest reason sales processes aren't adopted and followed is that they are not designed around this one simple truth . . .

> **As sales professionals, we don't earn commissions, or get quota credit, for anything that *we* do. We get paid, and retire quota, based on what our *clients* do.**

When they sign a contract, or they issue a purchase order, then we make some money. Isn't that the way it works?

Sales processes, like the one shown in Figure 6.1—and the overwhelming majority of process maps that companies try to get their salespeople to use—depict a series of stages, steps, and activities that *we* work through to try to sell something. But what is conspicuously absent from most of these are the stages, steps, and activities that our pro-

Figure 6.2 The Sales Process—Redefined

	Identify	Qualify	Validate	Propose	Close	Deliver
Things we do	Discover opportunity Compare to profile Conduct research Identify players Find out current vendors Initiate contact	Understand business disparity and impact Identify buyers and process Identify buying triggers Propose process of mutual discovery	Obtain executive sponsorship Conduct needs analysis Validate business results Prepare overview and value proposition	Deliver solution overview and value proposition Size & scope implementation Introduce pricing Demonstrate solution for technical approval	Provide references Manage "risk" in buyer's mind Leverage buying triggers Present final proposal to final approver Negotiate with contract signer	Smooth hand-off to client services Monitor delivery "as appropriate" Validate solution delivery & value derived Continue with follow-on sales
Things they do	Discover or acknowledge need Seek input on a solution Conduct research Identify possible vendors Initiate contact	Identify business goals & drivers Quantify impact & ROI Determine timing and budget Agree to process and definition of "success"	Coordinate buying process with P&L owner, legal, finance, contract signer, and final approver Produce valid justification for investment, ROI, and payback	Approval of solution overview and value proposition Begin planning implementation Confirm timing and budget Select vendor of choice	Check references All approvers "sign off" Final approver agrees to final proposal Contract signer signs contract or issues purchase order	Provide internal support & resources for project Validate solution delivery & value derived Pay their bills Re-engage for follow-on sales

spective clients have to work through in order to buy something. The truth is that the things we do at any particular step or stage in the process could be a complete waste of time if our client doesn't do what they need to do to move forward to the next step or stage in their buying process. Please take a look at the process model depicted in Figure 6.2, and notice the notation on the left-hand side indicating the "Things we do" and the "Things they do."

I'd like to pose a question: Is it possible that we could do every single thing that we are supposed to do in our sales process perfectly—execute flawlessly—and still not make the sale? Of course it is! Then let me ask you this. If the client did all of the things that they needed to do in order to buy, but we missed one or two of the steps we were supposed to do, could we still book the deal? Sure. So, in reality then . . .

It's not what we do in our sales process, but what the customer does in their buying process, that really matters.

This truth represents one of the major challenges of professional selling. We have to accept that we cannot control our customers. We can
only seek to understand them and learn how to positively influence their
thinking and behavior.

Your Customer's Buying Process

As salespeople, and especially as managers, we tend to ask the wrong
question. We ask, "What do we need to do to close this deal?" Unfortunately, that's not the right question because we could do three dozen
different things and still not get the deal done. What we should be asking is, "What does the customer need to do in order to buy?" Only
when we can answer that question are we ready to ask the follow-up
question, which is, "What do we need to do to get them to do those
things?"

If fully embraced, this attitude will result in a major shift in how we
think about the job of selling. We should look at each opportunity in
our sales pipeline, and instead of starting with, "What have we already
done, and what do we need to do next?" we should be asking these four
critical questions:

1. What Does This Particular Buying Process Look Like?

Buying and approval processes vary based on a whole host of factors. We
need to learn the specifics of exactly what it would take for our particular customer to make a purchase of the shape and scope we are planning
to propose. Here are just a few of the things we might need to learn:

- What is involved in getting funds released for a budgeted
  expenditure? Who has to be involved in that approval process?
- What would it take to get approval for an *unbudgeted* expenditure?
  Who would likely be involved in *that* process?
- Are they a small, privately held firm with one owner who makes all
  the big decisions?

- Are they a division of a huge corporation, which will have to look to corporate for final approval?
- What is the signing authority of the vice president (or whomever) we are selling to? At what point would she need to get the CFO involved in executing a contract?
- How and when does their legal department need to get involved?

2. Where Is This Customer in Their Buying Process?

Is your customer a day or two away from signing a contract? Or are they still "kicking tires" and thinking about buying something? Most of our active sales campaigns are probably somewhere in between. Our mission is to figure out where they are in their process, what they've already done or decided, and what they still need to do or decide before they can buy.

I want to emphasize here that we should *never* take any one person's "word" for what needs to happen before their company will be ready, willing, and able to buy. I have learned that every person I meet within a given company seems to have their own version or opinion of how decisions are made, how projects get approved, and what stage of a particular buying process they are currently in. Get as many different perspectives, views, and opinions as you possibly can and blend them into your own composite view of what their process is like and where they are *within* their process.

3. What Is the Next Reasonable Step They Need to Take?

If we can figure out where they are, and what still has to happen before they can buy, then we may be able to ascertain what would be a logical and reasonable next step for them to take. Years ago I heard a sales trainer say, "You should ask for the order on every sales call." Well, that's just silly! If we are selling a complex solution to a major business problem that costs $100,000 or $1,000,000 or more, it would be ludicrous to expect our customer to "sign" on our first visit, or even the second or third. The question is what is the next "reasonable" step that we could ask our customer to take that will move them toward point "B" on their way to point "C."

4. What Can We Do to Get Them to Take That Step?

If we can get an idea of what our customer needs to do next in their buying process, that helps us figure out what we need to do next in our selling process. Things don't happen in the same sequence, or on the same schedule, in every sales engagement. We have to be flexible enough to do what we need to do based on any particular customer's buying process, and where they are within that process. Only after we understand that, should our focus shift to "What are we going to do?" based on that information.

Selling with Specific Intent

If you choose to believe and internalize what has been said here, this has the potential to completely change everything about the way you sell. The most important takeaway of this chapter, and maybe this entire book, is . . .

> **Everything we do should be done with the specific intent of helping our client to do something they need to do in their buying process.**

Any action we take, or any move we make, that is not done with the intention of empowering, enabling, or encouraging our buyer to move one step closer to a purchase, is wasted energy. We only do the things that we do in our process so that they will do the things they need to do in their process. This might require us to think differently about how we do our job. Before we pick up the telephone to call—or before we drive over to see—our client, we should be asking ourselves, "What *exactly* is it that they need to do next in their buying process, and what *exactly* am I going to do on this call or on this visit to help them do that?"

Let's say you're planning to meet with the company president of your best prospect, who will—as far as you understand—provide the final approval to move forward with any proposal you might ultimately choose to submit. What do you want him or her to do? Not just in general, I mean what is it exactly that you want him to do during or after the meeting? This would depend on where they are in their buying process, wouldn't it?

Perhaps the best place to start then, would be to ascertain where *he* thinks they are in their evaluation or selection process. It is shocking how often it's *not* the same place that the director of information technology thinks they are. In fact, you'll probably find out some things in that very meeting that change your understanding of what has to happen before they can move forward, and it could very well change your whole game plan for that meeting, as well as others in the future.

We should go into every meeting with a plan of what we want the person we are meeting with to do during, or after, the meeting. Do you want him to:

- Endorse your plan to meet with, and interview, some of the other executives?
- Schedule a meeting where you can bring in one of your business analysts to get a better understanding of how the products and services you offer can help them reach their business goals?
- Introduce you to both their CFO and their legal counsel so you can work with the CFO to produce a valid justification for the investment, and with Legal to approve the terms and conditions of your standard contract?
- Commit to or schedule a time to meet with you again, after you have done your opportunity assessment, to present your findings and recommendations?

If you know exactly what you are there to accomplish, then your primary objective for that meeting is to make sure you get their commitment to do those things before you leave.

I want to encourage you to take this concept of selling with specific intent to the next level. Think about the purpose of every single thing you do with your client. What are you hoping to accomplish? Establish a clear understanding of the possible outcomes of every single interaction, select the outcome you think is most desirable, and focus on achieving that. But also, be prepared to handle all other possible outcomes. *Never* allow yourself to be surprised.

If you are going to provide additional information about your company, products, or services, what do you want them to *think* differently or *do* differently after you deliver this information? If you can't answer this question, *do not* share the information. You will be wasting their time and yours.

If you are planning to give a presentation, ask yourself, "What do I want the audience to think differently or do differently after they see this presentation?" *Never* present something that doesn't have a purpose. If the information you are presenting does not serve a specific purpose, and is not designed to work for you, then the best that can happen is *nothing*, and the worst is that it will be used *against you*.

Break it down one step further. Look at each and every slide in your presentation deck and ask, "What do I want the audience to think differently or do differently after they see this slide?" When I do consulting work with my clients who are preparing presentations for *their* customer's C-Level executives, my rule of thumb is: "If you can't explain exactly what purpose this slide is serving, then get it out of the deck." You might even want to throw them all out and make them earn their way back in. You and I, and our customers, don't have enough time as it is. We certainly can't afford to waste any of it doing things that don't serve a specific purpose.

I am asking you to think differently about the way that you sell. Before you pick up the phone to make your next customer call, figure out *exactly* why you are calling. What do you want your customer to agree to on this call? If you've come over to see them, what do you want them to do before you come to see them the next time? Your customers are not always willing or able to take the steps that you request or recommend. But if you don't ask, or worse yet if you don't even know what steps you would recommend if they were willing and able, there is no possibility that they will take them.

Before the next scheduled interaction with your customer, review what you know, and don't know, about:

1. Their selection, approval, and buying process.
2. Where they are in that process.
3. The next step they need to take in that process.
4. What you are going to say or do to get them to take that step.

Of course, gathering or collecting some of this information might be the main reason for having the next call or visit. That's fine. It's a never-ending process of learning, readjusting your plan accordingly, learning some more, and readjusting again. But always keep in mind that . . .

> If you or I drive over to see a client—or worse, get on an airplane to fly there—without knowledge of their buying process, where they are in their process, the things *they* need to do next, and what *we* are going to say or do to enable or inspire them to do those things, we are nothing more than a "professional visitor."

Keeping in Step with Your Buyer

Have you ever found yourself diligently working through a sales campaign—holding meetings, giving presentations, delivering proposals, and maybe even providing references—only to discover that the people within your customer's organization who have the authority to buy are still mentally back at the very early stages? Or they are still trying to decide whether this purchase is something they really have to take action on at this time? This has no doubt happened to all of us.

What goes wrong when this happens? I think we took our eye off of what we've been talking about here. We're no longer focused on helping our client move through a buying process. We've gotten too tangled up in our sales process.

Sometimes we find ourselves "pushing" a customer to move through their process faster than they want to. The primary cause of this is that we don't have enough opportunities in our sales pipeline. We end up putting pressure on what few prospects we do have to compensate for our own lack of planning. Unfortunately, the only thing worse than having a thin pipeline is trying to get a client to commit to buying before they are ready to buy, and damaging or ruining a relationship with one of the few prospects we do have.

The better we can understand our customer's buying process, or the things that have to happen before they can buy, the better we can stay aligned with our customer, and work with them where they truly are. Of course, we will try to help them see the value of moving forward sooner. Chapter 10 is dedicated to this endeavor. But if we need more business this quarter, and one customer simply can't or won't buy yet, we might need to accept it and work on finding some that can or will.

Facilitating the Buying Process

If you deal in complex solutions or big-ticket items, your customers probably don't have a defined process for buying what you sell. They don't do it often enough to develop a process, so you will actually be helping them to discover their own internal buying process as you go. Sometimes, we know the things that our clients will have to do to buy better than they do. We sell every day. We can see a pattern, client after client after client, of the things that companies typically have to do in order to buy the types of products and services we sell.

When all is said and done, we need to be flexible enough to do whatever it takes to get the deal done, as long as it is legal, ethical, and a worthwhile business investment for us to do so. Therefore, if we were to depict our sales process most accurately, it would probably look something like Figure 6.3.

We should be willing do whatever we need to, in whatever order or sequence required, to help our customer do the things *they* need to do

Figure 6.3 Facilitating the Buying Process

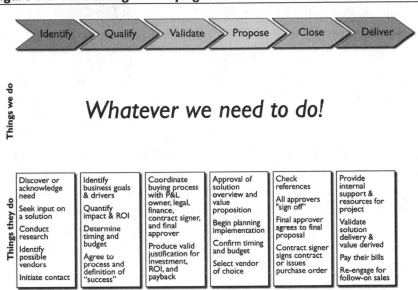

to buy . . . and then *use* what they have bought to achieve their desired business results.

As we work with our customers to help facilitate their buying process, we should keep a few things in mind:

1. We Should Try Never to Do "Something" for "Nothing"

I'm not suggesting we become greedy here. But if we invest our time and money to do things for them—like driving or flying several people in to do a demonstration—it's only fair that they have the right people in attendance, isn't it? I'm not even insisting that they have to match everything we do for them with something they do for us. Sometimes I just wish they would do something for themselves! We may need to "negotiate" or bargain with them at some point in the process to make sure that when we do what we are supposed to do, they will do what they are supposed to do.

2. We Have the Right to Choose to Do What We Do, Based on Whether or Not They Commit to Do What They Need to Do

Just because our customer wants us to submit a lengthy proposal, doesn't automatically mean that we have an obligation to do it. If they're not willing to let us speak with any of the people involved in the decision, how can we be certain it will provide the capabilities they need in order to achieve their goals?

If we can't find out whether or not they have the urgency and the means to buy, but they just want us to slip an elaborate proposal under the door and *hope* they like it and call us back, it may not be worth doing. If our prospect isn't willing to do the things they need to do along the way to make sure that our joint undertaking will be successful, you and I need to think pretty hard about whether or not we keep doing the things we need to do.

3. We Are Ultimately Not Responsible for What They Do or Don't Do

If you embrace this approach to selling, it is actually quite liberating. When you realize that you can't control your customers, and that all you can do is try to understand them and positively influence their behavior, it allows you to relax a little bit and disengage emotionally. We're not responsible for their inability or unwillingness to take the next step they need to take in their process. Yes, we work like crazy to figure out how to get them to take it. But if we do everything we can possibly do to help them, and they still won't move forward, it's not our fault. We might need to move on and start helping somebody who wants our help.

Documenting Your Process

The next two chapters are dedicated to better understanding how customers buy and to using that knowledge to develop a sales process that supports and facilitates any buying process. One of the things that is vitally important in developing a solid process is looking closely at the things you are doing now. What are the things that you do in every sales campaign that you know contribute to success? What are some of the activities that are required in special situations, and how do you know when a particular situation calls for one?

We want to begin to recognize the things we do all the time, or once in a while, that really don't directly impact our success. Some of these activities might be wasting energy, or worse, could be slowing us down. I urge you to immediately begin collecting the information you'll need to take your game to this next level. In so doing, you'll become instantly far more effective in every sales campaign in your pipeline.

The easiest way to begin is by keeping track of what you do in each sales campaign or each opportunity. Just the mere fact that you're tracking your actions will make you more efficient and effective. Think of it like a diary of each sales campaign. Look closely at the activities you have been engaged in for each sales opportunity and ask:

- What did *we* do during our most recent meeting or phone call?
    Topics discussed
    Questions we asked
    Information we presented
- Why did *we* do each of these things?
    What was the purpose or intent?
    What were we trying to get our customer to *think* differently
        or *do* differently?
- What did we recommend or ask *them* to do next?
    Specific actions to take
    Information (of theirs) to collect or provide
    Information (of ours) to review
- What did *they* agree to do going forward?
    Which of our requests did they agree to?
    What commitments did they make?
- What had *they* done since last time we met or talked?
    Which commitments, previously made, did they deliver on?
    What did *we* agree to do going forward?
    What commitments did we make?

Some will notice that this approach represents a slightly different way of thinking than they are used to. It's not uncommon to see participants in our workshops a little taken aback when they read this list of questions. Many of us have been conditioned to do whatever the customer asks us or tells us to do. The customer wants *this*, the customer wants *that*, and we run around jumping through hoops for a living. We're "professional hoop jumpers."

Too often, when we do leave a customer meeting with anything in the way of commitments, they are things that *we* have promised to do, provide, or deliver to them. This is another pattern of behavior we simply have to break. Our customer, also, should be making commitments about the steps they will be taking within their buying process between now and the next time we meet. To properly qualify opportunities, and stay in step with our customer, we have to understand what they are planning to do, and when they are planning to do it.

If we can't answer these questions listed above, it's either because we didn't have a reason for doing the things we did, or because we didn't recommend or ask our customer to take any specific action of any kind. If this is the case, we are not following a process at all. We are letting our client dictate the things that we do. If we begin documenting and evaluating the things that we've been doing and that is what we discover, then so be it. We can't change the past, but we can definitely change the way we think, and the way we sell, in the future. The remainder of this book is dedicated to better understanding how your customers buy, and the things we can do to influence their buying behavior.

CHAPTER 7

Anatomy of a Buying Decision

The entire area of business decision making has been the subject of a great deal of research over the last fifty years, and much has been observed about how individuals and groups make choices and decisions. What makes selling such a complex endeavor is that any particular buying decision may involve dozens of little choices and decisions that all add up to one big decision. There are often a lot of "moving parts" and variables that influence the many decision makers, and the larger the financial investment and the broader the business impact, the more decision makers and the more variables come into play.

For years I looked for a good way to define and explain "how customers buy" so that we, as sales professionals, could better understand the things that our clients think and do throughout a typical buying process. The model I now use was revealed to me in intimate detail one weekend a couple of summers ago.

Like millions of Americans, I enjoy backyard cooking on my propane barbecue grill. One night after work I picked out a nice, thick New York–cut steak and headed out back, arms loaded with all the accoutrements. I started the grill, let it heat up, placed the steak on, and went back in to cut up the salad.

Now, I can see the grill from the kitchen, so it's easy to keep an eye on things. But the next time I looked up, flames were shooting out from under the grill and up the front almost to the handle. As I ran out the door my first reaction was to turn off the control knobs, but there was too much fire, so I thought maybe I better try to "save the steak." After singeing the hair off my knuckles trying to open the lid, I opted to shut off the gas *at the tank* first, and then rescue my steak.

The steak wasn't fully cooked yet, dinner was ruined, and I thought, "Oh, great—just what I need—something else to replace. I don't have time for these distractions! I've got a trip coming up this week, and two different seminars to prepare for, blah, blah, blah, blah, blah." Later that night, I thought, "Maybe, if I just ignore it . . . pretend it never happened . . . the next time I use the grill it will work fine, and nobody will be the wiser." Tell me you've never thought something like that.

A few days later, after my short business trip, I went back to the grill with some marinated lemon-pepper chicken breasts. I figured if I didn't bring it up, maybe the grill wouldn't either. And you know what? Everything worked fine, and the chicken was cooked to perfection.

But Saturday, around noon, I decided to cook some hamburgers. Honestly, with the travel, the telephone calls, and everything else I'd had going on, I had completely forgotten about the incident earlier in the week. Or, maybe I was just in denial. That was, until the grill went up in flames again. But this time, it was worse. I very nearly caught my shirt on fire!

Now I had to make a decision. What am I going to do? I wasn't about to go vegetarian, or resort to cooking steaks in a pan on the stove, so mentally I laid out my options. I could probably just replace the element (the metal piece in the bottom of the grill that contains and distributes the fire) for a small amount of money. But my grill was getting kind of rusty, and broken down, so a new grill would be really nice. The year before, my neighbor installed a grill-top range in his kitchen, so I thought perhaps this would be a good excuse to invest a few thousand to upgrade my lifestyle, and even increase the value of my home. But as much as I travel, I didn't want to mess around trying to schedule a time to get the thing installed. Surely it would have taken a few weeks before it was all said and done.

So, later that day I jumped in the car and headed toward the store where I had bought my last grill. I had my mission, and my "flight plan," all mapped out. I would get the grill, stop at the grocery store to pick up some fresh steaks and burgers, swing back past the hardware store to get two fresh tanks of propane, and I would be all set to grill to my heart's content. There was only one problem.

I pulled into the parking lot, got out, and was halfway in the door before I realized that even though this was the right building, the store that sold me the grill was gone, replaced by a furniture store, which didn't sell barbecue grills. My next move was simple; where is the *next closest* place to find a barbecue grill? I drove down the road to another strip mall I knew about, but none of those stores sold grills either. That was enough fooling around. So, I turned around and drove clear across town to a department store I knew would have them.

Once I got there, found the grill department, and stood around for fifteen minutes, I literally had to go "track down" somebody to help me. I showed them the grill I wanted, but it was out of stock, and so were choices two and three. So, I took choice number four. It was smaller than I originally wanted, and it didn't have the little temperature gauge that I liked. Whatever! I had goofed around with this thing long enough, and at that point I just needed to get *a* grill and be done with it.

A few weeks later while laughing about this story with a friend, I recognized what I had been looking for. This little vignette is a perfect microcosm of what many of our customers think and do while in the process of buying something. While the motive to buy is not always to replace something that is broken, the pattern of thinking and behavior represents all the major aspects of a typical buying decision, which I will explain as we work our way through this chapter.

The Four Elements of a Buying Decision

Before you or I, or one of our customers, can buy anything, there are at least four things that have to be considered, and four decisions that have to be made. Sometimes, one person makes all four of these, but in medium to large businesses it's not unusual to see three or four different people, and maybe even a committee or two, that have some influence in the outcome of these four decisions. Every big decision involves, at least, these four smaller decisions, and each of these four may contain three, or eight, or thirteen components of their own. Please see Figure 7.1.

1. Action: "Do We *Have to* Buy Something *Now*?"

Individuals sometimes buy things because they want to, but companies—who are constantly concerned with controlling and minimizing costs—usually only buy things when they have to. Even if they determine they have to buy something in order to achieve a goal or fix a problem, they will often put it off until it becomes absolutely necessary. It's not procrastination. It's the reality of limited resources and unlimited opportunities, and the process of valuation and prioritization, which we discussed in Chapter 1.

If I could have kept on cooking steaks on my old barbecue grill, without burning my knuckles or catching my shirt on fire, I would not have taken the action to replace it. I even tried to ignore it for a while. Only when I realized I could not go on without the risk of blowing myself up did I decide I had to do something about it.

2. Course: "What Should We Buy?"

There is always more than one way to solve a problem or pursue a goal. Once a buyer determines that taking action is a priority, the next logical question is "What course of action should we take?" If deciding on a course of action involves more than one person, there will always be conflicting views, conflicting agendas, and differences of opinion involved.

Once my grill died, my options were to (1) quit eating steak and hamburgers, (2) cook them on the stove, (3) replace the element, (4) replace the whole grill, or (5) invest in a grill-top range. I quickly narrowed it down to numbers four or five as being the only two options I was willing to accept.

3. Resources: "Do We Have the Resources to Buy?"

Before a buyer can buy something, they must have—or be able to get—the money to buy it. Good business managers also look carefully to

Figure 7.1 The Four Elements of a Buying Decision

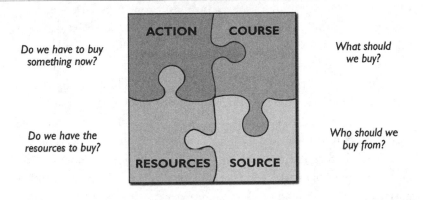

*Do we have to buy
something now?*

*What should
we buy?*

*Do we have the
resources to buy?*

*Who should we
buy from?*

make sure they have the resources, in terms of time and manpower, to actually implement and utilize what they buy before they buy it.

The reason I chose option four over five was not the money. It was more an issue of Time Value and Simplicity Value. I just didn't feel like ordering the range, finding someone to install it, scheduling the installation, and waiting a few weeks to get results. For me, it was just less hassle to go buy a new grill.

4. Source: "Who Should We Buy From?"

If a company determines that they have to buy something *now*, they know *what* they need to buy, and they have the *resources* to buy it and put it to use, they still need a *source* to buy from that can deliver what they need in a timely manner.

I naturally defaulted to my "incumbent vendor," the store that sold me the last grill, but when that didn't work out, my preferred choice became the next-closest store that sold grills. Once I did locate a new source, I decided to settle for one of the grills in stock. I wasn't willing to wait a week to order one, or run around to three other stores to try to find just the right model or to save a few bucks. I just bought one that was available.

These four decisions are interrelated, like the pieces of a jigsaw puzzle, and to get a complete picture of the overall buying process, we have to understand them all. One of these decisions really can't happen without the other. If taking action to solve a business problem is paramount, but a company doesn't have the resources to buy, then they can't very well take action. Likewise, if they have the resources to buy, and a great source to buy from, but no urgency to take action or no consequence if they don't, they'll probably put off buying for a while. All four decisions must be made in favor of buying before a buyer is ready to buy.

In a perfect textbook case of a buying process, these four decisions would happen in little airtight compartments, where one decision was completed before the next one began. Unfortunately, this never happens, and probably never will. But if we are going to stand a chance of understanding our customer's buying process, we have to start understanding how these four decisions *are* made, both in theory and in practice.

The Initiative That Drives the Buying Decision

Of all the things we need to learn when we discover a new opportunity, here's the most important: "Is there a goal, a problem, or an initiative that can drive a decision to buy?" In Chapter 2 we introduced the word *disparity* to describe the "gap" between where our customer is now and where they would like to be. We called their *current state* point "A" and their *desired future state* point "C." We also discussed the importance of Motive (a reason to leave "A" and move toward "C"), as well as the other five Action Drivers: Urgency, Return, Consequence, Means, and Risk. To go one step further in understanding how our customers make buying decisions, we should also consider the conditions surrounding, or the situation that causes, the disparity in the first place.

There are at least four situations our customer could face that would cause a disparity and a motive to buy:

1. A planned replacement of something they already have
2. An unplanned replacement of something they already have
3. A new purchase of something they need to "keep up"
4. A new purchase of something they need to "get ahead"

It is helpful to understand the circumstances surrounding the disparity because it can tell us a lot about the nature of the associated Action Drivers. A planned replacement will probably be perceived as very low *risk*, but the *consequence* of not buying at the planned time could be a strong *motive*. An unplanned replacement (i.e., something's broken) may carry a strong *motive* and a very strong *urgency*, so much so that the *payback or return* may not even be considered.

A new purchase to "keep up" with their competition—or to stay on schedule with their plans—might bring the *consequence* of falling behind if they don't take action. But if they've already fallen behind, they may not have the *means* to buy even if they did have a strong *motive*. A new purchase to "get ahead" may present a very compelling *motive*, but could be light on *urgency* or *consequence*.

In addition to understanding the Action Drivers involved in any buying decision, it is critical to find out "Where are these Action Drivers being driven *from*?" In the next section, we will explore the two types of buying initiatives we normally encounter: initiatives that originate and are driven from the bottom of your customer's organization, and those that originate and are driven from the top.

A Top-Down Initiative

In Figure 7.2, we can see what I am going to call a "top-down" buying process. Now, this model doesn't begin to illustrate the intricacy and all of the interrelationships of the four decisions, which happen both intermittently and simultaneously. But in the spirit of grounding this concept in some mutual understanding, I've found this model to be highly effective.

A top-down buying decision comes as a result of a project or initiative that originates at the top, from the leader of an organization, or from a small group of leaders. As a result of strategic planning or goal setting, an objective is defined that frequently requires a change in business process or infrastructure. To achieve these goals and objectives, certain actions have to be taken that might involve buying something, or at least considering the idea of buying something.

In a top-down initiative, which is driven by a desire to achieve a pre-determined goal or objective, the Action Decision is usually the first to be considered. The question "Do we have to buy something in order to achieve this goal?" is one of the first to be asked. Assuming the answer is "Yes," the next question is "What should we buy?" To answer this question, the people involved will use some variation of the cause-and-effect concept (introduced in Chapter 4) to explore various options and identify several possible courses of action.

Each option is then evaluated and the required resources (time, money, and manpower) are identified and considered. Assuming one or more of the possible courses of action is deemed viable, and the resources needed are available—or made available—the buyer will seek out one or more sources for whatever it is they need to buy. After multiple sources are considered and one or more qualified sources are identified, the issue of *when* to take action and make a purchase comes back to the forefront.

So, as Figure 7.2 shows, the process begins at the top with the decision of whether or not to take action. It then works downward through the three other decisions over a period of time, and comes back up to the decision of *when* to take action as the buyer approaches the "buy line." I struggled a bit with this model as I designed it, wondering, "Are the decision to take action and the decision of when to take it actually two separate decisions?" I've come to believe they are not separate. Let me tell you why.

Over the years I have asked hundreds of customers, "What bad thing would happen if you decided not to move forward with this purchase?" Many of them have said, "Oh, we've already decided we're definitely going to move forward with this." It's amazing how eager they are to tell you, "We're definitely going to buy." I've learned that this is actually a technique buyers use to get us excited so we will start jumping through their hoops.

When it was all said and done, a huge percentage of the people who told me they were "definitely going to buy," never did buy anything, from me or anybody else. So, how could they possibly have "made the decision," if they never did go ahead and buy? Please read this next sentence very carefully . . .

Figure 7.2 A Top-Down Buying Process

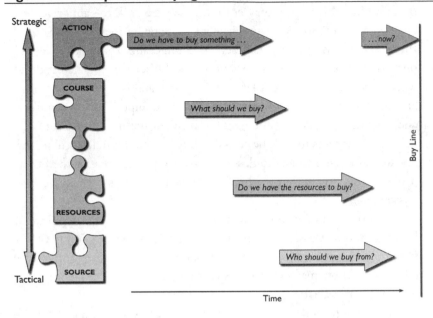

Until a customer has signed a contract, or issued a
purchase order, they have not made the decision to
take *action* and buy.

Until then, they are still thinking about it. So, the Action Decision,
or at least a portion of it, is always the *last* decision they make. A customer might collect information, explore their options, and consider
buying for six, or twelve, or eighteen months, but the decision to take
action is never truly *made* until the moment the pen hits the paper.

A Bottom-Up Initiative

Sometimes a buying decision originates deep within an organization.
Perhaps there is an engineering manager or a worker out on the shop

floor who says, "There's got to be a better way to do this." A grassroots initiative like this may or may not ultimately tie back to supporting or enabling the organization to achieve its strategic business goals. Sometimes, regardless of how much benefit could come from taking action on this kind of initiative, it goes nowhere. Other times, when it does work its way up to the right level of authority and is compared against all the other projects and initiatives that are competing for resources and funding, it just isn't good enough. It might not meet certain minimum requirements to even be considered. But even if it did, it still might not be staffed and funded unless it is able to displace one of the other projects currently "above the line" of available resources, which we discussed in Chapter 1.

Other times, a grassroots initiative that garners the right support and backing finds its way to the top and *is* deemed to be worth doing. Once in a while, it will even influence or change the strategic direction of the company. I know many companies that actively solicit ideas from deep within the organization.

There is a general business trend for companies to become "flatter," less hierarchical, and less dictatorial. As this trend continues, and as the philosophy of empowering lower levels of management to make critical decisions becomes more popular, we will probably see more of these kinds of projects undertaken. Rather than being driven by a corporate goal, a bottom-up initiative starts when someone at a lower level in the organization looks at a business process and asks, "How can this be done better, faster, or cheaper?"

It is also very common to see a grassroots buying initiative instigated by the question, "What tools or technologies are available that would enable us to do what we do better, faster, or cheaper?" Individual contributors (i.e., line workers) and frontline managers are always on the lookout for new products and services that would make their jobs easier. They subscribe to certain magazines for this express purpose. They belong to trade organizations, and join their key vendors' user groups to learn from others in their industry. They also eagerly walk the floors of tradeshows looking for new ideas to make their departments more efficient, more effective, and to make their own jobs easier. Plus, you can collect a lot of really cool, free stuff at those shows!

Figure 7.3 A Bottom-Up Buying Process

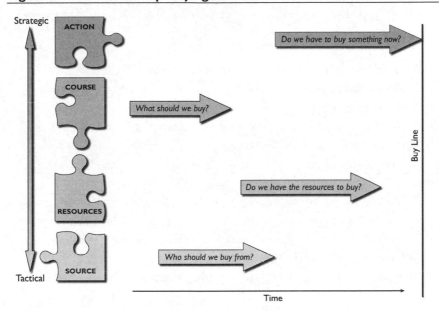

In this bottom-up sort of initiative, the sequence of decisions can be much different, as is shown in Figure 7.3. It often starts by asking something like, "What should we buy to make our jobs easier or be more efficient?" That is typically followed very quickly by, "Who should we buy from?" since all those magazines and tradeshows are chock-full of vendors brandishing their wares. In this type of a buying decision, the questions of, "Do we have the resources to buy?" or "Do we even have to buy anything?" are often left to the very end.

A bottom-up initiative can easily become an exercise in futility. You know the drill. Your prospect contacts you or stops by your booth at a tradeshow, tells you they are "definitely going to buy," and requests more information. We, of course, respond with literature, phone calls, site visits, and demos. We all have probably made the mistake of engaging in a full-blown sales campaign, assuming that a purchase was imminent, only to discover that senior management decided to "go in a different direction," or worse yet, never even took the time to consider it.

I've learned from years of observation, that top-down initiatives have a very high likelihood of resulting in a purchase. The only way one wouldn't is if management:

1. Decides not to take *action* to pursue the goal after all.
2. Figures out some other *course* of action to achieve the goal without buying the products or services you sell.
3. Decides that the return on invested *resources* isn't worth the risk.
4. Can't find a good *source* and/or decides to make whatever they need themselves.

Bottom-up initiatives, on the other hand, have a very low likelihood of resulting in a purchase. Rather than being "on the list until they are crossed off," they have to earn their way onto the list by displacing some other project or objective, and by beating out dozens or even hundreds of other grassroots initiatives that are all competing for limited resources.

Winning the Battle but Losing the War

In our Power-Prospecting for New Business™ workshop, we talk about the importance of proactively prospecting for new business opportunities. When we initiate communication with a prospective customer, we can call at any level we want. We may not start off, for some very specific reasons, by calling the CEO directly, but we can start as high up in the organization as we choose. Using this approach, we can learn about the goals, objectives, and initiatives that are already on the minds of executives and align our sales campaign to support the achievement of those goals.

When a prospect contacts us—by visiting our website, stopping by our booth at a tradeshow, or circling our number on an "information request" card in a magazine—at what level do those inquiries usually originate? Is it usually the chairman of the board? The CFO? How about the executive vice president of sales and marketing? No, it's usually the procurement manager, or an individual contributor of some kind. There's nothing wrong with that. I want all the inquiries I can get, but let's recognize them for what they are.

When someone at a lower level in our prospect's organization contacts us, we know that we are probably dealing with one of two situations: it's either a bottom-up initiative in its early stages, or a top-down initiative in its late stages.

If, when we "get a lead," we immediately react by positioning our products and services as superior to our competition, explaining the many unique advantages and benefits, and working to become the vendor of choice, it could turn out to be a complete waste of our time. The most important takeaway from this discussion is that we can't afford to expend all of our resources to win the *source* battle, only to find out later that we lost the overall war.

One of the most frustrating experiences for any sales professional is to win the Source Decision, but find out later that:

1. They don't have the *resources* to buy, or at least not right now.
2. Management decided to "go in a different direction," or pursue a different *course* of action.
3. Management decided not to take *action*, or at least not at this time.

Please notice on both Figures 7.2 and 7.3 the vertical arrow on the far left-hand side. At the top it says "Strategic" and at the bottom, "Tactical." We should remember that the Source Decision is actually the least important decision from our customer's point of view. They may well believe that any one of several sources will suffice.

We can't afford to wallow around in the Source Decision with the misconception that *if we can just win that*, we've won the deal. Here's a truth we should all take to heart . . .

> **Using our sales resources to try to win
> the Source Decision is useless, and in fact
> irresponsible, unless we have strong evidence
> or reasons to believe that we can win the
> Resource, Course, and Action Decisions,
> as well.**

We have to learn how to engage our clients on a different level. We should have an approach to our territory that involves calling *them* and calling *higher* within the company so we can discover top-down initiatives earlier in the overall buying process. The earlier we call, the more likely we can help to influence and shape their vision of the ideal solution. But when they call us, we should be asking questions about the Resource, Course, and Action Decisions so that we can put together a solid plan and strategy for how to win. Learning to work our way up from the Source Decision to start engaging our customers in the more strategic decisions they will make is one of the most valuable skills we could possibly develop. To get there, and to be effective, we will need to better understand how those higher-level, more strategic decisions are made.

The Action Decision

In making the Action Decision, there are a lot of factors your customer will consider and questions they will have to answer for themselves. To get in step with our buyer, we need to know the answers to these just as much as they do. In a top-down initiative many of these questions will already be answered, but in a bottom-up initiative, you can bet these are the questions that management will be asking when the proposal finally hits their desk.

To help answer the larger question of "Do we have to buy something now?" your customer will consider the following factors, and seek to answer the associated questions (please note the six Action Drivers that we have talked about throughout this book):

- **Disparity:** "What is the goal, objective, need, pain, problem, obstacle, disparity, or gap we are trying to address?"
- **Motive:** "Why do we have to take action on this right now?"
- **Urgency:** "Is there a deadline (either internal or external) by which we must take action?"
- **Payback:** "What kind of return-on-investment can we expect? How soon? How certain?"

- **Consequence:** "What bad thing will happen if we don't take action?"
- **Means:** "Do we have the money to buy, and the manpower to make this investment successful?"
- **Risk:** "What is the downside of taking action? What could go wrong?"
- **Prioritization:** "Of all the initiatives we need to act on, which are the most important right now?"

The Action Decision is by far the most critical because if this decision can't be resolved, none of the others really matter. Top-down initiatives begin here, and *every* buying decision has to end here, so our knowledge and understanding of where our customer stands on the Action Decision is one of the most important things we can know about any opportunity. But as important and as overarching as the Action Decision is, it is highly reliant on the other three decisions as well, because . . .

A buyer cannot take the *action* to buy until they have a *course* of action to take, the *resources* available to buy, and a *source* to buy from.

Therefore, successful resolution of the other three decisions becomes an important factor that influences how and when the Action Decision is ultimately made.

The Course Decision

In evaluating the various courses of action available, your customer will have many new variables to consider. Note that some of these questions relate to the six Action Drivers, but there are also several additional criteria. I like to refer to these as Choice Drivers, because they are the factors that buyers use to differentiate between options and that ultimately drive the choices that they make.

In answering the question, "What should we buy?" the following factors and their questions may come into play:

- **Delivers Result:** "Will this course of action enable us to achieve our desired results?"
- **Feasibility:** "Are we certain this solution will work for us?"
- **Proven:** "Has it been done successfully before?"
- **Make vs. Buy:** "Is this something that we could do or make ourselves?"
- **Risk:** "What are the chances of success or failure if we follow this course of action?"
- **Time to Benefit:** "How quickly can we start seeing results?"
- **Prioritization:** "Of all the possible courses of action, which one is the best?"

Sometimes business managers get confused. They end up focusing more on "*What* they're going to do" than "*Why* they're going to do it." Anyone can fall prey to this. What starts out as an objective to increase customer retention, repeat business, and top-line revenues, ends up as an initiative to implement a Customer Relationship Management (CRM) system. I always get worried when I hear a customer start to refer to a project or an initiative by the name of a solution as opposed to the name of the goal or result they are trying to achieve. An example would be when the objective of increasing gross revenue becomes known as the "CRM Project."

When the customer loses sight of the reason for taking action—their "C"—and instead becomes fixated on "B," they begin to focus on the wrong decision. They sometimes take their eye off the Action Drivers that are really driving the initiative and start to focus on the subtle choices between vendors and their products and services.

This kind of thinking is what causes them to produce multi-hundred-page RFPs (requests for proposal), and engage in a long, drawn-out selection process. This is never a good thing, because a nine-to-twelve-month selection process isn't good for anybody. It costs both the customer and the vendor enormous amounts of time and money, and they delay any results that the customer might hope to achieve. The bigger problem is that our customers begin basing their choices and decisions on the wrong criteria; features, functions, and slight differences in products become paramount; pricing becomes the central issue. When this happens, no one benefits.

If I'd had three days of free time, and I was worried about saving a few bucks, I could have driven around to a dozen different stores until I found just the right barbecue grill with all the features I wanted. Then I could have played one store against the other until I got the best possible price. But the opportunity cost (the value lost by not using that time in a more productive way) would have been enormous. The same is true for many of your customers.

When you start to see your customer behaving like this, there is usually one of two reasons: it is either a bottom-up initiative that doesn't stand much chance of ever being funded, or it's a top-down initiative that has gotten bogged down under its own weight. Either way, we have to find out if the people who will make the final Action Decision and the Course Decision are focused on the right things or not. If they aren't, we might be wasting our time. In Chapter 9 we will address how to reach and engage these executives who make the higher-level decisions.

The Resources Decision

Taking action requires resources. Without the right resources, your customer can't buy even if they want to. The Resource Decision involves an evaluation of Economic Value and Risk, Payback or Return, availability of funds, and so on. It's not just about money. It takes people to head up projects, and other people to do the work, as well as managers or committees to provide oversight and accountability. The Resource Decision should include a close look at all the resources an organization would need to expend to buy, implement, and make use of a solution.

The question, "Do we have the resources to buy?" considers the investment of time, money, and manpower by looking at the following:

- **Budgeting and Planning:** "Have we planned for, and allocated funds for, this investment?"

- **Availability of Funds:** "Do we actually have the money on hand, or the financing in place, to make this investment?"
- **ROI Requirements:** "Does this investment meet the minimum hurdle rate (ROI or Payback) to even be considered?"
- **Portfolio Management:** "How does this investment impact our overall investment strategy and exposure to financial risk?"
- **Manpower:** "Do we have the people and the bandwidth to make this project successful?"
- **Oversight:** "Is there some person, or a committee, who will take ownership of, and responsibility for, the success of this project?"
- **Prioritization:** "Of all the places we could invest these resources, which is the best right now?"

The Resource Decision can get complicated, especially for a bottom-up initiative that has to prove its value to senior decision makers. A top-down initiative may get funded because it's "what the CEO decided was the right thing to do." But bottom-up initiatives are typically scrutinized very carefully. They often require return-on-investment analysis, which looks at the proposed project as financial investment. A bottom-up initiative will likely need to meet certain minimums or thresholds just to be considered, and then will be compared against other uses for the resources being requested. The more we know about the way our customer evaluates and justifies investment in projects, the more we can do to make sure our project earns approval.

The Source Decision

Earning the coveted "vendor of choice" label is an important milestone in any sales campaign. However, it doesn't guarantee a sale. It only makes it *possible* to sell something. As your customer considers their options for a source to buy from, they will probably ponder some of the following aspects about each source, and the specific products and services offered by each. They'll also be asking themselves some of these questions:

- **Vendor Relationship:** "Who do we already know and trust that can provide this solution?"
- **Reputation/Stability:** "Will this vendor be around to support us after the sale?"
- **Functional Fit:** "Does their product or service have all the functionality we need?"
- **Technical Fit:** "Does their product or service meet all of our technical requirements?"
- **Total Value Package:** "Which vendor offers the best total package: high value and low risk?"
- **Delivery:** "Can this vendor deliver what we need on time and on budget?"
- **Prioritization:** "Of all the sources we could buy from, which one is the best?"

If we were to look at the Source Decision all by itself, and not in relation to the other three decisions discussed earlier, we might conclude that this is where the sale is made. But over the years I have observed that winning the Source Decision only gives you the *chance* to win the other three. And more important, if we are focused solely on winning the Source Decision, we will end up spending most of our time talking about our "B," rather than the customer's "C."

In fact, I have observed that if we don't seek to fully understand how our client has made, or will make, the decisions that relate to Resources, Course, and Action, we are perceived as a "vendor" at best, and are sometimes not considered to be "partner" material. Some might call me crazy, but I contend that . . .

The best way to win the Source Decision is to help your customer to make the best possible Resource, Course, and Action Decisions.

Then we are truly adding value to our customer's buying process.

Helping Your Customer over Their Buying Hurdles

It has been very helpful to me, and to many of my clients, to think of the buying process and all the little choices and decisions therein, as a series of hurdles that our customer has to jump over to get from wherever they currently are, to where they are ready to buy. It's our job to not only know where they are in the process, but also to do all we can to make sure they will be able to clear each hurdle along the way.

These buying hurdles, which can vary greatly based on the industry you are selling to and the nature and scope of what you sell, represent the "little decisions" or choices your client makes during their buying process. Your customer must resolve these little decisions by answering questions such as, "Are we certain this solution will work for us?" and by conducting a feasibility study or research on possible vendors. These hurdles become the milestones along the path to winning the big decision.

There is no set number of buying hurdles. Every customer type, and indeed every customer, will have a unique set of hurdles based on the nature of their company, their industry, and the type of product or service they are considering buying. But as I mentioned in Chapter 6, there are similarities in buying processes from company to company.

For use in our *Structuring the Deal to Close*™ workshop, we have constructed a number of different examples of the buying hurdles for customers from a variety of different industries. We use these examples only to help participants think about, "What are the hurdles that a customer in my market has to get over to buy the products and services I sell?"

Please take a look at Figure 7.4 as an example of the buying hurdles that *might* be involved for a typical manufacturing company selecting and buying an enterprise software solution. Note that the letters A, C, R, and S, which appear under each hurdle, indicate which Decision (Action, Course, Resources, or Source) each hurdle relates to.

The following is a list of these hurdles within this sample buying process. Please take a minute to read through these. This is only an example, and may be quite different from the hurdles your customer will need to get over in order to evaluate, select, and buy the products and services that you sell. Again, the letters in front of each one indicate which of the four decisions each hurdle pertains to (Action, Course,

Figure 7.4 Helping Your Customer over Their Buying Hurdles

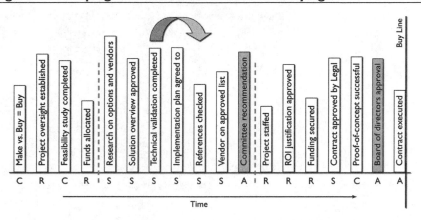

Resources, or Source). The dotted lines after hurdles number four and eleven will be explained in the next section.

1. C—Make vs. Buy = Buy
2. R—Project oversight established
3. C—Feasibility study completed
4. R—Funds allocated

---

5. S—Research on options and vendors
6. S—Solution overview approved
7. S—Technical validation completed
8. S—Implementation plan agreed to
9. S—References checked
10. S—Vendor on approved list
11. A—Committee recommendation

---

12. R—Project staffed
13. R—ROI justification approved
14. R—Funding secured
15. S—Contract approved by Legal
16. C—Proof-of-concept successful
17. A—Board of directors approval
18. A—Contract executed

Our sales strategy, and our game plan, for any opportunity needs to be predicated on our knowledge of our customer's buying process. So, the question is, "What are the hurdles that your customer has to get over in order to buy, and be successful, with what you sell?" These hurdles, and the order in which they need to be cleared, will vary based on:

- Whether it's a top-down versus a bottom-up initiative.
- Whether you are selling to a new prospect versus an existing customer.
- Whether you are selling a product versus a service.
- Whether you are the incumbent vendor versus a potential new vendor.
- The size of the financial investment.
- The scope of the impact of your solution.
- The standards and policies of the organization you are selling to.
- The culture of the organization you are selling to.
- The strength of certain Action Drivers, such as Urgency (they have to decide quickly), or Risk (they are forced to be extra careful), etc.
- Whether or not they have recently bought something similar.

The point here is that our job is to identify every hurdle that might be involved in our customer's buying process and begin preparing now for how we are going to help them clear those hurdles. If being added to the preapproved vendor list is required, for example, then let's start early to get that taken care of and out of the way. We should try to get the "normal" hurdles, which we see in every buying process, out of the way as early as possible. That way we'll have more time to deal with any unexpected hurdles that may suddenly appear out of nowhere later on.

By keeping track of the things that we are doing *right now* in our current pipeline opportunities, we can begin to observe and formulate a list of "What hurdles do our customers typically have to get over in order to buy?" I would suggest developing and maintaining a list of all of the typical hurdles, which you see in the vast majority of buying processes, and the specific "things that we do" to help our clients get over them.

I also recommend making a separate list of each hurdle that you may have seen only once or twice, or that one of your coworkers experienced once. As you build your expertise and knowledge of helping your clients clear their standard hurdles, you should also carefully record how you—or someone else on your team—helped a customer to clear one of those "unusual" hurdles. Let's leverage everything we can possibly learn to make us more effective and better prepared to deal with the next "surprise" hurdle when it comes along.

Two Big Mistakes We Can't Afford to Make

Too often, when a prospect contacts us and says, "We're going to buy," we lead with our solution and focus on trying to win the Source Decision. Please take a closer look at Figure 7.4, or the list of buying hurdles above. We should take the time to understand what critical decisions *may or may not* have already been resolved *before* the customer started "Researching options and vendors" at hurdle number five. Some of these critical strategic decisions—appearing before the first dotted line—may include:

1. C—Make vs. Buy = Buy
2. R—Project oversight established
3. C—Feasibility study completed
4. R—Funds allocated

The first big mistake we should avoid is jumping in at the point where our customer has conducted some research and contacted a few vendors, without finding out what has *already* been done or decided. Until we find out what has already happened *before* they contacted us, we simply don't know enough to properly qualify the opportunity, let alone put together an effective strategy and plan to ensure a successful sales campaign.

If they have not yet explored the *make vs. buy* question, for example, we might spend months winning the source battle, only to watch them decide to craft some sort of homemade solution on their own. Likewise, if project oversight has not been established, or funds have not yet been allocated for the project, there may never actually *be* a project at all.

Beginning with the fifth hurdle in Figure 7.4, there are six Source hurdles in a row:

5. S—Research on options and vendors
6. S—Solution overview approved
7. S—Technical validation completed
8. S—Implementation plan agreed to
9. S—References checked
10. S—Vendor on approved list
11. A—Committee recommendation

Assuming we help our client clear these hurdles, we could win the Source Decision. But that's not all it's going to take to win this deal.

The second big mistake we can make is working our heart out to help our customer clear hurdles five through eleven so we can win the "Committee recommendation," and then *hoping* they can figure out how to clear the rest of the hurdles (appearing after the second dotted line) on their own. If we spend all of our time and attention on winning the source battle, without preparing to—and helping our customer to prepare to—get over the hurdles that come *after*, our customer could stumble on one of these later hurdles, as we watch all of our time and effort go right down the drain. We have to know exactly what it's going to take—and be ready and willing to do whatever *we* need to do—to make sure our customer gets over every hurdle, including "Board of directors approval" and "Contract executed."

12. R—Project staffed
13. R—ROI justification approved
14. R—Funding secured
15. S—Contract approved by Legal
16. C—Proof-of-concept successful
17. A—Board of directors approval
18. A—Contract executed

In the next chapter, I will show you how to use the framework that has been presented here to sort out the various steps and stages your customer will have to go through to be successful in their overall buying process. Once you understand the specific hurdles your customer has to get past in order to buy, and then to achieve the business results they want to achieve, you'll be ready to develop a rock-solid sales strategy and a plan to help them get there.

CHAPTER 8

Reverse-Engineering the Buying Process

The term reverse-engineering is quite familiar to some, but not to all. It's the process of analyzing a finished product, or the end result of a work process, in order to determine the way in which it was made or completed. Reverse-engineering is usually done to replicate a product or process, to redesign it to make it more efficient to produce or execute, or to deliver a higher-quality result.

In our pursuit of a successful sales campaign, we can use this approach to better understand all the things that would have to happen before our client would be ready to buy. But in order to be a partner to our client, as opposed to just a vendor, we need to make sure that they can also use whatever it is that we sell to obtain their desired business results.

This concept is consistent with the principle that Stephen Covey articulated in his landmark bestseller, *The Seven Habits of Highly Effective People*, when he reminded us to "Begin with the end in mind."[1] The best buying decisions are made in reverse; that is, they are made based on a clearly defined objective or desired outcome. Therefore we should start by trying to understand the end result that our customer is trying to attain—their ideal point "C."

Figure 8.1 shows the Customer Results Model (introduced in Chapter 2) from a process perspective. The activities and the actions our customer takes to move from "A" to "B" constitute a "Selection and Buying Process." The activities and actions to move from "B" to "C" make up an "Implementation and Utilization Process." From our client's point of view, the former is useless without the latter. They have to be able to use what they buy to get what they want. So, if we are to use the concept of reverse-engineering successfully, I believe we should begin where our customers begin, by focusing on point "C," and then helping them to figure out how to get there from here.

It's very easy to lose sight of the real reason behind an initiative to buy. It's easy for us to lose sight because the way we earn commissions, retire quota, and earn the right to keep our job, is to close business. It's also easy for our clients to lose sight of their desired results because of all of the activity involved in a typical buying process. After a few hundred phone calls, dozens of meetings, and endless demonstrations and presentations, it all kind of runs together.

One of the ways we can keep ourselves and our customers focused on our common objective is to develop a plan of all the things that have to happen between the point where we find them, point "A," and the point where they achieve, or at least begin to see, the results they are looking for, point "C." I like to remind my workshop participants that we have to . . .

"Sell beyond the close." Because our customer isn't done when they sign the contract, and if we are selling the value of business results, neither are we.

There could be just as many, or even more, milestones and hurdles to get over after we pass point "B" and money changes hands, as there were before.

To apply everything we covered in Chapters 6 and 7, we need to construct a plan, or a road map, of the things our customers have to do before they can *buy*. But I want to stress that part of earning their trust and providing a complete solution is using that same diligence to help them plan exactly how they will *use* our solution to arrive at point "C" on time and on budget.

Figure 8.1 The Processes That Lead to Point "C"

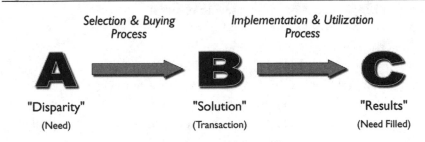

Framing the Opportunity

As we seek and identify new sales opportunities, we are looking for a prospective client who has a business objective they want to achieve, or problem they have to solve, and is both driven and able to take action to do something about it. Granted, it could take a lot of work on our part just to help them get to that point, but once they're there, we can begin to frame the opportunity as a shared objective and a project we can work toward together. Then, beginning at the end, we work with our customer to reverse-engineer a series of actions or "hurdles" that lead to a successful conclusion.

Step 1: Establish Urgency

As early in the process as you deem appropriate, begin asking the "When?" questions that relate to the Action Driver of Urgency. I try to ask these questions during the very first conversation, especially with an executive. As soon as you begin discussing the goals they are trying to achieve, or the problems they are trying to solve, make sure and ask:

- "When was this goal established or initiative adopted?"
- "When did you first realize this problem needed attention?"
- "When do you need to get this done?"

- "When do you need this problem solved?"
- "When do you need to start seeing results?"

What we would like to discover through this line of questioning is a deadline or a time-bound trigger of some kind, which can drive an urgency to take action. It's sad, but true, that if your customer can get by without taking action, that's probably what they will do. But if we are able to identify and leverage what some refer to as a "compelling event," we are much more likely to be successful.

Please keep in mind, this is not, "When do you want to buy?" or "When do you plan to make the decision?" Those are questions about point "B." They indicate to your customer that you are "in it for you." It makes people feel uncomfortable to have to tell you when they are going to decide. Keep your questions focused on outcomes, and *when* they want to achieve their desired results.

The most compelling buying triggers are tied to promises that have been made *outside* the organization you are selling to. A personal mandate from a senior vice president (SVP) to get a new system in place by September 30 can easily be displaced by some other urgent issue the SVP is faced with. On the other hand, if that same SVP makes a promise to her biggest customer that a certain new system—perhaps one that enables the customer to check order status via the Web—will be in place by September 30, it is far less likely to be "bumped" by the next issue that comes along.

Step 2: Establish Motive

Once our customer has given us a time frame for arriving at point "C," the next thing we need to explore is the motive that makes it compelling and important. We learn about their motive to take action on a project by asking, "Why?" Let's assume that they have told us that September 30 is when they need to be "up and running" and starting to see the results that they are looking for. Our next question could be one of these:

- "Why is September 30 your ideal time frame to be operational?"
- "What is it about September 30 that makes it important?"
- "Why would you pick September 30 instead of August 31?"

In order for a sales opportunity to be well qualified, our customer has to have a pretty good reason to take action sometime *before* September 30, so they will be able to start seeing results by then. Without a strong motive that is tied to a time-bound trigger, deals can drag on forever. We should start early, and constantly be looking for any event, occurrence, or urgency that reinforces a motive to buy.

Step 3: Establish Consequence

So, your client wants to be "live and in production" with their new system (or process) in place by September 30. They might even have a good reason "Why?" But we have one more critical question to ask. We need to know if there is any consequence to not getting this done in the time frame they have established. We should ask:

- "What bad thing will happen if you aren't 'up and running' by September 30?"
- "What will your biggest customer say if you don't have this done by September 30?"
- "Have you figured out how much it could cost each month that this is delayed?"

When several budgeted projects, as well as a few dozen unbudgeted grassroots projects, all start competing for the same limited capital and resources, something's got to give. Managers start asking, "What can we put off for a month or two?"

In some cases, it's not simply a matter of which deadlines carry a consequence, but which ones carry the greatest consequence. The conversation sounds like this:

> *"If we push this project back, then we will make certain people mad, and if we push the other one back, we make these other people mad. Which of these two choices does the least long-term damage?"*

Nothing can insulate our sales campaign from these harsh realities, but let's do all we can to understand what we're up against, and where we stand, before it all "hits the fan."

To frame an opportunity, and understand its chances of coming to closure, we work with our client to understand what they are trying to accomplish, and the urgency, motive, and consequence to get it done. I tell participants in my workshops to repeat those three words silently in their mind when they are exploring a new sales opportunity . . . Urgency, Motive, and Consequence . . . Urgency, Motive, and Consequence.

We need to constantly have our radar on, monitoring the frequency for "When?" "Why?" and "What if you don't?" Each time we meet with a new person who plays a role in the buying process, we should try to add their perspective of Urgency, Motive, and Consequence to our composite understanding of the Action Drivers at work in the opportunity.

It has been my experience that only about 20 percent of the opportunities in any given sales pipeline carry an urgency, motive, and consequence that can be tied to a certain date or point in time. This doesn't mean that the other 80 percent of your opportunities are "no good." But a project or an initiative that does not carry these will normally be "bumped" from the list by another initiative that does. To be most effective . . .

> **We should spend 80 percent of our time and effort on the 20 percent of our opportunities that carry a strong urgency, motive, and consequence, because these are the deals that *can* close.**

Reverse-Engineering "B" to "C"

Once we frame the opportunity with what they are trying to accomplish, as well as "When?" "Why?" and "What if you don't?" we can begin our reverse-engineering process. First, we step backward through the events and actions that need to take place during the Implementation and Utilization Process.

You are the expert here; or someone else on your team is. Your client will look to you for guidance and advice on how to use the products and services you sell to achieve their desired business results. You will provide an estimate on how long it will take to implement your solution. Depending on what you sell, there might be project planning, installation, customization, development, pilot testing, prototypes, or whatever.

It's important to begin to let your customer know what's involved in making your solutions work even early in the process. The last thing you would want to do is submit a proposal that includes months of implementation or set-up time when their expectation was weeks. This is all part of properly managing client expectations.

The more your client can understand about the Implementation and Utilization Process, the better. Now, I don't mean we want to overwhelm them and scare them with an elaborate implementation plan in the first meeting. What I am referring to here is dealing with the fear of "What's going to happen after we buy?" Let's keep in mind that . . .

People are naturally afraid of the unknown. We should try to eliminate as many unknowns about the Implementation and Utilization Process as we possibly can.

The more comfortable and confident your customer feels about your ability to help them get from "B" to "C," the less anxiety they will have about moving from "A" to "B." You might want to start by just offering a rough estimate. Depending on what's involved with implementing your solutions you might say, "Most of our clients allow 90–120 days to complete the implementation." Then you can fill in the details later on as you understand more about the specifics of the project and their available resources. Be careful not to set unrealistic expectations. It's better to err on the high side for implementation time than to tell them ninety days, only to have it end up taking ten months.

Here again, resist the urge to propose what you can do to help them until they have had a chance to tell you everything about what they want to accomplish. Make sure they have said all they want to say and are now ready to listen. Through interchange and discussion you'll come up with the beginnings of a timeline that you can share with the client when it seems like they are ready to hear and understand it. Here's an example of what this might look like:

June 1	Commence implementation with a project team planning meeting
June 20	Requirements and specifications completed
July 15	Customization and development completed
July 30	Installation and configuration completed
Aug 15	Integration with existing systems completed
Sept 1	Pilot testing completed
Sept 12	User training completed
Sept 30	Go live

Depending on the complexity of what you sell, you may be able to offer this high-level sketch fairly early on. For others, it will take a team of people a number of weeks to hash this out. In the latter case, you may only be able to say, "We should allow at least 120 days for implementation." Obviously, when we create an actual project plan there will be dozens of little deadlines and hundreds of little tasks that will be part of the overall implementation plan. This is just a skeleton view, for now.

What we are trying to do is establish the fact that in order to start seeing results by September 30, we will need to get started by June 1, which means they will need to work through their Selection and Buying Process before then. Some customers will come to you with their own timeline, but if they do, make sure their expectations are appropriate and realistic. One common mistake customers make is underestimating the time it takes to properly implement solutions. If we don't take the time, even if it means risking a confrontation with our client, to properly reset expectations, we can easily set ourselves up for a mighty upset customer somewhere down the road.

Reverse-Engineering "A" to "B"

Assuming we can arrive at some sort of timetable that is realistic and acceptable to the client, the next step is to figure out what has to happen before June 1. I mentioned before, we sometimes know more about the steps of a buying cycle, and the hurdles they will have to clear along the way, than *they* do. I prefer to hold back a little. Try framing the next question like this:

> *"If we were going to start the project on June 1, that means we would have to earn your trust and reach an agreement before June 1. If we were able to do that, what are some of the things that would need to happen between now and then?"*

We don't want to be too presumptive. We want to gently lay the question out there and make it easy to answer. I remember one sales manager of mine who used to constantly say, "You have to ask the tough questions." He's right. As you have read, I encourage salespeople to ask as many tough questions as they can possibly think of, but there's no reason you have to be "tough" about it. We're not interrogating a felony suspect here. We are having a conversation with our client about how we can help them reach their goals.

Notice that the question is posed in a hypothetical fashion: "If we were to . . ." Asking questions in a hypothetical fashion allows you to explore the possible answers without you or your client having to commit to anything. Customers use this technique all the time. You may have heard it called "buying signs." Your customer will say, "If we *were* to move forward with this project . . ." to ask you a question without committing to anything. Well, we can use that same psychology to learn what we want to know, too.

Your customer may have quite a number of milestones and hurdles in mind, such as a proposal, a demonstration, a presentation to executive management, and so on. Take note of whatever they have to say. I personally like to use a whiteboard or a flip chart for this.

> *"So, let me make sure I've got this right, Mr. Johnson. You said:*
> - *Product demonstration*
> - *Proposal*
> - *Presentation to executive management*
> *Is there anything else?"*

> *"Yes, I think we would also want to . . ."*

Hear them out. The idea here is that we'd like them to share with us everything they think needs to happen between now and when they will be ready to buy. But just because they say something does not mean that we have an obligation to do it. And it doesn't mean it has to happen in the order they originally propose. We have a say in the matter. Also, as I said before, we can't afford to take any one person's word for it. We need to get a composite view of many opinions and perspectives. Only then can we get a good picture of *all* of the things that will need to happen along the way.

Once we have an idea of what our client sees as the steps and stages between where they are now, and where they will be ready to move forward with the project, then we can add our own ideas about what makes a buying process successful. You might want to introduce a "needs analysis" as something that is required before any demonstration or proposal can be made relevant to their business situation. They might remember that a "reference visit" is something that they know their boss is going to insist on, for example. Let's assume that after some additional discussion, we come up with a rough draft of a Selection and Buying Process that looks like this:

- Needs analysis
- Product demonstration
- Reference site visit
- Proposal
- Presentation to executive management
- Finalize agreement

Now, we have something to work with.

Reordering the Activities Accordingly

The next thing I like to do is get things in the proper order. Your customer's idea of a selection process tends to favor their purposes, and in many ways their purpose is "de-selection." In most cases, the products or services you sell are much like those your competitors sell. Sure there

are some technical or functional differences, but your customer probably couldn't tell the difference. And as long as either one will do the job,
they probably don't even care.

By requesting things like demonstrations, references, and proposals,
your customer hopes to be able to narrow the field of competitors
through a process of elimination. But if it costs us thousands of dollars
and hundreds of man-hours to participate, we might want to negotiate
reordering things a little, and maybe even requesting some additional
information up front.

I have learned, the hard way, that some customers simply buy wrong.
They want you to lead with "B" (your solution) and *they* will tell you
whether or not they think it is the right one to take them to "C" (their
desired destination). In some cases they won't even tell you what that
"C" is. I hesitate to be brash, but these kinds of deals are not worth par-
ticipating in. This would be just as silly as calling up a car dealership
and saying, "I am in the market for a new car. So, I am asking the top
five dealerships in town to drive whichever car they think is right for
me over to my house. Then I'll decide which one I like best." You have
the right, as a business professional, to insist on certain conditions
before you invest thousands of dollars trying to sell something.

Here are some suggestions about how you can sell your ideas of
reordering things to better suit your purposes.

1. Insist on Meeting Up Front with All of the People You Will Be Presenting To

I have encountered buying committees or gatekeepers who would not
allow any access to those who would make the final decisions. They
think they're being smart, but they could not be more mistaken. If you
and I can't get an understanding of what those decision makers perceive
as point "C," and the value they hope to derive when they get there, our
chances of hitting the target are just about as good as shooting up in
the air and hoping that a duck is flying over.

By meeting with the executives up front, you will have a much better idea of what to look and listen for during your needs analysis, opportunity assessment, or discovery process. Then, you will be able to tie

your functional capabilities to the goals and objectives that they told you were important, and connect the dots between what they want to do and what you can do to help.

Every big sale is just a series of little sales, and if we can't make the sale of why we should meet the people who understand "C," so that we too can understand it, then what chance do we have of making the larger sale? If our customer wants us to present to a group of executives, I carefully sell them on why I need to meet each person they expect to have in that meeting *individually* before the presentation, and preferably very early on in the process. Keep in mind that if they are extremely resistant to our request to meet with executives, it might mean that the project is part of a bottom-up initiative, and executive management may not know a thing about it. We will talk about this further in Chapter 9.

2. Push the Product Demonstration Toward the End

Many customers will want to "see your product" as soon as they possibly can. Sometimes it's because they are trying to bolster a grassroots campaign and they think "seeing" the product will help to garner support for the initiative. Other times they simply want to see which one "looks" the best.

If your product offering is visually and aesthetically superior to your competitor's product, you might be able to get away with showing it early, but as a general rule, "seeing" the product is part of the deselection process. Especially in the software business, which is where I spent most of my selling career, showing the product almost always results in a number of objections about things "they don't like." Here are some classic examples:

- "This isn't the way our current system does it."
- "We don't look at shipments by warehouse; we look at them by customer."
- "We would need to customize the interface to display other data that this doesn't show."
- "This data pertains to flavored juices. We don't sell flavored juices, we sell fashion apparel. I assume your system is incapable of handling apparel data, right?"

The interesting thing about software is that it can be made to do or show almost anything the customer wants it to. But the chances of it looking exactly the way they want it to look in an up-front demo— before we do any needs analysis or discovery—are nil. Take it from a guy who has made this mistake too many times. Learn how to sell them on the idea of doing a more customized demonstration *later on* in the process. If they get a "bad taste" up front, you will be pushed to the back of the line of potential vendors, you won't be given the same access to people or information you otherwise would, and you may never be able to recover.

There are some cases where a customized product demonstration, or what some vendors would call a proof-of-concept, can be quite an expensive undertaking. I have often insisted on presenting the findings of a needs analysis along with a detailed value proposition, which includes product pricing, before doing a custom product demo. My rationale is, "If you agree with our findings, and you feel the value proposition justifies the estimated investment, then we will move forward with the demo to 'prove out' the solution we propose. Does that seem fair to you?" We certainly don't want to invest all the time and money to develop a prototype or proof-of-concept only to hear them say later, "That's just way out of our price range."

3. Only Use References as the Last Step Before Commitment

It's really easy for your customer to say, "Give us a few references." It doesn't cost them anything. It's a great way to get us off balance and to start jumping through their hoops. We can't allow that kind of precedent to be set. For many years I have maintained this policy:

> *"If you want to talk to one of my existing clients, that's no problem. But I cannot ask my customer to take their time to speak with you, or host a visit, unless it is the last hurdle we need to get over before you are ready to move forward. I have a lot of happy customers, and you can talk to any of them you want. But I don't have so many that I can afford to exercise them for a 'maybe.' If you decide to do business with us, I will treat you with the same respect. I would not waste your time to provide a reference for a*

prospect unless they were in a position to finalize their decision as a result. Does that seem fair to you?"

I've never had a customer who took issue with that. In most cases they simply want to know if you actually do have happy customers. To provide this "warm fuzzy," you might want to produce a partial list of existing clients that you can share, or several written customer testimonials in either a case study or a letter format.

I often ask my best reference clients if I can conduct a short interview in which I will ask them a few key questions, then write a letter "to me" on their behalf, and e-mail it to them for approval. If they approve of the letter, they can print it on their letterhead, sign it, and mail it back to me. I always keep color copies of a dozen or more of these testimonial letters ready to go and often include them in information packs to new prospects.

Some companies organize scheduled conference calls, or even scheduled site visits, with key reference clients that their sales reps and their invited prospects can participate in. But here is a very important point to remember . . .

There are a finite number of things that your prospect thinks they *want* from you in the Selection and Buying Process. Now, you and I might know that they actually *need* our guidance and advice, our domain expertise, and the like. But sometimes they think that all they want are specifications, functionality, price, availability, and references. If we give them everything they want too early, they might not see a reason to meet with us again. We need to try to leverage these things they want, to get some of the things we want such as access to executives, other decision makers or influencers, Finance, Legal, and so on.

4. Never Present a Written Proposal Without a Verbal Agreement First

One of the most uncomfortable situations in selling is submitting a final proposal and waiting for them to "get back to you." The days or weeks that elapse seem like years and are a leading source of gray hair and ulcers among sales professionals. To reduce the anxiety, and to make sure your proposal hits the bull's-eye, insist on reviewing the proposal verbally before you submit it in writing. This allows you to gauge their reaction, handle any concerns or objections they may have, or clear up any ambiguities that might exist.

There are situations where a client will demand that a written proposal be submitted before any response is provided. But here again, if they won't even talk to us, what makes us think they are going to turn around and buy from us? If your customer won't sit down with you to go over everything to make sure it's right before you type it up, take that as a sign that you are not positioned to win. That's why we need to sell them on the idea right up front. Tell them, "This is how we do our proposals. We meet with you to review the proposal, work out any kinks, come to an agreement, and *then* we go back and type it up. Does that seem fair to you?"

For years I have insisted on this as a rule of thumb: I will not type up anything that hasn't been verbally agreed to first. If you aren't in a position to be that bold, at least catch the spirit of the suggestion and work in that direction. What I've found is . . .

> **Submitting written letters, plans, or proposals that have not been verbally agreed to first can destroy your momentum in a sale, and can even damage a relationship if your customer doesn't understand or agree with what they read.**

Take the time to review things verbally before you put them in writing. That way, when you do submit the written version, you don't have to sit around wondering what they thought about it. It's worth the trouble, and you'll find yourself having to write a lot less when you've already explained things in person or on the phone. What you write will simply be a confirmation of what you've already mutually agreed to.

5. Add in Any Major Steps or Events That Seem to Be Missing

There are certain steps that you *know* are critical in a successful sales campaign. You will have other chances in the future to suggest additional steps along the way, but if you see a big one that is missing, it's best to bring it up and get it on the table early on.

A couple of examples might be meeting with Finance to talk about options for financing, or meeting with Legal to review standard contract language and at least start the dialogue around specific terms and conditions that you know might be contentious.

Heeding these guidelines and others that you know to be true about how customers buy in your market, you can present these steps once again slightly rearranged. Now the process looks more like this:

- Meet with key executives to understand desired results
- Needs analysis and opportunity assessment
- Meet with Finance to discuss financing options
- Present findings and value proposition to executive management
- Meet with Legal to iron out contract issues
- Verbally review proposal
- Product demonstration/proof-of-concept
- Submit final proposal
- Reference site visit
- Finalize agreement

Ideally, we would like to get verbal buy-in on this "rough draft" of the things we will do together moving forward. The plan is obviously not complete yet, but it's important that we have some degree of shared understanding and shared expectations to make sure that we are both on the same page. Then we can go back to the office and take this plan to the next level.

Further Defining the Process

In Chapter 7, we talked about developing a list or a "set of the hurdles" that represent the milestones that customers in your market typically have to get over in order to evaluate, select, and buy the types of products and services you sell. As we maintain and enhance this standard model of a buying process, we can compare each opportunity against it to make sure we are not missing anything. Most of the events and activities identified to be part of any particular buying process will relate to the standard hurdles that we know customers in our market typically need to get over in order to buy.

We need to leverage each and every event or interaction to learn more about their buying process, both what will need to happen, as well as *who* within our customer's organization will be involved. We should also use each event to further qualify the opportunity to make sure that they *can* and *will* take action once all of the hurdles are cleared.

In Chapter 7, I pointed out that we must take the time to ask key questions to understand which hurdles they may have *already* cleared, or at least started working on, *before* we got involved in the process. These buying hurdles listed below (from the sample buying process presented in Chapter 7) represent some of the little decisions that are often made, or at least considered, *before* our customer starts any aspect of vendor evaluation or Source Decision. Here are some of the questions that can help us to better determine whether we are dealing with a top-down or a bottom-up initiative. The answers to these questions will also reveal where your customer is in their overall buying process. The A, C, R, and S before each hurdle indicate that hurdle is an element of the Action, Course, Resource, and Source Decisions, respectively.

Standard Buying Hurdles	Questions We Can Ask to Better Understand
C—Make vs. Buy = Buy	"Is there any chance you might just decide to make this yourself?"
R—Project oversight established	"Who will ultimately have responsibility for the success of this project?"
C—Feasibility study complete	"How did you decide that this is the best approach to addressing this issue?"
R—Funds allocated	"Is this something you've budgeted for, or will you have to go through a capital requisition process?"

We should use any needs analysis or opportunity assessment we conduct to evaluate our customer's specific functional business needs to better understand their buying process as well. If we have the opportunity to meet with decision makers and influencers in our discovery process, we can weave in a few questions about the buying process as we go along. We can also use an early meeting with Finance to discuss where they are with the allocation or appropriation of funds, as well as what will need to happen before they can get the funding secured.

As we work through the various events and meetings, we also want to understand as much as we can about the other "small" decisions they will be faced with moving forward. We should ask questions about the other buying hurdles they will probably have to clear, *after* they complete the vendor selection and the Source Decision, but *before* they can actually pull the trigger and buy. Some good questions might be:

Standard Buying Hurdles	Questions We Can Ask to Better Understand
R—Project staffed	"How does your company make decisions about the allocation of manpower resources?"
R—ROI justification approved	"How do you plan to justify the investment?"
	"Will you have to submit a ROI analysis with the Capital Appropriation Request (CAR)?"
R—Funding secured	"What is the process to secure the funding?"
S—Contract approved by Legal	"Your legal department won't have to get involved, will they?"
C—Proof-of-concept successful	"Who gives the thumbs-up on the proof-of-concept?"
A—Board of directors approval	"Will the final approval come from your CEO, or does the board of directors (BOD) have to approve something of this size?"
	"When is the next scheduled BOD meeting?"
	"How does this decision get onto the docket?"
A—Contract executed	"If we get that far, who will actually sign the contract?"

In addition to *what* needs to happen, we also need to start building our knowledge of *who* will be involved in the various stages of the process. Some sample questions might include:

- "Who has to submit the Capital Appropriation Request?"
- "Who approves that request?"
- "Who has to sign off on the legal aspects of the contract?"

Figure 8.2 Your Customer's Organization Chart

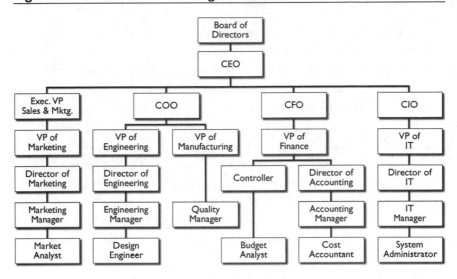

In fact, it is helpful to simply ask, "Who will be involved in that?" after every one of the questions recommended above.

The names and roles of the individuals involved should be collected and arranged into an organization chart that you maintain and add to as you learn about and meet more of the "players" who will make or influence any aspect of the decision. A thorough organization chart, like the example in Figure 8.2, is one of the most important documents of a successful sales campaign. You're probably already drawing these out for each of the qualified opportunities in your pipeline. But I would like to offer at least one suggestion . . .

As you develop and maintain your client's organization chart, make note of not just the name and title of the people you meet and learn about, but the role they play in the process. Try to get as clear an understanding as possible of exactly what function they will serve in the overall process, as well as an understanding of their unique perception of value. What do they stand to *gain* if you win? What do they stand to *lose* if you win? It's not just, "Have you met them?" and "Do they like us?" The question is "What are they in a position to influence?" and *"What's in it for them?"* We will need this information as we build out our plan moving forward.

A Process of Mutual Discovery

As we develop our understanding of all the things that are going to have to happen in our customer's buying process, we can start to put together a bulletproof sales campaign. We turn all the events and activities we have identified into an overall game plan, which we and our prospective customer will work through together. I recommend managing every qualified sales campaign just like you would manage a project, complete with milestones and assigned resources from both our company and our prospect's company. Figure 8.3 shows the activities of the sample buying process we reverse-engineered earlier in this chapter in project form.

You could call this a project plan, a sales plan, a closing plan, or whatever strikes your fancy. I like to call it a "Process of Mutual Discovery." The name itself helps remind me, and my customer, that we are constantly in discovery mode every step of the way. Customers seem to like the name, because it emphasizes the fact that the plan is a way for us to learn about them, and for them to learn about us, to further explore whether we can accomplish our mutual objective.

For some readers, this will not be a brand-new idea, but I want to emphasize the most important aspect of this specific approach. Please take one more look at the Process of Mutual Discovery in Figure 8.3. Notice that this is not a plan of how to get to point "B," which ends when we receive a signed contract. This plan defines all of the things that have to happen to get your customer all the way to point "C." This is vital.

Why would a customer have any interest in your plan to get the deal closed? Wouldn't that kind of be a slap in the face? That's not what they care about. They want business results. Building and sharing your plan to help them get from where they are right now to *where they ultimately want to be* communicates that you have the right shared interests and that you intend to be around after the ink dries on the contract. Your client will notice the difference, and they will perceive you in a very different light than your competitor who is focused only on closing the deal.

I share my Process of Mutual Discovery with my client whenever I feel the time is right. We certainly don't want to present the idea before we've earned a certain level of trust. It takes a little time to earn the right to propose a joint plan like this. We need to have found someone

Figure 8.3 A Process of Mutual Discovery

	Proposed Process of Mutual Discovery			
Date	Event	Our personnel	Client personnel	Completed
Feb. 23	Met with technology specialist	B. Stinnett	K. Denneau (IT Mgr.)	✔
March 4	Met with business process owner	B. Stinnett	J. Aziz (VP Mktg.)	✔
March 11	Meet separately with key executives to understand and clarify desired results	B. Stinnett C. Martinez	R. Harris (CEO) D. Rand (Pres./COO) J. Aziz (VP Mktg.)	
March 18	Technical needs analysis and opportunity assessment	B. Stinnett M. Francis D. Chang	J. Aziz (VP Mktg.) E. Crantz (CIO) K. Denneau (IT Mgr.)	
March 25	Meet with Finance to discuss financing options	B. Stinnett J. Carter	A. Jones (CFO) D. Ryan (Finance Mgr.)	
April 3	Present findings and value proposition to executive management	B. Stinnett M. Francis	R. Harris (CEO) D. Rand (Pres./COO) J. Aziz (VP Mktg.)	
April 14	Meet with Legal to review standard contract	B. Stinnett	T. McCarthy (Counsel)	
April 24	Verbally review proposal	B. Stinnett C. Martinez	R. Harris (CEO) D. Rand (Pres./COO) J. Aziz (VP Mktg.) A. Jones (CFO)	
May 6	Product demonstration/Proof-of-concept	B. Stinnett M. Francis D. Chang	D. Rand (Pres./COO) J. Aziz (VP Mktg.) E. Crantz (CIO) K. Denneau (IT Mgr.)	
May 10	Submit final proposal	B. Stinnett	D. Rand (Pres./COO) J. Aziz (VP Mktg.)	
May 17	Reference site visit	B. Stinnett M. Francis	J. Aziz (VP Mktg.) E. Crantz (CIO)	
May 26	Finalize agreement	B. Stinnett C. Martinez	R. Harris (CEO) A. Jones (CFO)	
June 1	Commence implementation with a project team planning meeting	B. Stinnett D. Chang J. Johnson F. Cappozzi	D. Rand (Pres./COO) J. Aziz (VP Mktg.) E. Crantz (CIO) K. Denneau (IT Mgr.)	
June 20	Requirements and specifications completed	B. Stinnett D. Chang J. Johnson	J. Aziz (VP Mktg.) K. Denneau (IT Mgr.)	
July 15	Customization and development completed	J. Johnson F. Cappozzi	K. Denneau (IT Mgr.) S. Rossi (Sys. Admin.)	
July 30	Installation and configuration completed	J. Johnson F. Cappozzi	K. Denneau (IT Mgr.) S. Rossi (Sys. Admin.)	
Aug. 15	Integration with existing systems completed	J. Johnson F. Cappozzi	K. Denneau (IT Mgr.) S. Rossi (Sys. Admin.)	
Sept. 1	Pilot testing completed	B. Stinnett J. Johnson	J. Aziz (VP Mktg.) K. Denneau (IT Mgr.)	
Sept. 12	User training completed	Our Training Dept.	Client User Community	
Sept. 30	Go live	All	All	

who knows the goal or objective they are trying to accomplish, *why* they want to accomplish it, and *how* they can afford the investment of both time and money resources to get there. Ideally, this person would be an executive with substantial authority to allocate both money and people resources, but in a bottom-up campaign, you may not have that early on. Find somebody who stands to gain something important if the project is successful and who is willing to fight for what they want. Then present your plan as a tool to help them make the internal sale they will have to make.

There are several things that make this approach to managing a sales campaign very effective:

1. It Helps Keep Us on Track

As you meet more of the decision makers and influencers, and learn more about the hurdles you're going to have to help your client get over, the sheer overload of information can sometimes become a blur. Mapping out the process enables us to sort things out, think about what we are doing, and do a better job of selling with specific intent.

2. It Forces Us to Look Ahead

It's very easy to get caught up in all the meetings, e-mails, and phone calls involved in a sales campaign. It's even worse when you are trying to manage three, or five, or eight deals at a time. Having a codified plan that defines what we need to do, and what our client needs to do, helps us both to stay focused on the bigger picture of the overall campaign, rather than getting mired down in a competitive "feature and function" battle.

3. It Helps Us to Stay Aligned with Our Buyer

If we use this plan as a dynamic, living document that changes as we go along based on new information and understanding of what our client is doing, and planning to do next, it helps us keep in step with our buyer throughout the process.

4. It's a Tremendous Qualification Tool

It has been my experience that you get one of three reactions when you share your plan with the client: (1) they think it is a great idea, they take part ownership of it, and they adopt it for their internal selling purposes, (2) they are somewhat "ho-hum" and indifferent, or (3) they want nothing to do with it. Their reaction can tell us a lot about where we stand, and about where they stand in terms of their own internal buying process.

In a complex buying decision, especially a bottom-up initiative, there will probably be more internal selling going on than external selling. All our actions as a vendor will be a small part of everything that has to happen in order for a project to be approved, staffed, and funded.

Normally about a third of my prospects love the idea of a documented Selection and Buying Process. They take full or partial ownership of the plan. They help to make sure it includes all the hurdles we will be helping them to clear, and that all the right people attend the meetings, and so on. Another third of them aren't necessarily impressed, but if you ask them for information to build the plan, they will provide you with *some* of it. The final third hand it back, change the subject, or otherwise communicate, "We are not doing that."

Their reaction to your plan is one of the best ways I know to find out which clients want our help to make a great buying decision and reach point "C." Of course, just because they don't turn a backflip when you show it to them doesn't mean it won't help later. Just keep using the plan for your own benefit. You can show it to some of the other players in the buying decision later on. Many of those clients who are not overly impressed initially come around later, after they've met with some of your competitors who seem to be focused more on making a sale than helping the customer reach their goals.

5. It Helps to Justify Access to the Right Executives

Notice that in the column labeled "Client personnel" of the process shown in Figure 8.3, we specify who needs to be involved in these various activities and events. To begin with, you may not even have the names of the people in these various roles. That's fine. Just put the title or the role in for a place holder.

This way of requesting executive access is remarkably effective. I have never found a better way to gain access to the "right" people. It is really quite surprising how much less resistance you will encounter. Think about the difference here. In one scenario you hand your customer a piece of paper that defines a certain event, shows where that event fits in the overall scheme of things, spells out the purpose of the event, and lists the personnel who should be in attendance. In another scenario you ask, "Would you please set up a meeting with your CFO." In the former, it only makes sense that the CFO should be there. In the latter, it seems like you are just trying to go over their head. You may not be able to appreciate how effective this is until you try it yourself, but I'll share one of many examples of how this has worked for me.

I met a woman at a tradeshow who was the vice president of information systems (IS) for a midsize construction company in New York City. She had been hired by the president and owner of the company for the express purpose of buying and implementing an Enterprise Resource Planning (ERP) system.

At first she was very resistant to any request for access to those who would be involved in the final decision. It was one of those, "Just send me your questions via e-mail, and I will get the answers and e-mail them back to you," routines. I couldn't blame her. She started with fourteen potential vendors, and she was just trying to do her job without tying up everyone's time answering questions from vendors.

After a couple of meetings, I showed her the skeleton of a plan I had put together. It was very incomplete at that point, but she saw the value right away. It was as if a lightbulb went on for her. She helped me figure out the additional hurdles we needed to clear. She took joint ownership of the plan and began arranging meetings with all the right decision makers that needed to be involved. It was an amazing change to observe.

She told me later on, "You know, we had no intention of going with your company when we started out. Your system seemed too big, cumbersome, and expensive for us. But when you showed up with your process, it seemed to make so much sense. You helped us define exactly what issues we were trying to solve. From there you quickly determined what pieces of your overall solution we should spend our time looking at. You helped me think about a lot of the decisions we would be faced with that had nothing at all to do with the solution, but with resource allocation, funding, and the strategic direction of the company. Most of all, you made my job easier because after we mapped out the steps along the way, and who needed to be involved in each step, I just printed out a bunch of copies and went around from office to office saying, 'I need you on this day. I need you on that day.' You made it very easy to buy from you."

Now I must admit, not every client I have shared this process with has responded with this level of enthusiasm. For many of my customers, it simply helped them to better clarify and document the plans they already had. Other customers have used it in a more limited fashion, to organize meetings or plan resources. And some just yawned and said, "Thank you for your time." But if this plan served no other purpose than to justify, or simply provide a good reason for, gaining access to key decision makers, it would be well worth the effort.

6. Finalizing the Agreement Is Just One Step Along the Way

Because the process that we use includes activities and events both before and after point "B," finalizing the agreement is just one step along the way. When your customer understands that you're "in it with them" all the way to "C," closing the deal is not such a scary event. Yes, it's important, and there will most likely be negotiation and certain objections that arise when it comes time for them to commit, but your focus—and your customer's focus—will be on getting the agreement worked out so you can move forward together. The act of closing will carry a totally different dynamic.

This idea, just like every other tool or technique, doesn't work every time. But *when* it works, this is *how* it works. Your own results will impress you more than any success story I can tell. But please remember, a good two-thirds of the customers who you share this with probably *won't* jump all over it, but for the one-third that do, your chances of winning that business will increase exponentially. As one of my workshop attendees pointed out, "By developing and providing this kind of process, we're not only providing "B," we are providing the arrows (the process) that connect "A" to "B," and "B" to "C." Give that man a star!

Six Reasons Clients Don't Move Forward

If, or when, your customer doesn't want to work with you to put together a plan, or doesn't jump right into the plan you propose, there is usually a specific reason why they don't. I have found the following six issues at the root of most customer hesitation to move forward with you on a Process of Mutual Discovery. If you've shown them your plan and asked, "Is there anything we need to change about this plan, or are you ready to move forward with the next step?" but did not get a "Yes!" it might be that:

1. The Plan Isn't Right

Sometimes we don't listen well enough, we don't really understand their buying process very well, or the timing of the plan isn't right. Somehow what they told us, and what we propose back, just doesn't match up. So, when you sense their hesitation, make sure and ask, "What about the plan itself? Does this match with what you told us in terms of the steps involved and the timing and so forth?" Maybe they will suggest a change or two. Or maybe they will say, "No, this is pretty much what we told you. But . . ." You might need to move on to the next potential objection.

2. We Have Confused "B" with "C"

Once we learn our product and solution set thoroughly, and once we develop a well-rounded "problem knowledge," it's easy to start broadcasting solutions before we fully diagnose the problem. We can inadvertently start positioning our *solution* as their desired outcome instead of what the solution is going to enable them to do, and the results they are trying to achieve. You might need to clarify by asking, "Have we misunderstood what you are trying to accomplish here? The objective is _____ (fill in the blank), right?" If that's not the problem, then move on to the next possible issue.

3. The Desired Result or Point "C" Isn't Very Compelling

Sometimes, things look good and sound good, but not quite good enough to take action on. There might be other uses of capital and resources that are simply more compelling than the project you are part of. There just may not be a very powerful motive to make the change, or there is no consequence to the status quo. Or, despite how great "C" looks, the perceived risk is just greater than the perceived return. Perhaps you could ask, "It sounds like the payback or the return on this project just isn't that compelling right now. Is that what's holding you back from moving forward?" If not, try the next one.

4. The Customer Plans to Reach Point "C" with Someone Else

It is entirely possible that your plan is great, but some other vendor has provided a plan or a solution that is more closely aligned with their vision or is perceived to be lower risk. Despite all we do, we don't lead in every deal, so maybe we should ask, "Are you leaning toward another solution to solve this problem, or maybe another provider has a better plan?" Sometimes they do have someone else in mind. Other times, that isn't it, but they still aren't sure they are ready to take the next step. Keep digging.

5. You Are Dealing with the Wrong Person

One mistake that we all have probably made is asking the person we think is our buyer to "buy-in" to our plan, when he or she doesn't have the authority to do so. We might be asking the wrong person. If the person we are dealing with really doesn't have the authority, it would make sense that they are going to be hesitant to commit to working with us, wouldn't it? We need to be very careful if we decide to ask a question about this. We might try, "You know, John, maybe you would feel more comfortable if we took the time to garner a little more support for the project before we jump into a process like this. Maybe we should get a few more folks on board. What do you think?"

What we wouldn't want to do is make them feel as though we don't respect their position by coming across with something like, "John, it sounds to me like you really don't have the juice to make any decisions around here." Be careful not to insult somebody who you want as an ally. We'll need all we can possibly get.

6. The Next Step You Are Proposing Isn't the "Next" Step

Perhaps the most common reason that our customer isn't ready to start working through the milestones and clearing the hurdles as they have been defined, is that the next step we have proposed simply isn't the *next* step. Something else internally or externally may need to happen before they can move forward. Sometimes they have to meet with three more vendors in round one before they can proceed with any vendor. Other times, they need to report back to the committee to get guidance or approval to move forward. We could try asking, "I'll bet there is something else that needs to happen first, right?"

When this happens, then that new hurdle just becomes one more line item on the plan. You'll simply need to "Insert Row" and plug the new task or the new activity in wherever it belongs on your table or spreadsheet. You will probably insert dozens of rows as you work with your client through the Selection and Buying Process, and as pointed out earlier, the few milestones we defined in the Implementation and Utilization Process will probably be replaced by a more complete implementation plan once we get to that point.

Whenever you hit a bump in the road, a brick wall, or a really big pothole, think about these six issues above. Asking questions around these six is a helpful way of troubleshooting the process to try to determine where things have gone wrong and how to get back on track.

Selling Your Process

This process of managing a sales campaign is so effective, and delivers such benefit in terms of managing your own time and resources, that it's worth using even if your customer has no interest in it. For years I have used this kind of a plan for every complex sales opportunity I've pursued. I start piecing it together from the very first interaction I have with the client.

One of the techniques that I have found very effective is to print out the plan and take it with me starting with the very first meeting. Now, in that first meeting—where all I know are the few names and facts I was able to pick up during a preliminary phone call—the plan will be skeletal at best. But as the meeting progresses, I make my notes about other people who the customer happens to mention on my "plan sheet." If they mention certain dates, or an upcoming event, or anything that binds the process in time, I make notes of that on the sheet as well. I construct the plan on a preprinted sheet right in front of them. After a couple of meetings, in which I have very obviously used the plan as a mechanism for capturing and organizing what I have learned, clients will often ask, "What is that you are writing on there?"

Sometimes the best way to sell something is not to sell it at all, but to create curiosity about it. Sure, you can present it to your client for their consideration whenever you feel the time is right. But before that, just use it for your own benefit, in plain sight. They might surprise you by asking about it before you even bring it up. I've seen this happen many times.

Regardless of how you approach it, your customers will only be as interested and as excited about it as you are. I believe if you use this idea the way it has been presented, and you share your plan with a few customers, you will be amazed at how well it will be received.

If you were the customer, it would be pretty hard *not* to be impressed if a vendor took the time to understand your internal policies, your business processes, and your organizational structure, and rolled all of that into a step-by-step plan of how to help you reach your business goals. I encourage you to . . .

**Sell your process, and let your process sell
your product.**

According to the customers I have worked with over the years, this method of selling is quite different from what they are used to seeing. Oh, I didn't win every deal, and neither will you. But you will win more than your share if you're willing to do the work. It's one of the best ways I know to differentiate yourself from your competitors. Try this approach for yourself, and you'll soon be wondering why you weren't selling this way all along.

CHAPTER **9**

Elevating the Buying Process

I doubt there is a suggestion more frequently made to sales profes-sionals than, "sell higher." Throughout this book I have tried to pro-vide highly actionable ideas and tools to help you learn how to think *about* the things that executives think *about*, and to leverage that per-spective as you construct and conduct your sales campaigns. Now, let us get specific about *why* selling higher is so critically important, as well as *how* to elevate your sales campaign and help your customer to elevate their buying process.

When opportunities find us, and we react to them, it is almost inevitable that we engage at a relatively low level within our prospect's organization. Even in our proactive prospecting efforts, where we make the first move to contact our customer when seeking potential business opportunities, our first successful "connection" might happen at a mid-management level or even lower.

As sales professionals, this situation of selling bottom-up is a very common one to find ourselves in. Participants in my workshops ask more questions on this one topic than on all other topics combined. So, I have dedicated this entire chapter to "How and Why to Sell High."

Why Sell High?

Selling higher really means earning access to those who will be making the Action Decision. "To buy, or not to buy," *that* is the question. And it can only be answered by the person or persons with the authority and responsibility to make these critical decisions on the company's behalf. These are the same individuals who will prioritize the various goals and objectives the company is trying to achieve. They ultimately decide which course of action to take, and they decide where to draw the line of available resources. In short, only *they* know what *we* need to know in order to mount a successful sales campaign. Never forget that . . .

> **Until we meet and understand those who will make the final Action Decision, we really can't know much about what it will take to win the deal, or even if there is a deal to win.**

Selling higher is not optional. It's the only way to really be successful at our job. If we can't elevate our sales campaign and get through at the higher levels of our prospective customer's organization, we will never really know:

1. Is It a Top-Down or Bottom-Up Initiative?

Many of the people involved in a Selection and Buying Process never actually know whether or not the initiative that is driving the buying decision originated at the executive level or is a grassroots campaign. I have seen many selection committee members and even some committee chairmen just as surprised as I was when their management decided to "move in a different direction," which means they decided to pursue a different course of action or to forgo action altogether.

2. What Is the Business Disparity (Goal or Problem) They Are Trying to Address?

For those who are assigned to the selection process of choosing the best vendor or source, the goal is to make a well-informed, quality Source Decision. In a high percentage of cases, they have not been told, nor have they ever bothered to ask, "Why?" the company would consider such a purchase. In some corporate cultures, when your boss tells you to do something, it can be career-limiting to ask "Why?"

3. What Is the Desired Outcome or Result at Point "C"?

For many of the lower-level buyers involved in source selection, their point "C" is actually point "B." Once they sort through all the responses to their request for proposal (RFP), watch all the demos, weigh all the evidence, and make their recommendation, they're done. Understanding how the solution will be used, what kind of return is expected, when it is expected, and what bad thing happens if things don't work out as planned, simply may not be part of their job description.

4. Does the Project Tie to and Support Corporate-Level Goals and Objectives?

Very few companies that we sell to do a really good job of communicating how the contribution of the various business units and functional departments support and contribute to the overall success of the company as a whole. Most individual contributors, many managers, and even some directors, are not privy to how their goals and objectives fit into the overall corporate strategy. If they don't know, how can they possibly help us understand?

5. What Action Drivers Are at Work—Motive, Urgency, Return, Consequence, Means, and Risk?

When we ask a manager, "When do you need to start seeing results?" they typically answer, "As soon as possible." Some even think that we will "jump higher" if they say, "We need these results yesterday!" If you've ever gone through one of these "we need it yesterday" drills, only to have executive management say, "Come back and see us in six months," you'll know the folly of qualifying an opportunity with a low-level buyer.

Please read this next sentence very carefully . . .

A sales opportunity qualified with anyone other than the person or persons who will make the final Action Decision is *not* qualified.

Sure, collect the "opinions" of all the people who influence the buying decision, build relationships at all levels, use all the information you gather to create a composite picture of what it's going to take to win the sale, but don't rely too heavily on anything unless it comes from the mouth of the person or persons who make the final Action Decision.

6. Who or What Are We Competing With?

At the lower levels, where the Source Decision is made, our competitors are other companies that sell the same things that we sell. As far as our low-level buyer is concerned, if we can offer a better price than XYZ Corp., we've got the deal. Who are they kidding? We will compete in the Resource Decision with every other potential use of the money and manpower required to buy and implement our solution. We will compete with alternate courses of action, any of which may increase revenue or reduce costs just as effectively, or even more reliably than we can. And in the end, even if the initiative that our solution is a part of is deemed worth pursuing, they might decide to delay taking any action. We might find ourselves placed on the "back burner" for a while. Typically, only the executives making the higher-level decisions know who or what we are really competing with.

7. What Resources Can or Will Be Made Available to Ensure the Success of the Investment?

Quite often the selection committee is told, "You select the best vendor or the best source for this solution and recommend it to us here in senior management. We'll take it from there." Can you imagine how demoralizing it would be to tell the committee, "You spend a few months selecting, and then we'll see if we can even afford to do it or not." I know that some buyers are purposefully blowing smoke when they say, "We're definitely going to buy." Other times, they are just repeating what they have been told or led to believe by their management.

8. Is There an Executive Predisposition to One of the Vendors or Sources Being Considered?

The CEO, or someone else sitting around the table making the Action or Course Decision, may have been a loyal customer of one of your competitors at their last company. Heck, they might even have a brother-in-law who works for them! We can't assume that all vendors will be on a level playing field when it comes to the more strategic, higher-level decisions, even if we win the source battle and are recommended by the selection committee.

One of my clients shared a story with me about a $50 million contract his company had lost at the very last minute, when their prospect's CEO decided that it was less risky to go with my client's competitor because of brand recognition and reputation. This happened despite a brutal eighteen-month selection process that cost my client hundreds of thousands of dollars to win. No one from my client's firm had ever met their prospect's CEO. Their prospect's CFO had convinced them it was not necessary, and that the CEO would yield to the recommendation of the committee. Ouch!

9. Where Are They in Terms of the Action Decision and the Buying Process as a Whole?

To properly plan and execute a successful campaign, we need to know more than just the criteria for selecting the best vendor. We need to know:

- What facets of the Action, Course, and Resource Decisions have already been decided?
- What questions are still on the table?
- What specific hurdles of the Action, Course, and Resource Decisions will be left until after the Source Decision is made?

The Source Decision is always a subset of the larger buying process, and the final Action Decision always comes later. If we can't get an understanding of what it will take to win the Resource and Course Decisions, as well as what else has to happen before they can decide to take action and buy, winning the Source Decision could be an exercise in futility.

10. Are They, as an Organization, Willing to Work with Us?

We have talked about the importance of selling your buyer on a Process of Mutual Discovery, or a plan to help them get from point "A" to point "C." But we need to sell that plan at a high enough level so that we have some assurance that once we reach point "B," they will, in fact, buy and continue on with us toward point "C." Let's realize that without buy-in at the executive level, any commitment made by a lower-level decision maker is unreliable at best. A manager or director may be empowered to speak for a senior executive, but they are very seldom given the authority to commit for one.

So you see, it might not be that the manager or director you are selling to won't tell you what you want and need to know to properly qualify an account and mount a successful sales campaign. Much of what we really want and need to know is never told to them in the first place. The problem here is that it's OK for them to operate without knowing these details. It is not, however, OK for us.

A director of finance can invest his own time as well as the time of the people on his staff, several from IT, one or two from HR, and even an outside consultant or two for the next twelve months in order to make a well-informed and bulletproof Source Decision. If they, as a committee, make their recommendation to senior management, and then senior management decides to wait six months or to go in some different direction entirely, no one is going to be upset with that director of finance or anyone else on the committee. They were just doing their job.

Unfortunately, if we invest the same twelve months of our time, the time of our pre-sales consultants, business analysts, and sales managers trying to make the sale, only to find out the executive team had no intention of taking action on this initiative at this time, we'll probably be fired. Or, at least we should be. Gaining access to, selling to, and qualifying at the executive level is paramount to our consistent sales performance and success.

I have watched too many sales professionals over the years become frustrated and even angry when they hear that, after all their hard work, "The CEO (of their prospective client's company) decided to put the project on hold for six months." I have been that angry rep myself, too many times. Our customers don't purposefully lie to us or waste our time—well, other than one or two I've met along the way. More often, the circumstances surrounding the Action Decision simply changed over time. Or, maybe we operated on the assumptions of a lower-level player who "coached" us based on bad information, while all along the CEO had a very different perception of Urgency, Motive, and Consequence.

One could argue, "But they should have asked the CEO and made sure before they wasted our time like that!" Probably so. But let's not forget that their motive to understand the CEO's decision criteria and perception of value is very different from ours. They don't stand to get fired or miss their quarterly quota when the CEO delays the purchase, the same way that you or I do. It is ultimately our responsibility to reach that CEO, or whoever will make the final Action Decision, and try our best to understand how she thinks and what she thinks *about*. Any choice we make to take someone else's word for it is at best a risk, and at worst downright foolish.

A Proactive Strategy

I recommend a proactive strategy when it comes to reaching executive-level decision makers. We should start today to reach out to every C-Level executive within every existing company we sell to, as well as within our best prospective new customers. If what you sell has no relevance to some of these C-Level executives, then identify the five or six executive roles that are most relevant to you. If you sell consulting services to the marketing and advertising departments, then your five or six target people might include the chief marketing officer (CMO), VP of advertising, VP of channel marketing, or whatever. If you manage a broad territory with hundreds of potential accounts, then narrow it down to the top twenty best prospects and reach out to the right five or six executives in each.

When we are proactive, and we make the first attempt at communication, we can call at any level we want. You might choose to start out calling lower in the organization to learn more about their company before you approach the executive, but be careful you don't get stuck down there. I suggest at least attempting to reach the key senior executives of all your target accounts, before anyone at their company has a chance to call you.

You may choose to use mail, fax, telephone, voice mail, e-mail, or whatever, but reach out to them and try to at least make the acquaintance of all the top executives you can. It is often easier to get past gatekeepers when they aren't currently evaluating potential vendors than when they are. If we do our homework, and the research I described in Chapter 1, we may be able to provoke or instigate a top-down initiative, or at least a commitment to explore the possibilities.

A Reactive Strategy

If we don't at least attempt to meet with the key executives proactively, but instead wait until an opportunity finds us, we are often stuck selling bottom-up. Once they call us, we lose the chance to be proactive, we end up reacting to opportunities, and it's possible to lose a great deal of control over how we engage the client. They are in a position to dictate how we sell to them, if we allow it. One of the most common questions that salespeople struggle with is, "What do you do when you have made a connection or developed a relationship with a lower-level person, and you know you need to sell higher?" Well, let's face it. There are only three things that you *can* do . . .

Option #1: Just Sell at the Lower Level

One approach is to just do what they tell you to do. Show up, give your presentation, show the product, submit a proposal, and hope like crazy that they call you back. You know what, that's a depressing way to live. That's if you *can* live. You probably won't sell much . . . Oh, maybe something here and there. But even if you could pay your bills on your base salary alone, that's not what you signed up for, and your boss won't be able to justify having you on the team for long.

Can you win *some* business selling low? Sure. You can play the numbers game. Put out ten proposals, and close one. Put out twenty proposals, and close two. Cut your price 40 percent and you might even be able to close three. But if you were happy with that approach, you wouldn't be reading this book. Let's just say that selling low is pretty risky. You could end up wasting a lot of time on deals that aren't deals. You can't build relationships with strategic decision makers you never meet. You may also never know what other products and services or other initiatives you are competing with, and therefore you can't proactively do anything to be more competitive.

Option #2: Go over Their Head and Call Their Boss

Another approach is: When your prospect contacts you, you ask to meet their boss, they say "No," and you call her anyway. This is an even riskier approach! If you would have called in at a high level a week earlier, they probably wouldn't even have known about it, let alone cared. But once they call you . . . too late! Now, you have to play by their rules. Or, at least they *think you do*.

There are circumstances where the "go over their head and call their boss" strategy is the only option left. If you are called into an opportunity very late in the game, or if you simply aren't given any opportunity to learn about their business, or meet with any of the people who will make the strategic decisions, there's not much else you can do. You can either play by their rules, as in approach number one, or you can risk it all by calling high anyway.

There are several other techniques, which we will discuss, that should be tried first. I would suggest making this approach your last resort. Only use it if you have exhausted all other options and you are willing to risk damaging any relationship you may have, or may hope to have, with the lower-level person.

If you think the lower-level person won't find out you called over their head, prepare to be surprised. More than once I thought I was being clever by leaving a voice mail, or sending an e-mail, to someone's boss on the sly, only to have the boss forward it to the person who originally contacted me. The lower-level person then proceeded to lecture me on "how we do things around here."

Option #3: Earn Your Way Up to the Higher Level

The third approach, which will come as no surprise to you as the one I recommend, is to earn your way past the gatekeeper to get access to higher levels. This is not as complicated as some would make it out to be. It's relatively simple; it's just not very easy. Even the most experienced sales professionals find themselves "stuck" from time to time. It is this approach that we will explore here as we look at several techniques and tactics, as well as the psychology involved in making this work for you.

The Psychology of a Gatekeeper

I believe it helps to put ourselves in the shoes of the lower-level person in order to understand the dynamic of what and whom we are dealing with. The reason a gatekeeper is a gatekeeper is that he or she has been given a specific job to do. One type of gatekeeper is the administrative assistant. It might seem to us that the job description of an executive assistant is, "Don't let anyone through under any circumstances." That is probably an exaggeration. It's more like, "Screen out all the garbage calls, but if you find a good one, put it right through." I've found the best way to sell past the gatekeeper is to *sell to* the gatekeeper. Treat them with the same respect, and sell the value of your company, your people, and your solutions just as you would if you had the executive on the line. If the gatekeeper finds you worthy of getting through, they will often even help you with your approach.

Now let's look at the other kind of gatekeeper. This is a lower-level person in some unit or department who calls you to request information, a demo, or a proposal. If they have been given the task of calling you by their boss, then they believe it is their job to prescreen you. In fact, the specific instructions from their boss may well have been, "Call a few possible sources, and when you find one or two good ones, then I will get involved." That's standard management practice. So, let's realize that pressuring them to speak to their boss, or worse yet calling over their head can make them look bad. It looks as if they didn't do their job. What we have to do is change this psychology around. We need to figure out a way to make them look good.

Have you ever been in a client meeting, or in a conversation on the phone, when the person you are talking to interrupts you to say, "Could you hold that thought just a minute? I'd like my boss to hear this"? I'll bet that's happened to all of us, hasn't it? What happened there? We probably stumbled onto something that the boss has been asking about or complaining about. Or maybe we said something that reinforces what the person we are meeting with has been trying to explain or communicate to their boss for some time. This does not have to be an accidental occurrence.

One of the main reasons we spend so much time in our workshops talking about value, how our customers perceive value, and the cause and effect of business value, is to help each of us to be more effective asking the questions that prove we are worthy of meeting their boss and other senior executives. When we start asking questions about Urgency, Motive, and Consequence, and how the specific objectives that he or she has been personally tasked with link to and support the higher-level goals of the company, we are perceived as someone who deserves to be talking to management.

The Right Mind-Set

We should go into every meeting, or every phone call, with the intention, and the expectation, of earning access to other people within the company, and especially at higher levels. Starting with the first meeting, use the techniques we have discussed, and a few more still to come, to try to get beyond the person you are meeting with and meet the next person.

Here's a helpful rule of thumb that has served me well: you need to get beyond the person you are meeting with or talking to, and on to someone at a higher level, within three meetings or extended phone conversations. It has been my experience that . . .

> **If you can't "make the sale" of *why* you should be meeting with more people at higher levels in your customer's organization within the first three meetings, you probably never will.**

You end up establishing a precedent that is very hard, if not impossible, to overcome.

If you meet with the same person four, five, or six times, and they still won't give you any access, they must have a reason. It could be they want certain information from you so they can get credit for providing it. Just as often, the reason they won't let you meet senior people, is that the project or the solution they are investigating or considering is tied to a bottom-up initiative, and the senior managers and executives don't even know about it yet.

I can think of no more important piece of information we could ever learn about an opportunity than where the initiative originated. If that is unclear to us, or if we are plain wrong, everything we do could be completely misdirected and ultimately a waste of time and energy. Our objective should be to get up to the level where the Action Decision will be made as quickly as we possibly can. It's important to realize that this is good for our client, too.

If a top-down initiative has trickled down to a lower-level person who is then asked or told to research and meet potential vendors, the executives would probably like a reliable recommendation sooner rather than later. If our sales efforts help to ensure that the criteria they use to select a source are consistent and congruent with what is important to the executives, then we have helped our client make a great Source Decision. On the other hand, if by our efforts a grassroots, bottom-up initiative is properly aligned with and tied into the higher-level corporate goals and objectives, then we help to make the internal sale that inevitably has to be made to get a bottom-up initiative approved, staffed, and funded.

Eight Techniques for Selling Your Way to the Top

So, how do you get past the low-level gatekeepers and get access to the higher levels? Here are a few proven techniques you can leverage to "make the little sale" of why you deserve to meet your customer's boss, their boss's boss, and the senior executives of the company. Most of these techniques leverage concepts that have already been introduced in this book. Here are a few practical examples of how to use them in your effort to elevate your customer's buying process.

1. Leverage the Business Value Hierarchy™ Model

A gatekeeper might block you from gaining access to those higher up in the corporate structure for a number of reasons. One is that they may not trust you, or they simply may not like you, but more likely it's that they assume you are going to ask the same exact questions, and talk about the same products and services with their boss, that you have talked about with them. If you are selling in broadcast mode, and wowing them with advantages and benefits, instead of asking questions about possible business disparities, cause and effect, and cross-organizational impact, they would look silly bringing you to their boss. They were told to gather all that detail and sift through it on the boss's behalf. We have to start asking questions about, and sharing ideas about, how we might be able to help reach their boss's goals, or to solve their boss's problems.

Whatever the subject matter of the conversation, whether it be the problems they are experiencing or the goals they are trying to attain, we should be asking questions like . . .

"Why is this objective so important right now?"

or

"What are the effects that this problem creates?"

. . . in order to understand the cause-and-effect relationships that link the issue at hand to the higher-level goals and objectives of the company. As we build our business acumen, we will understand more about *what causes what* in business, so that when we converse with our customers—and they talk to us about the business issues they are faced with—we will be prepared to ask the right questions. We'll be asking questions not just about the issues they face at their level, and the impact those issues have on their world, but the effect that these issues cause for their boss, and how they impact their boss's world. We need to be able to link everything that our products and services do, all the way up to increasing revenue, reducing costs, and better utilizing assets, in order to maximize our client's profitability.

In our workshops we help participants make the transition "from sales rep to profit advisor," by helping them to understand the linkages between the functional capabilities of their products and services and the business issues facing the various executives within their customer's business. We want to be able to translate the value of what we sell to increased profit to our customers, and ultimately trace the value of every feature and function of our product or service to the specific line item on our client's Balance Sheet or Income Statement. Sounds like a tall order, doesn't it? Well, that's the power of the Business Value Hierarchy™ (BVH) concept, and why it is such a powerful tool in the hands of sales professionals who learn to use it.

In Chapter 4, I offered a number of practical applications for the BVH model, both during discovery and presentation, several of which were specific to earning access to executives. Even during somewhat casual conversation, when our client happens to mention that they are concerned about poor customer satisfaction, for example, we can explore a possible link to executive-level business issues by asking questions like:

- "Is that causing a problem with customer retention? How is your chief marketing officer (CMO) affected by this?"
- "Is this having a negative effect on revenue? What does your vice president of sales have to say about that?"
- "Has this caused any increase in accounts receivable or any problem with collections? What has your CFO done to try to deal with that?"

- "Is all this impacting overall profitability? What is your CEO planning to do to correct this before it winds up causing your company to miss your quarterly earnings estimate?"

You may want to look back to Figure 4.4 in Chapter 4 to see the visual representation of these questions.

When we ask questions about real business problems, and the people that are affected by them, we demonstrate our business savvy and our value as a potential partner. Then if we can start to weave in a few stories about how we have helped other companies within our customer's industry deal with similar problems, as well as some of the results we were able to help them achieve, the psychology begins to change. The customer starts to think, "Wow. These guys have done this before. Maybe if I got this guy in front of my boss, or the CMO or CFO, they would be impressed and I could look like a hero for finding him."

I am in the business of making heroes out of gatekeepers. I want to make them look as good as I possibly can. When you go to the meeting with their boss, make sure and say, "Here are some of the ideas John and I came up with last time we met." Give *them* all the credit you can.

2. Focus on Point "C"

One way to prove that you deserve to be speaking to those who will make the Action Decision is by staying focused on learning all you can about point "C," their desired outcomes and results. I honestly believe that until we hear the description of what point "C" is, and what value they hope to derive there, from the mouth of the person or persons who will make the final Action Decision, I still don't know how to properly position myself to win.

How can I possibly craft a solution that is "dead on" and hits the bull's-eye for the final decision maker if they won't describe it to me in their own words? Did you ever, as a kid in school, play that game where the teacher whispers something in the ear of one student, and then she whispers it to the next student, and so on, and so on, until it comes out at the other end as something completely different than what was said to start with? That's what happens when visions of "C" trickle down through an organization in a top-down initiative. It's even worse when it starts from the bottom-up and we have no clue whatsoever as to what's important to the executives.

I have learned through common sense, trial and error, and direct experience how to ask key questions that help me earn access to senior decision makers so I can learn what I need to know to start positioning myself to win. You can too! The questions vary based on what you sell, the market you sell to, and how a typical customer in your market makes buying decisions. Therefore, as my sales role and the types of buyers I sell to have changed over the years, so have the questions I use to gain access.

At Sales Excellence, Inc., we use a combination of inbound and outbound approaches to identify new business opportunities. One of the most common situations we encounter is when a sales manager plans a quarterly or annual sales meeting for his or her team and then decides to dedicate one or two days to sales skills training.

The chore of locating several potential vendors is inevitably handed off to an assistant or someone in the marketing or human resources department. That's who goes out to a search engine, types in "sales training," and finds our website. That person then calls us with a standard list of questions:

- "What kind of programs do you offer?"
- "What is the duration?"
- "What will our people learn?"
- "How much does the program cost?"

The worst possible thing that we could do would be to answer any of these questions. If we were to simply answer those questions, our name would go into a hat and stand very little chance of ever getting pulled back out. When I take the call, I handle every one of these inquiries in the same exact way.

First, I hear them out. I listen to anything and everything they are willing to tell me about their company, the details of the meeting, how many people will attend, what other kinds of training may have been provided recently, and so on. When I can tell they are getting tired of talking, I say, "I'll bet you called to ask us:

- What kind of programs do you offer?
- What is the duration?
- What will our people learn?
- How much does the program cost?

Is that right?"

They frequently think I am a mind reader. Then I tell them, "I would love to answer all those questions for you, but unfortunately I can't."

"Why not?" they usually ask.

"Because before I can propose the right solution, I have to understand a few things first, such as:

- What is the highest-level goal or objective we are trying to address here? What would we be trying to accomplish with this workshop?
- Is this goal or objective measurable? And if so, how is it measured? How can we gauge our success? What metrics can we use to measure the effects of this training three months or six months after the event is over?
- What changes in attitudes and behavior must take place in order to see marked improvements in these measures or metrics? Put more simply, what do we want participants to be able or willing to *think* or *do* the day after this training session that they couldn't or wouldn't *think* or *do* the day before?"

Not one person who has ever called our office has known the answers to these questions. Ninety-five percent of the time, the person from marketing or HR says, "Well, we will have to get the vice president of sales on the phone to answer that." Even the occasional VP of sales who picks up the phone to call us themselves has to go back and think a little bit before they can answer these questions adequately. The questions are designed specifically to have that effect.

These kinds of questions, which are focused entirely on our customer's "C"—and have nothing at all to do with our "B"—force executive-level conversation and brainstorming. They also encourage our involvement in the discussion and the creation of the ideal training workshop or program. At Sales Excellence, we find that when we earn that kind of access to sales executives and we work together to craft a solution, we can close 80 percent of those opportunities. When their sales executives won't engage in a discussion about what "C" means to them, or when we have three phone conversations with the marketing or HR person without being granted access to those who will make the Action Decision, we move on to the next opportunity. Period. Even if they did want to hire us, the chances of getting them to "C" are nil. How can you possibly hit a bull's-eye you don't have?

You will need to craft your own questions that force interaction with the strategic decision makers in your particular selling environment. To make them effective, make sure they are focused squarely on understanding the "C" your customer wants to achieve, and not on finding out what kind of "B" they want to buy.

3. Develop a Process of Mutual Discovery

In Chapter 8 we talked about how to leverage a Process of Mutual Discovery plan to gain access to executives. I will reiterate here that following this approach, you will be forced to speak with executives to get a complete picture of all the things that need to happen before the customer can buy. Gatekeepers tend to understand this better when you request access in the context of completing your process map than if you just say, "I want to meet your boss." If they like your process, which is to fully understand and document *their* process, they will be much less guarded and often will help you get the access you need to create an accurate model of their internal decision process and policies.

Once the process is produced, even in the early drafts or revisions, your customer will much more easily understand why you need certain decision makers involved in certain meetings, and often will help to make sure the right people are invited and attend.

4. Share a Reference Story or a Case Study

I have made it a habit to collect success stories as told at the level of the person who will ultimately be responsible for the success of the initiative at hand. This is usually at the vice president–level or higher. Learning to tell the stories using terms and measures and lingo that VPs can relate to earns you access to other VPs.

When possible, we should collect stories as told by the CEO or another C-Level executive. Stories about how other CFOs have used your products and services to achieve goals and objectives that are top-of-mind issues for CFOs helps you earn access to other CFOs. Plus, once you get there, you can talk about how the functional capabilities of your products and services translate into value in the eyes of a CFO.

I encourage my clients to make their success stories both value specific as well as *role specific*. If you have a happy customer, who uses your solution across their business enterprise, work hard to collect success stories about how your solutions have delivered tangible business value to the CEO; the finance executive (CFO); operations executives (president, plant manager, or COO); sales and marketing executives; and (if appropriate) information technology (IT) executives. That way you can tell your story in the language of whichever executive you are meeting with.

Reducing inventories, for example, conjures up different ideas and feelings depending on the role of the person you're talking to. A finance executive might see it as a way to save money on carrying costs and overhead. An operations executive might be interested in freeing up working space on the shop floor, while the vice president of sales and marketing might see it as a threat that could result in more back orders, lower order fill-rates, and problems with customer satisfaction and retention.

One more point here. In this situation, don't use a preprinted reference story or case study. The second you show the lower-level person the printed sheet, they will take the sheet to their boss, instead of you. You are the storyteller. You go tell the story. Then you can ask a few questions and more important . . . listen!

5. Bring Your Boss to the Meeting

Most customers understand that when you bring your director or vice president to the meeting, they need to invite their director or vice president as well. But we can't assume they will know to do this. We may need to bargain with them, or strike a deal of some kind. Perhaps you bring your boss to talk about their request for a customized proof-of-concept demo, and, in exchange, they bring their vice president of operations, who is the person who will have the final say on the success of that proof-of-concept.

It doesn't necessarily have to be your boss. You might decide to bring an implementation specialist to meet the people who will be involved in their implementation. You could bring a business analyst to meet their executives and get very specific about how you can help them accomplish their objectives on time and under budget. Or, if it applies in your market, bring your leasing partner, or whoever can have a discussion about financing, to meet with their CFO or VP of finance to discuss their finance options. Leveraging the other players on your team can help to justify accessing and meeting with other people on their team.

6. Trade Something They Want for the Access You Want

We've already talked about the principle of trying never to do something for nothing. Sometimes the best thing we could ask for in return for what they want is access to their key personnel. If your client wants you to come over to conduct a site survey or needs analysis, you might respond by saying:

> *"If we did take the time to come over and walk around your manufacturing plant, would you be willing to arrange a meeting right afterward with the one person who is going to be held financially accountable for the success or failure of this project? Before we could put together a solid value proposition, we would need to understand exactly how they will justify, plan for, allocate, and secure the funding; how they plan to account for the investment; as well as exactly how the payback and return will be measured. Because without knowing that, any proposal we would submit would be like shooting in the dark. Does that sound fair to you?"*

Start thinking about these kinds of "trades" early on, while you still have things they want. Once they've seen your demo, called your references, and have your quote or proposal, they may not want anything else. Think ahead, so you don't run out of things to trade.

7. Insist on Executive-Level Answers to Specific Qualifying Questions

I have a set of four high-level qualifying questions that have served me very well for many years, especially in my days of selling seven-figure technology solutions. I often share these in our workshops, because they work particularly well when we get a surprise call from a relatively low-level contact, and especially if they want us to invest our time and energy to complete an unannounced RFP. You can use these in one of two ways, depending on what you are comfortable with.

One way to use these questions is to ask them of the person who has contacted you. You might preface them something like this: "We are excited to be considered for this project, Mr. Thompson. I wonder if you would mind if I ask you a few specific questions before we agree to complete the RFP?"

1. **"What is the highest-level goal you are trying to achieve, or problem you are trying to solve?"** We are asking about the Action Decision with this question. What we want to flesh out is whether this is a top-down or a bottom-up initiative, and whether or not they have identified a particular business objective (point "C") that is important enough to take action on *now*.
2. **"What other courses of action have you considered, or are you considering, to solve this problem?"** With this question I want to determine if this person is even aware that there are other initiatives and other courses of action competing for the same resources, or if they are just blindly doing what somebody else has told them to do.
3. **"How do you plan to justify and account for the investment?"** Here, I am clearly asking about resources. I want to see where they are with the Resource Decision, and if the individual I am dealing with is prepared to explain to their CFO why *this* project should be staffed and funded, instead of a dozen others.

4. **"What bad thing would happen if you just did nothing?"** This is a great all-around qualifying question that normally reveals information about the Action Drivers—and especially the consequences—fueling the initiative. Their answer can also reveal indications of where they are in their overall buying process.

What you'll find is that the person who calls you normally doesn't know the answer to any of these questions. After that becomes apparent, we can say, "Well, Mr. Thompson, before my boss will allow me to invest a bunch of time and money in this opportunity, I have to be able to explain to him why I think we should. I'm sure you can understand that." If we get a "Yes," we can continue on with, "Do you think you could help me get a hold of somebody who would know some of these things, so I can be a little more prepared when I go to my boss with this opportunity?" This is a very effective approach for getting high-level access very quickly. I like to think of the answers to these questions as prerequisites to the investment of our sales resources.

The second way to use these questions, which also works exceptionally well, is what I call the "reality check." Again I want to remind you, if you don't feel comfortable with this approach, just leave it on the shelf. Personally, I have spent too many man-years chasing my own tail, desperately trying to win the Source Decision of some ill-begotten, bottom-up initiative, which never did find its way to an executive's desk. The reality check has been an exceptional qualification technique to avoid this.

This scenario works well when a RFP just shows up in the mail unannounced, or when it comes to you by way of a partner, such as a consulting firm that has been retained by the prospect to help them create and distribute the RFP. Once you've had a chance to look it over, make note of the clause that is almost always present, which says, "Do not call anyone at our company except the person whose name is given herein," which is usually a low-level contact or the chairman of some selection committee. Then, completely ignore that note and immediately place a call directly to the CFO of the company.

You might get the CFO live, but more likely you'll get an assistant. Explain that you received the surprise RFP and before your boss will let you invest the time to respond to it, you have to ask the CFO four quick questions. The conversation could be as short as five or ten minutes, only more if the CFO has more she wants to say. Once you get her on the phone, very politely ask the four questions above.

I have never met a CFO who has ever had a problem with my phone call or with these four questions, and I have used this approach dozens of times. Some of the opportunities proved to be valid, and we responded and competed as best we could. But at least we knew it was a real deal! I can also tell you that I remember at least a half-dozen times that the CFO had no clue whatsoever about any RFP, or any project or initiative of this kind currently under consideration. Using this simple but effective technique, I have saved myself a lot of time and heartache by *not* chasing several bottom-up initiatives that were destined to "die on the vine."

The key, here, is that I didn't ask anyone's permission to make the call. When you ask permission, they say "No," and then you do it anyway, somebody usually gets mad. When you don't ask permission and you call, they normally only get frustrated. But this is very often worth the risk to make sure that the response or proposal you will invest hours or maybe even days worth of time in, is a responsible use of your company's time and money.

8. Sell Wider

One of the most effective ways to sell higher is to sell wider. There are several reasons for this. First, I have found many gatekeepers who work in operations, for example, are much less afraid of the idea of me calling their CFO, than calling their COO, who is their boss's boss's boss. They often have much less fear of being reprimanded for not "blocking me." The second reason is once you get two different units, two departments, or two different "brand teams" involved in an initiative, the person who will make the final Action Decision usually becomes someone who has oversight and responsibility for both groups.

If I am engaged in a sales campaign with my customer's operations department, for example, and I am able to get some people in sales and marketing or finance excited about what our solution can do to help them, too, then the decision is usually pushed up to the president or CEO level. When we can proactively drive the Action Decision up a layer, it provides one of the best reasons I know to ask for access to that Action Decision maker. If it starts out as an operations-only initiative, and the COO is identified as the "final decision maker," the gatekeepers tend to guard him with their lives. But when you and I can cause a change in their buying process, such as a change in who will make that final Action Decision, then our request to meet with the new decision maker is almost always met with far less resistance.

Another benefit of learning to sell wider is the potential to tap into other budgets and resources. Your client's operations department might have spent all the money they budgeted for the year, but maybe Finance has some that they could free up, if we could make a good business case for why it would be a good investment to do so. Maybe Finance could combine their resources with those of Operations to afford an investment that neither could afford to make on their own.

By far the best-kept secret for appropriating the funds needed to invest in enterprise-wide solutions is the sales and marketing department. If you can use the Business Value Hierarchy™ model, and the cause-and-effect-of-business concept, to demonstrate how your solutions can not only save money (reduce costs) for operations, but can actually drive new sales (increase revenue) for the sales and marketing department, it is amazing how often Sales and Marketing can get the funding they need. Companies perceive investments to cut costs and investments to drive revenue completely differently. You try it. Start looking for creative ways to help your customers *sell more*, as opposed to just *spend less*, and see how quickly they find the money they need to take you up on it.

The most important thing about selling wider, however, is the political and relational clout we earn by meeting with and building relationships with more people who can derive value from our business solutions. In the final analysis, it is the *collective perceived value* of what we offer that will be weighed as they make the Resource, Course, and Action Decisions.

As illustrated in Figure 9.1, the more business disparities we can convert into business results, the greater the collective perceived value of what we sell.

Figure 9.1 Turning Many "A's" into Many "C's"

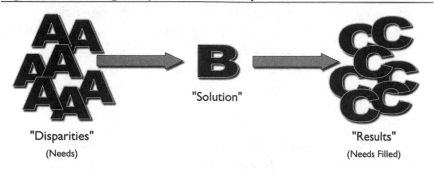

"Solution"

"Disparities"   "Results"

(Needs)   (Needs Filled)

The more "A's" we can identify, and the more "C's" we can deliver, the more likely we are to win all the little decisions and the big decision as well, because . . .

> **The best way to influence a *collective perceived value*
> is to identify and deliver more desired results for
> more of the people involved.**

Selling wider enables us to broaden our relationship base within our customer's company. If we are selling to and building relationships with only one or two people within our client's organization, we are exposing ourselves to a huge risk. What happens when our one "hero" quits, gets promoted, or gets fired? What if our one internal "champion" can't make the internal sale? Do we just go down in flames with them?

The importance of developing many relationships between the personnel of our company and the personnel of our client's company cannot be overstated. It is crucial, especially in the case of our best customers, to build strong working relationships with multiple people throughout our company and theirs in order to weather any unforeseen storms that can, and usually do, come up along the way.

These are just a few suggestions that I hope you can put to use in your endeavor to make the "little sale" to earn access to higher levels. But remember, once you get to the boss, you've only got three meetings to try to get through to that person's boss, or to someone else in the company, before you get stuck again. This is an ongoing process. We should continue to try to meet with more people, and build more relationships, both higher and wider within our customer's organization for as long as we continue to do business with them. It might be tough to accept but this is true . . .

If every time we go see our customer, we meet with the same person who already likes us, and who already wants to buy from us, we are not really doing our job.

We need to meet with and earn the trust of the people who we haven't met yet, or who don't like us, or who are determined to buy from our competitor. These are the people we really need to be selling to. The more people you meet, learn to understand, and build relationships with in your customer's organization, the more you will be able to influence *how* and *why* your customer buys.

CHAPTER 10

Accelerating the Buying Process

Do you want to increase sales revenue? There are two ways to do it. One is to increase sales velocity by increasing the number of opportunities that flow through our sales pipeline and "close" in any particular month or quarter. If we put twenty deals through the pipeline last quarter, and we were able to put twenty-five through this quarter, then we would have increased sales by 25 percent, assuming they were similar in average size.

The other way to grow revenue is to increase the average size of each sale. If we could increase our average deal size from $50,000 to $60,000 and we could close just as many, we would see a 20 percent increase in gross revenue. I often ask new clients which one they want to focus on. What do you suppose they say? You guessed it. "Both!"

There are many specific techniques and approaches that can be used to increase average deal size. One of the most important is reducing price erosion, which simply means to quit giving away so much in discounts and price reductions. Negotiation skills is an entire subject area unto itself that we will not formally explore here, but I would like to point out that . . .

> **Our effectiveness in negotiations is determined by how well we establish and influence the perceived value in our customer's mind throughout the entire sales campaign.**

If our customer arrives at the end of their buying process without believing that we offer value that is superior to our competition, we've got nothing to negotiate *about*. That's one of the reasons we spent so much time on understanding how customers perceive value in the first half of this book.

There are several other specific techniques that are equally valuable both in increasing deal size and increasing sales velocity. We will discuss several of them here, and I will point out certain instances that apply as we go, but this chapter will be focused primarily on maximizing sales velocity. It is a vitally important aspect of sales success in today's marketplace, because any situation that erodes profit margins—such as an economic downturn, or increased competition—has a negative impact on profitability. If we earn less profit on each transaction, then to increase total profit we have to increase the frequency of transactions. Some industries call this increasing "turnover." That's what this chapter is about.

We are going to be talking about the specific strategies, tactics, and techniques for accelerating our customer's buying process. This acceleration is good for us *and* good for our customer. Many companies, and especially technology solutions manufacturers, have gone to tremendous lengths to make their solutions easier to install, quicker to implement, and faster time-to-benefit. Why do we do that? Why do we, as vendors and suppliers, give so much attention to how "fast" our customers can see Return of Payback? Because customers demand it, right? Once they buy, they want to get to point "C" as fast as they possibly can.

Every day that we can drive out of our customer's Implementation and Utilization Process adds real Economic Value to their bottom line. The faster we can help them get from point "B" to point "C," the faster they see returns, the faster the investment pays for itself, and the faster they can free up capital for the next investment. But if our customers start out at "A," and the destination is "C," then every day that we can drive out of the Selection and Buying Process (the time it takes to get from "A" to "B") is just as valuable, isn't it? Accelerating the buying process creates value for our customers because it helps them get to "C" faster. But the flip side, of course, is Risk. They can't afford to buy too fast because a mistake could actually set them back and make the entire journey to "C" that much longer.

Shortening the Average Length of Sales Cycles

One very common measure that companies use to gauge sales velocity is the average length of a sales cycle. This is normally measured in the number of days it takes to work an opportunity through the sales pipeline and close the deal. There is a big difference, however, between shortening sales cycles and accelerating a buying process. The length of a sales cycle is a measure of the "things *we* do." Accelerating your customer's buying process speaks to changing the rate at which they do the "things *they* do."

Measuring Sales Cycles

Before you can shorten your average sales cycle—or rather have evidence to show that you've shortened it—you have to measure the length of each sales cycle accurately. Many companies use their Sales Force Automation (SFA) or Customer Relationship Management (CRM) system to track the length of sales cycles. A common approach is to simply count backward the number of days from the date the deal closed to the date the opportunity was first entered in the system. An alternative method is to count back from the close date to the date the opportunity was first forecasted. Either of these approaches does leave some room for "creativity."

If I am a sales rep, and I am being judged or compensated on the average length of a sales cycle, what's to keep me from "sandbagging," and not entering the contact info, or the forecast, until I get closer to the date that I think the customer will be ready to buy? This is not an indictment on any sales rep. The point of this example is that the measurement can be manipulated and can be quite subjective. If we can change the total elapsed time by simply changing when we start the clock, we may not actually be shortening anything.

There is one facet of measuring the sales cycle, however, that does have tremendous merit. It is based on the truth that . . .

> **Where performance is measured, performance improves. Measuring any human activity will cause those being measured to be more effective and efficient.**

It's human nature to want to do better over time. So, sometimes just the mere fact that we are measuring makes us work smarter and look for ways to drive time out of the process.

When I consult with clients to maximize sales force effectiveness, I recommend measuring sales cycles separately from prospecting cycles. A prospecting cycle is how long it takes to find, identify, and frame a sales opportunity. Then once the opportunity is framed, the sales cycle measures how long it takes to close the deal.

As a sales rep, you or I might spend twelve months networking and leveraging acquaintances to gain access to the CEO of a particular company. We might also need to meet with that CEO or other key executives more than once before we mutually discover a goal or an objective they are trying to achieve that we can help them with. A long average prospecting cycle is not such a bad thing if it promotes building relationships over time and earning access at levels that we might never reach if we wait for the director of IT to stop by our booth at a trade show.

My rule of thumb for when to start the clock ticking on a sales cycle is the day on which I am given an end date. That is, the date on which I frame an opportunity and the prospect tells me *when* they want to arrive at their desired point "C." Anything that happens prior to that is part of the prospecting cycle.

By breaking the whole process into two distinct measures (1) length of prospecting cycle, and (2) length of sales cycle, we can better identify where we need training, coaching, and/or changes in behavior to improve results. And human nature being what it is, as soon as you start measuring, you start seeing improvements.

Measurement is another reason the Process of Mutual Discovery is such a tremendous tool. When you map out the steps and hurdles involved in helping your customer move through their Selection and Buying Process, you will actually be preprogramming the duration of your sales cycle. Sure, there may be setbacks or additional hurdles that pop up along the way, but when your client works with you to plan out the process, the predictability and accuracy of sales forecasts improve dramatically.

Working the Right Opportunities

I often tell clients whom I consult with that the quickest way to reduce the *average* length of your sales cycles is to quit working on a bunch of those old junky deals in your pipeline that can't or won't close. Spend that time looking for some new opportunities that can close more quickly. Create for yourself a "Profile of the Ideal Client" that defines the characteristics of a great sales opportunity: one that is in an industry for which you have strong references, one who is big enough to afford what you sell, and one who has certain requirements for which you have a strong solution.

In the Enterprise Resource Planning (ERP) business, we used to only work with prospects who already had an ERP system, and who had an observable and measurable business disparity that could drive the need for an upgrade. We learned, the hard way, that selling to a company who had never been down that road before was often more trouble than it was worth. When I sold Supply Chain Management (SCM) software, one of the defining characteristics of a good prospect was a company that had multiple manufacturing plants that could make the same product, or multiple warehouses from which they could ship the same product. The need to make extremely complex decisions about where the most cost-efficient place is to make something, or where to store it and ship it from to better balance supply with demand, was one of the key preexisting conditions that made SCM not just interesting, but critical.

I'm not saying that you shouldn't pursue new markets or prospects that are less than perfect, but if the objective is to shorten the average length of your sales cycles, find your "sweet spot" and sell there.

I urge you to look closely at each opportunity in your pipeline and ask, "Is this where I should be spending my time?" I know it's hard to walk away from anything that has even the slightest pulse, but we have to use our time wisely. Use the suggestions presented throughout this book to carefully qualify each opportunity. Take a clean sheet of paper and go down through the deals in your pipeline. Make each one earn its way onto a fresh list.

1. Ask, "What goal or objective is this prospect trying to achieve, or what problem are they trying to solve? What is their desired point 'C'?"
2. Look for the six Action Drivers: Motive, Urgency, Return, Consequence, Means, and Risk, and make sure they are really strong enough to drive a purchase.
3. Identify *what* and *who* is involved in your customer's buying process, where they are in that process, and what else has to happen before they would be ready to buy.
4. Determine who you believe will make the final Action Decision, and then do what is required to earn your way to that person or persons. If you exhaust every possibility, but cannot get there, don't bank too heavily on winning that deal. Invest your time and effort in deals you can win.

With a little diligence and reflection, we can reduce the average length of sales cycles substantially. But let's be reminded that all of the suggestions thus far in this chapter do not in any way address how to accelerate our customer's buying process. For most of us, this requires a paradigm shift. It is akin to the change in thinking we made to focus on *what our clients do* in order to buy something, as opposed to *what we do* in order to sell something.

Shortening the length of our sales cycles is important, in that it speaks to our own effectiveness and efficiency, but we shouldn't stop there. We need to learn to drive time out of our customer's buying process in order to help them reach point "C" faster, as well as maximize our own sales velocity, gross revenue, and profitability.

Ten Ways to Accelerate Your Customer's Buying Process

Once we are measuring the right things, and we know we are working the right opportunities, we can start to apply specific techniques for accelerating our customer's buying process. Please let me emphasize, we are not talking about pushing customers to buy before they are ready. All of these suggestions are put forth as a means of helping our clients to drive time out of their Selection and Buying Process, so they can more quickly see the desired results and derive the business value they are looking for at "C." It just so happens to be good for us, too.

As we work through these suggestions, be on the lookout for ways that you can apply these ideas to specific situations within the accounts that are in your current sales pipeline. Some of these ideas will apply to one specific account or another, while others apply to them all. I've tried to put the really "big ones" first, but other than that they are in no particular order. They are all important, time tested, and extremely effective.

1. Sell Higher

Remember earlier in this chapter when I said that our customers want to get to point "C" as soon as they possibly can? Well, that statement needs a little clarification. The *executives* within our customer's organization want to get to "C" as soon as they possibly can. The individual contributors (line workers) and the frontline managers within our customer's organization want to get to "C" as soon as they can. Middle managers often don't. I know what you're thinking, "That doesn't make sense," right? Actually, it makes all the sense in the world.

If you look at a typical organization structure, you'll often see three strata as it relates to a desire to leave "A" (the status quo) and venture out to "C" (a desired future state), as shown in Figure 10.1. This is not universally true, but executives are often very interested and eager to take action to move toward their defined goals and objectives. That, in fact, is their job. They are typically hired for, measured against, and compensated for their ability to achieve the company's high-level goals and objectives.

Likewise, those who work as individual contributors on the "front line," as it is often called, are typically happy to embrace change and progress, especially if it makes their job easier to do, less monotonous, less dangerous, or whatever. It's often the people in the middle who want to hold back. Many managers, directors, and even some vice presidents, see change and progress as a threat to their existence, with the potential to render them obsolete, unnecessary, or redundant.

Unlike senior executives, who are paid to take risks, middle managers are paid to avoid risks. They are seldom the ones who get the glory if a project or initiative succeeds, but they're the first ones to be blamed if it fails. To them, a long and arduous Selection and Buying Process involving a dozen vendors and a twelve-month evaluation, as well as a major Implementation and Utilization Process with lots of committees and consultants to manage, means job security. Who can blame them for slowing things down? If we were in their shoes, we would probably do the same thing.

One of the things we should guard against, in our desire to sell higher, is to work our way up to sell to middle management, and stop there. Instead of simply saying, "sell higher," we should probably be saying, "sell as high as you possibly can," because we might have to sell two, three, or four levels up, before we get to someone who understands point "C," is focused on it, and who is willing to take some risks to get there. It isn't always the CEO, or even the CFO, who we need to be selling to, but it's someone who is high enough that they are motivated to get beyond the buying process and get to the results.

2. Influence the Scope of the Project or Initiative

In the last chapter we talked about the tremendous value of selling wider, and of identifying and offering solutions to solve more problems for more people. But there is one aspect of this we should be cautious

Figure 10.1 The Strata of Your Customer's Organization

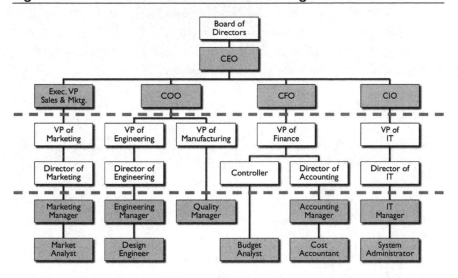

of. Sometimes, when we get more and more people and departments and budgets involved, the buying decision becomes exponentially more complex, both for us and for our client. We should be careful not to make the buying decision so big that it forces the customer to step back, think about it for six months, and then form a committee to go out and conduct a twelve-month investigation.

This is always a judgment call. I will often drive the opportunity wide enough to get the backing and support of several key executives to ensure we can obtain the staffing and funding resources, and then turn around and refine or narrow the scope of the project so that the decision is as low risk and simple as possible. Sometimes, in order to clear the hurdles of the buying process, it is beneficial to start with a pilot implementation, or some limited commitment on the buyer's part, in order to get our foot in the door and prove the value of our solution.

Be very careful in how you influence the scope of the project or initiative. If you sell too little, it might be a year or more before they decide to buy more. But likewise, if you try to sell too much, you can cause the buying decision to get bogged down, or stop altogether. Also, be cognizant of how your competitors are positioning themselves. If they come to your prospective customer with the idea of a limited scope pilot, but you are still proposing the whole enchilada, they might choose the pilot because it exposes them to far less risk. We don't want to become the "me too" vendor, constantly reacting to your customer's interest in what your competitor is proposing.

3. Neutralize Competition

One of the things that adds a great deal of time to any buying cycle is your customer having to go through the motions with a large number of vendors. Neutralize competitive vendors by leveraging your strengths against their weaknesses. Learn the differences in functional capabilities, and find out if there are real business issues that your customer is faced with that cannot be addressed by your competitor's solutions.

Knowing this difference is one thing; helping your customer arrive at your conclusion is another. We talked a bit about competitive differentiation in Chapter 3, when we discussed Intelligent Positioning and how to ask the right questions to better understand how your customer perceives value. Avoid negative "bashing." It almost always works against you. But you can lay traps for your competitors to fall into.

If you know, for example, that your product has far less chance of breaking during your customer's assembly process, you might ask:

"Do your people ever accidentally break one of these parts during assembly?"

"Yes. They do."

"What happens when they break one?"

"Well, of course we have to throw it away and replace the part, but what's worse, sometimes when that part breaks, we have to take the whole assembly apart just to replace the broken part."

"Really? What happens then?"

"Well, sometimes the whole line ends up getting backed up, and then we have to hurry to complete the work on time, which leads to other

mistakes along the way. Once in a while it can even hold up a shipment."

"Wow! How often does one of these parts break?"

"Oh, it happens several times a day."

"Really? Well, do you have any idea how much it costs you in time, rework, and expediting costs each time one breaks?"

"No. But I can tell you it's a major pain in the neck . . . and other places."

"So, it sounds as though reducing the chance that one of these parts would break could be pretty important to you. Is that right?"

"Yes. It sure is."

"Well, you'll be happy to know this is one of the main reasons our customers tell us they prefer to use our components rather than our competitor's."

You get the idea. Leverage your strengths against your competitor's weaknesses, and help your customer arrive at your conclusion.

4. Crystallize the Implementation and Utilization Process

One of the main reasons customers hesitate to move away from "A," or stall out before they get to "B," is that they don't fully understand how they are going to get from "B" to "C." While doing a one-on-one coaching session with one of my clients, he shared a story that illustrates this point very nicely.

He had been working with a prospect for almost a year trying to sell about $150,000 worth of software and services and deliver a highly customized solution designed to shorten his client's new-product development cycles and shorten time to market. They had conducted multiple software demonstrations and met with all the various people involved, but the vice president of R&D kept putting off his final decision.

Finally, in desperation, my client asked him, "I don't mean to be pushy, but we've met quite a few times and it seems we're not getting any closer to moving ahead with this project. Can I ask, is there an order in our future?"

The VP said, "Actually there are still some things I don't totally understand. Once we buy this, where are you going to do this development work? Will that be done here, on-site, or will it be at your facility? Will my people be able to review your progress and have input along the way, or will we not be able to see it until it's done? When the development work is done, will my people be able to test it before it gets installed to make sure it's going to do what we want? And if we need to make some changes after the initial install, who will make those, my people or yours?"

What he was asking for was a simple implementation plan, which my client was happy to provide. Once he did, and the customer could clearly see and understand the path from "B" to "C," he was happy to move through point "B" right away. The lesson here, for all of us, is to spend as much time as it takes helping our customers understand that we're selling "C," not "B." Then we have to take the time to make them as comfortable as possible with our plan to help them get there.

5. Work Your Plan in Parallel Instead of Serial

In Chapter 8, we talked about developing a Process of Mutual Discovery to help our client get all the way to point "C." The documented plan defines the steps, events, and milestones of your customer's buying process, but no one says you have to take only one step at a time.

Once your customer feels comfortable with your proposed process and your plan for helping them get where they want to go, you might explore their interest in compressing that timeline a bit. Please refer back to Figure 8.3 in Chapter 8. You could ask:

"Why was it you wanted to wait until September 30 to start seeing results? I was going over our proposed plan, and it occurred to me that we could do some of these steps in parallel, instead of serial. For example, the same day that we come to meet with your CFO to discuss financing options, we could

have a quick meeting with Legal to go over the terms and conditions of our standard contract and agreement. I will be there anyway, and it could save us some time."

It is usually easy to determine whether or not your buyer has an interest in expediting the plan. Some will be very receptive, and others won't. We just need to make sure we are asking someone who is above that imaginary line we discussed earlier. They need to be high enough in the organization that they're motivated to reach point "C" faster and have the authority to reset the agenda, as compared to someone in middle management who would naturally be opposed to accelerating the plan, or who couldn't do anything about it even if they did like the idea.

6. Keep Your Sales Opportunities "Moving"

Are the opportunities in your current sales pipeline "moving" or "stopped"? It's really easy to tell the difference. Take a look at your day planner, or personal digital assistant (PDA), or whatever you use to schedule appointments. Do you have a date and time on your calendar for each opportunity when you will next meet or speak to your customer on the phone? Do they have that date and time on their calendar too? I'm sorry to inform you, but if you don't or they don't, your sales opportunity is not moving; it's stopped.

I'm not trying to be mean here. We all battle with this constantly. A couple of the opportunities in my own sales pipeline are stopped right now. But when you or I allow any active sales campaign to stop, we are taking a huge risk. It's possible that it will never start up again. I like to think of it as if I am a doctor, and my patient has gone "flat line" on me. If we let an opportunity stay flat, we sever any momentum we may have generated. And if it stays flat too long, that opportunity will die, or at least sustain serious brain damage. If an opportunity that you believe in has stopped, get it moving again immediately! Call your customer right now and get on their calendar. Shock 'em back to life. "Clear!"

Get an appointment scheduled with every qualified opportunity in your pipeline . . . today! Do not let another day go by. When it comes to scheduling the next step with your customer, the sooner the better.

Even if the scheduled meeting is a month out, get it on the calendar because . . .

It's easier for you *and* your customer to keep a previously scheduled appointment than to schedule a new one.

It's also harder for your customer to cancel a scheduled appointment than to simply ignore your request for a new one.

Remember, this practice is good for your customer, too. They probably want to reach some resolution on the buying decision at hand as much as you do. Keeping the next appointment booked helps them stay focused as well.

At the end of every meeting with every prospect, schedule your next meeting or event before you leave. You know what happens if you don't. You call them the following week, and their assistant says, "I'm sorry, Mr. Johnson is in Europe all this week." So you call the following Monday and you hear, "I'm sorry, Mr. Johnson was in Europe all of last week and he has back-to-back meetings all day." So, you wait a few days, because you don't want to appear desperate. When you call again the assistant tells you, "I'm sorry. Mr. Johnson is out until Tuesday of next week." On Tuesday you connect with Mr. Johnson and schedule your next appointment for the following Tuesday. Meanwhile, four weeks have gone by with no forward motion.

Some of the excess time in our sales campaigns is our own darn fault. To drive time out of the process, keep your opportunities moving. Book your next appointment or correspondence at the end of every meeting or phone call.

7. Make the Most of Every Meeting or Phone Call

With a little effort and forethought, we can make every meeting and every phone call much more productive. In many of our workshops we discuss the importance of pre-call planning and post-call review. We actually start with the review first.

In the case of most of the opportunities in your current sales pipeline, you've already had some interaction with your customer, either on the phone or in person. Let's start with a review of who we've met with and what we've learned. Here are some of the questions we should ask ourselves:

- What do we know about their corporate goals and objectives?
- Are there major problems that could keep them from achieving their goals?
- Do they currently have a plan to achieve them?
- Do *they* see any gaps in their plan to achieve them?
- Do *we* see any gaps that they don't see yet?
- What do we know about the Action Drivers of Motive, Urgency, Return, Consequence, Means, and Risk?
- Who and what would likely be involved in a buying decision?

We should also begin to develop an organization chart to depict who we've met with and who else within the organization we might still need to meet. Once we have a clear picture of where we stand, then we can plan our next meeting or correspondence with the specific intent of learning critical information we don't yet know, meeting additional decision makers and influencers, and helping to identify and clear the hurdles of their buying process.

We then develop a pre-call plan to define exactly what we should do and ask next, while constantly looking forward for what else has to happen to get beyond point "B," and on to point "C." The kinds of questions we ask ourselves as we plan our next meeting are:

- What is the purpose of this meeting or phone call?
- What are we trying to accomplish?
- What do I need them to agree to or commit to?
- What do I need to learn about their business goals?
- What do I still *not know* about their buying process?
- Who else do we still need to meet and begin building a relationship with?
- Who or what are we competing with?

The more progress we can make in each meeting or on each phone call, the more time is "driven out" of the overall buying process. I've never met a customer who wants to be pushed, but many of them don't mind at all being led a little faster, as long as we remain focused on their desired outcomes, very respectful, highly predictable, and worthy of their trust.

8. Mitigate the Perceived Risk of Moving Forward

Risk, whether real or perceived, exists in every relationship. For a customer, especially those that are considering buying from a *new* vendor for the first time, Risk becomes more real and more formidable the closer they get to making a commitment or passing through point "B." So, as we have talked about more than once, we should do all we can to minimize the risk our customer perceives in doing business with us.

However, let's not forget that purposefully introducing risk—or what I often refer to as FUD (fear, uncertainty, and doubt)—can and will be used against you in a highly competitive sales campaign. I have gone up against some competitors who seemed to have made it into an art form. I'd rather invest my time mitigating the perceived risk of buying from me than fueling the perceived risk of buying from my competitor. When throwing FUD, just like when throwing mud, you usually end up getting it all over yourself.

We need to be prepared to defend ourselves against any FUD missile our competitor decides to launch. As we talked about in Chapter 3, prepare for and expect the most common objections you may encounter. Predetermine what your countermove will be. Prepare your rebuttal. Keep your helmet on, mouth guard in, and chin strap buckled. Never allow yourself to be caught off guard.

9. Give Your Customer a Way Out

There are several specific approaches that can be used to reduce both perceived and actual risk in a brand-new buyer/seller relationship that help you to earn trust at the same time. I offer two of them here (numbers nine and ten on this list) for your consideration. These suggestions are certainly not practical in all situations. Please use them with dis-cretion. You may not have the authority to leverage these ideas, and those who can grant you that authority may not approve of their use. Like everything else in this book, this is a smorgasbord. Take what you can use, and leave the rest on the shelf.

Any buyer is naturally more willing to take a risk if they can change their mind later. In fact, if we offer them a satisfaction guarantee or some other way out, we could eliminate the perception of risk alto-gether. Here are the first of two suggestions that have worked for me in a variety of selling situations.

Many years ago, I happened across an opportunity to sell a high-end computer workstation to a prospect over 3,000 miles away from my office. I spoke on the phone with the vice president of engineering who would be the final approver for the purchase of a single $35,000 work-station. But if he liked it, he would be replacing thirty more over the next two years. He told me he had eleven different quotes at a wide range of prices from vendors all across the country.

We talked on the phone several times over a two-week period, and as we talked I sensed that he was extremely confused about the variables that would cause the price of a workstation to range 30 percent or more, and especially why mine was one of the highest-priced options he was considering. He told me that he was getting pummeled with calls from the other vendors, each with a bigger discount or offering to match the lowest bid. Somehow I could sense an intense dread of buying the wrong thing just because it was cheaper, and tremendous frustration with the lack of time he had to fool around evaluating the differences. He was just too darn busy to go through a lengthy evaluation process.

Finally, one night I woke up and sat straight up in bed with an idea. The next morning I convinced the owner of our company to let me send one of our fully configured workstations to this VP with a simple ver-bal understanding, "If you like it, send us a check for the asking price. If you don't, send it back."

Some would say, "You're crazy. You shouldn't have taken that risk." Well, maybe not, but he did send us the check. Then he did over a $1 million worth of business with us during the next two-and-a-half years, and our relationship continued even after he left that company and

moved on to a new one. His story became one of our best customer testimonials, and he acted as a reference for over $2 million in new sales
to other customers.

What I did for him was eliminate the massive amount of time he
would have to spend researching and understanding the minute differences between the various options and deciding which one was the very
best choice. My approach allowed him to move past all that minutia, but
offered an exit strategy if he found out later he had made a mistake. He
knew that if he wasn't 100 percent happy, he could just send it back.

Please be warned: Be very careful about whom you decide to take
this kind of risk with. Not everybody is honest, whether they are a seller
or a buyer. Some would-be customers are devious, and I've even met a
few who seemed to be downright malicious. These are the kind of
clients you'll wish later you never had. Sometimes you're better off
walking away from an opportunity if you feel your prospective customer is not honest and ethical.

10. Shoulder Some of the Risk Yourself

Another idea that can inspire a customer to move forward with you in
the face of perceived risk is your willingness to shoulder some of the
risk yourself. In a perfect world, we would never take any risk, but in
the highly competitive world of business, Risk is a part of every
interaction.

Too often, when our customer is reluctant to make the commitment
to buy, we think that we need to "sweeten the pot" to get them to move
forward. We may know logically that they *should* buy, but they hesitate,
stall, or simply stop moving forward for some reason. We often
assume—based on the Value Equation presented in Chapter 3—that
their perceived value of what we are offering is not equal to or greater
than the money we are asking them for. But we should also remember
that any reduction in perceived risk increases perceived value. Mitigating risk could be the best way to balance the equation.

About sixty days after I started Sales Excellence, Inc., we got a call
from one of the world's largest information technology (IT) outsourcing companies. They were interested in a sales prospecting workshop
that could be customized and integrated with their existing training cur-

riculum. They had already invested millions in sales process consulting, methodology, and training, but they had a gap in the area of prospecting they felt needed to be addressed.

As we worked with them to define the shape and scope of the course, I interviewed several executives, sales managers, and various members of the sales team and developed a workshop that was just what they told me they wanted. However, in my gut I started to feel the old, "We're a big global company and you guys are a little start-up," objection getting ready to happen. I did the best I could to handle the objection before it became an objection, but with few references and no global clients, how much handling can you do?

When it finally came down to it, the committee did, in fact, get nervous about working with a small and young company. It appeared the whole opportunity might come to a screeching halt when I received a call letting me know that the committee wasn't willing to commit to our agreement as proposed. They just weren't sure about engaging a start-up company for this critically important project. However, they said, if I was willing to travel to their headquarters at my own expense to do a pilot workshop "for free," there might be a potential upside of lots of future work if things went well. I decided to counter with a different idea.

I said, "I will come and deliver a pilot program for you that will be exactly what your sales organization has told me they want and need. If you are not absolutely blown away with it, you can send me home without a check. No charge! But if this workshop *is* what we have already agreed it should be, I need to be paid my normal rate as well as my travel expenses." They agreed, I delivered, and they loved it! After we tweaked the content a bit we delivered fifteen additional workshops across the United States and Europe during the following six months, all at full rate. They remain one of our best clients to this day.

Sometimes all your client needs is to see that you are willing to shoulder some of the risk yourself. In this situation, I didn't feel as though I was at any risk at all, because I knew they would like the workshop. How could they not like it? The entire program sprang from the minds of the people I had met with and interviewed. I just needed to help them get over their own mental hurdle by changing the rules of the game a little. I have used this type of approach in many different forms over the years to reduce perceived risk and thereby impact the Value Equation in my favor. But again, this technique should be used with extreme caution.

I want to emphasize here that I did not offer to do the work for a lower price, or to do the first one "for free." Price was obviously not the issue, since they gladly paid the regular rate once they saw the final product. One axiom that we all need to live by is . . .

> **Never ever do anything, or give your customer anything, for free. When you give something for free, it immediately strips it of all perceived value.**

It might be possible to discount what you sell far enough that the Value Equation eventually swings your client's way so that they think, "Well, at 40 percent off, perhaps it's worth the risk." But typically, all it does is erode your profit and communicate to your buyer that you were overcharging to start with. Then, in their mind, anything else you propose in the future should *start out* at 40 percent off! Learn to be creative about how you can alleviate perceived risk to increase perceived value without trying to balance the Value Equation by dropping your price.

This list of ten is certainly not exhaustive. In many ways, this entire book has been about accelerating your customer's buying process by understanding and influencing how and why your customers buy. I firmly believe that if you simply start to *think about* different ways that you can accelerate your customer's buying process, you'll come up with many more ideas of your own.

Making These Ideas Work for You

At this point I want to encourage you to take a minute to look at the list of "Good Ideas" you have captured as you have worked your way through this book. Or, perhaps just flip back through the pages to remind yourself of some of the major tenets. My hope is that a few of these ideas and suggestions will find their way into your work, and that you will take the time to learn to use them effectively.

Change is never easy, and neither is success. Some of these techniques and approaches may feel a little uncomfortable the first time you use them. But I assure you they will work, just as they have worked for me, and are working for thousands of sales and marketing professionals all over the world who have participated in our workshops and seminars. The proof, however, is in making them work for you.

Learning to *Think Like Your Customer* starts with being willing to think differently than you think right now. It involves learning what your customers think about, how they see the world, and the things that influence their behavior. Once you begin to *think* from the standpoint of *how* and *why* your customers buy, you will never sell the same way again.

Notes

Introduction

1. Strategic Selling® is a registered service mark of Miller Heiman, Inc., 1595 Meadow Wood Lane, Suite 2, Reno, NV 89502.
   Solution Selling® is a registered trademark of Solution Selling, Inc., a Sales Performance International company, 6230 Fairview Road, Suite 200, Charlotte, NC 28210.
   SPIN Selling® is a registered trademark of Huthwaite, Inc., 22630 Davis Drive, Suite 100, Sterling, VA 20164.

Chapter 1

1. Stephen R. Covey, *The Seven Habits of Highly Effective People*, New York: Fireside, 1989, p. 237.

Chapter 2

1. Amos Tversky and Daniel Kahneman, "Prospect theory: An analysis of decision under risk," *Econometrica*, 47, 1979, pp. 263–91.

Chapter 5

1. Daniel T. Gilbert and Patrick S. Malone, "The correspondence bias," *Psychological Bulletin*, 117, 1995, pp. 21–38.
2. Amos Tversky and Daniel Kahneman, "Judgment under uncertainty: Heuristics and biases," *Science*, 185, 1974, pp. 1124–30.

3. Albert Mehrabian, "Communication without words," *Psychology Today*, vol. 2, no. 4, 1968, pp. 53–56.

4. Michael Ross and Fiore Sicoly, "Egocentric biases in availability and attribution," *Journal of Personality and Social Psychology*, 37, 1979, pp. 322–36.

Chapter 8

1. Stephen R. Covey, *The Seven Habits of Highly Effective People*, New York: Fireside, 1989, p. 99.

Index

About the Author

Bill Stinnett is the founder and president of Sales Excellence, Inc., and is a highly sought-after speaker appearing at sales meetings, conferences, conventions, and annual sales kick-offs worldwide. He is the creator of several popular programs, including *Selling at the C-Level®*, *Power-Prospecting for New Business™*, and *Selling Business Value™*. His clients include General Electric, Microsoft, Verizon, American Express, EDS, Harvard Business School, and many others. For more information, or to request Bill for your next event, please call 1-800-524-1994 or visit www.salesexcellence.com.

He can be reached via e-mail at: bill@billstinnett.com.